CROSSWORDS

CROSSWORDS

SOLVE &
UNWIND

SIRIUS

SIRIUS

This edition published in 2024 by Sirius Publishing, a division of
Arcturus Publishing Limited,
26/27 Bickels Yard, 151–153 Bermondsey Street,
London SE1 3HA

ISBN: 978-1-3988-4397-4
AD012307US

Printed in China

1

Across

1 En-graved letters?
4 Make your move
7 Incidentally, in IMs: abbr.
10 Lapse, perhaps
11 Up for payment
12 Cry with a pointed figure
13 Any means possible: 3 wds.
16 Soon, in a stanza
17 "How's ___?"
18 To the most extreme degree: 2 wds.
20 Oversupply
23 Elvis Presley's "___ Las Vegas!"
26 Inflation victim?
27 Straight, unobstructed path: 3 wds.
31 Pub request
32 Do the deck
33 Statement to the judge
35 Kate Middleton's sister
39 Lunkhead
42 Chaotic places
43 Baseball pitches that drop at the last second
46 Player for pay
47 Heartache
48 Manage, with "out"
49 Hitherto
50 "Does she or doesn't she?" item
51 Took a breather

Down

1 Fixer-upper
2 O'Henry specialty
3 Evidence
4 "Much ___ About Nothing"
5 Terse
6 Engineering college designation
7 Produced illegally
8 Granting that, in brief
9 Vessel for making lo mein
14 Roguish guy
15 Maid's cloth
19 Spanish rivers
21 "Guh-ross!"
22 Pre-schooler
24 Armed services org.
25 Exec's "now," initially
27 Napkin holder
28 "___ be seeing you"
29 Can skip: hyph
30 Neighbor of Formentera
34 "Perfect!" NASA-style: hyph.
36 May and telephone
37 Beer Barrel dance
38 Wit or good looks, e.g.
40 Vulgar
41 Gift horse location
43 Bug, with "on"
44 More than annoyance
45 Spelling or quilting event

2

Across

1. Part of a footnote abbr.
4. Train stops: abbr.
8. ___ Kosh B'gosh (clothing brand)
9. Woman's legwear
12. Want ad palindrome, initially
13. Reorganize, especially for the purpose of updating
14. Free from restraint
16. Hound's trail
18. Shows a response
20. Biol. energy sources
21. Author Umberto
22. Groundbreaking tools
23. Dangerous conditions for drivers: 2 wds.
27. Wait in hiding
28. ___ Aviv
29. Department of Transportation agcy.
30. Sportswear brand
34. Bath ___
36. TWA exec Carl
37. Continue: 2 wds.
39. He played Davidson's love interest in "The Crying Game"
40. Soft drinks brand of Pennsylvania: hyph.
41. "Mighty ___ a Rose" (song)
42. Zaire's Mobuto Sese ___
43. Darwinian ancestor

Down

1. Heart of France
2. "That ___ of the strangest things I've ever seen": 2 wds.
3. ___ rhythm, brain waves pattern
4. Duration
5. Item worn around the neck
6. Brokers, briefly
7. Compulsive buyer
10. Affected: hyph.
11. At a slant
15. Rink dancers: 2 wds.
17. Blog feeds, initially
19. "Lark" or "park" sound: 2 wds.
23. Asian and swine, e.g.
24. Capital of Zambia
25. Biceps band
26. Preceded: 2 wds.
31. Alfalfa's sweetheart on "The Little Rascals"
32. Lots: 2 wds.
33. King cobra or black mamba
35. "Admiral Graf ___"
38. Strong tree

3

Across

1 David Copperfield's field
6 Sleeps in a tent
11 Destructive hurricane of 2011
12 Scarlett's last name, in "Gone With the Wind"
13 Puff on a cigar
14 Items being sold
15 Way off in the distance
16 High tennis shot
18 Cobb of baseball fame et al.
19 Verb suffix
20 ___ whim: 2 wds.
21 Gardening tool
22 Even scores
24 Gofer's job
26 Customers
28 Maryland or Massachusetts, once
30 Put one foot in front of the other
33 Gold: Sp.
34 Cut, as a tree
36 Flightless bird of Australia
37 ___ de Janeiro (Olympics city of 2016)
38 Ending for lime or lemon
39 Soaked
40 Biology classification
42 Separate
44 Lifeless
45 On the ___ of (about to)
46 Way of doing something
47 Computer key

Down

1 Person without a social group
2 Big name in men's suits
3 "Syriana" and "Ocean's Eleven" actor
4 Sign, as a contract
5 Half of the band Gnarls Barkley (anagram of ECOLE)
6 House for mooers
7 "Now I've got you!'
8 Billionaire with her own "Living" magazine
9 Attack, as a predator does: 2 wds.
10 Talked back to
17 Like two of the jacks in a deck of cards
23 ___-mo camera
25 Some football linemen: abbr.
27 Hurriedly: 2 wds.
28 Welsh ___ (cute dogs)
29 "Murder on the ___ Express"
31 Come to the forefront
32 Golf club used on the green
35 Work with a loom
41 Web address: abbr.
43 Be the author

4

Across

1 "Nightmare" local: abbr., 2 wds.
6 Sketch show with Aries Spears and Michael McDonald: 2 wds.
11 Big name in cameras
12 Ontario tribe members
13 Not subject to any more changes
14 1970s music style
15 Lycee student
17 Sony handheld device, initially
18 Letters on a car sticker
20 At any time
22 "One Day ___ Time": 2 wds.
23 Close (of a victory): 3 wds.
26 Red or blue, e.g.
28 Skip about playfully
29 They're boring
31 "... ___ shall die": 2 wds.
32 Botanist Gray et al.
33 ___-a-brac
34 Big bang producer, for short
36 Gold standard
38 Words before hearts, e.g.: 2 wds.
40 Cooked in hot fat
43 Monte ___
44 Pilotless plane
45 It'll shock you
46 Man in Monterrey

Down

1 Northern helper
2 Flowers around your neck, in Hawaii
3 Perrier and Evian, e.g.: 2 wds.
4 Cornrow's place
5 Story
6 Hospital transports
7 "Exodus" character
8 Imbalance
9 Gumshoes
10 After-dinner drink letters
16 "Oy ___!" (cry of dismay)
18 "Pleasantville" star William H. ___
19 Ancient colonnade
21 "Bambi" character
23 Suddenly run toward, as an exit: 2 wds.
24 Sonoran Indian
25 Idle or Clapton
27 Switch settings
30 Where to hear Xhosa, initially
33 Washington County, Vermont city
34 Diplomat's talent
35 Org. that oversees many golf tournaments
37 Country postal addresses, for short
39 Cheer for a flamenco dancer
41 Brian whose albums include "The Ship"
42 The, in Germany

5

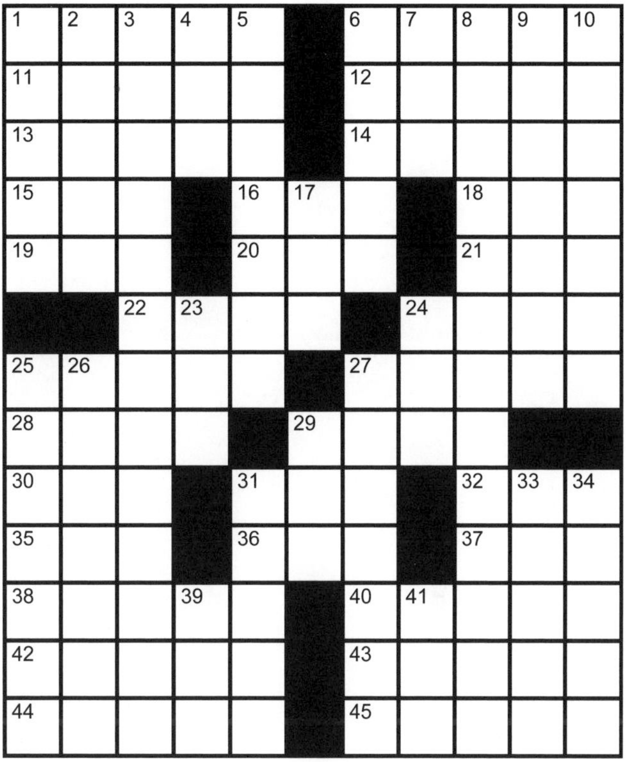

The crossword grid appears here with numbered cells.

Across

1 Pretended (as though)
6 Teens who wear black makeup, e.g.
11 What a plane or ship carries
12 Not urban
13 Friend, in Mexico
14 Cheri formerly of "Saturday Night Live"
15 Word before room or center
16 Aisle
18 iPhone program
19 Reindeer's relative
20 Newsman Rather
21 Spinning kid's toy
22 Walk off the job
24 Chunk of ice floating in the sea
25 Reason
27 Daily ___ (the same old thing at work)
28 Section
29 Be a chef
30 Reading and Short Line, in Monopoly: abbr.
31 In addition
32 Clairvoyant's ability, supposedly
35 Back muscle, for short
36 Unusual
37 Narcotics watchdog: abbr.
38 Bagel choice
40 Having debts
42 Torment
43 Like the gods Thor and Odin
44 Dings
45 Key word

Down

1 Without ___ in the world: 2 wds.
2 Desert animal with humps
3 "Who's buried in Grant's tomb?" for example: 2 wds.
4 Omelet ingredient
5 Critical, as a situation: 3 wds.
6 No longer a child
7 Not safe, in baseball
8 Abuse: 3 wds.
9 Whale hunter's weapon
10 Succumbed to a wet floor
17 Cracklin' ___ Bran (Kellogg's cereal)
23 Country north of Mex.
24 To and ___
25 Amount that can fit in a Ford, say
26 Put in order
27 "That was a funny joke!": 2 wds.
29 Popular fish for fish 'n' chips
31 Awards for Broadway actors
33 Hearing, taste or touch
34 Beeper
39 Canadian province: abbr.
41 Took first place

6

Across

1 Fall behind
4 Animal in the family
7 Bobby of hockey
8 "This feels good!"
9 Kia or Miata
12 Head honcho, initially
13 You, for one
15 "OK, I give up!"
17 Uncooked meal
18 Takes the wheel
20 At that point
21 Cheer
22 Ms. Morrison
23 Cloak wearer, perhaps
25 One of 435 in D.C.
27 Took off
28 "Silence!"
30 Kim's Hollywood ex
32 Utah ski resort
33 Bone ____
36 Decreases
38 ____ ghost (hallucinates): 2 wds.
39 Attendance
41 Father
42 Mimic
43 ____ Lanka (country near India)
44 Mike and ____ candies
45 "Lost" network
46 Little bit

Down

1 Point
2 "____ we all?"
3 Business with carts: 2 wds.
4 With 26-down, question they may ask you at a 3-down: 2 wds.
5 Piece of corn
6 "____ is the last straw!"
9 Another question you may be asked at 3-down...which boils down to the same question as 4-down: 3 wds.
10 Wise goddess
11 Get under control: 2 wds.
14 No purebred
16 Melissa ____, who cursed at the Oscars
19 Power for trains
23 Drink brand named for a mountain
24 Palindromic exercise: hyph.
26 See 4-down
29 Goldie of "Cactus Flower"
31 Before
34 Japanese city
35 Went into the water
37 Sammy who hit 66 home runs in 1998
40 City, in slang

7

Across

1 Relaxed personality classification: 2 wds.
6 "I don't ___ bit!": 2 wds.
11 Fleshy extension hanging above the throat
12 To have, in Le Havre
13 Forgoing personal pleasures: hyph.
15 Animal welfare org., initially
16 Largest city in Mich.
17 "Zip-A-Dee-Doo-___"
18 "___, With Love" (Sidney Poitier movie): 2 wds.
20 Alteration of a corporation's structure: abbr.
23 Pre-entree course
27 El ___ (weather phenomenon)
28 Plantation in "Gone With the Wind"
29 Kind of blade
31 "What a shame": 2 wds.
32 Corral: 2 wds.
34 Publishers' hirees, for short
37 Ozone depleter, shortly
38 Long-lived
41 Shade of turquoise: 2 wds.
44 "All ___ Need Is You" (Sonny & Cher album): 2 wds.
45 Cleo of jazz
46 Belief system
47 Dwindle

Down

1 Scornful expression
2 First name in fashion
3 Afghan monetary units
4 Little creature who helps Santa
5 Reprimand to Fido: 2 wds.
6 Slender predatory insect
7 Wall-climbing plant
8 Reason to be turned away by a bouncer: 2 wds.
9 "Johnny Mnemonic" costar Meyer
10 Cry of frustration
14 Suffix with appoint or assign
18 ___ movements (military maneuvers)
19 Betray, in a way: 2 wds.
20 Genre of popular music, initially
21 Kiddie-song ending letters
22 Canadian province: abbr.
24 Refrain syllables
25 Southern constellation
26 Pop
30 Put on tape
31 Short-handled farming tool
33 Org. for Seahawks and Saints
34 Grander than grand
35 Does and bucks
36 Except for
38 Mixed bag
39 Bergman in "Casablanca"
40 "Groove Is in the Heart" singers ___-Lite
42 Hook shape
43 Place to get some drinks

8

Across

1 Put one foot in front of the other
5 The San Diego Chicken, e.g.
11 Spoken
12 Video game place
13 Homer Simpson's older daughter
14 Make less messy
15 Connect-the-____ (pencil and paper game)
16 Has the power to
17 Work with acid
19 Get-rich-quick scheme
23 Many different kinds of
26 Pie ____ mode: 2 wds.
27 Put up, as a building
28 Camera company
30 Fix, as an election
31 Material for a cyclist's clothing
33 Grocery store containers
35 Highfalutin'
36 Not her
38 Reverberating sound
41 Evaluate
44 Smear, like paint
45 Sewing kit item
46 "Do ____ others..."
47 Made fun of
48 Townshend or Sampras

Down

1 Auction cry
2 Threesome
3 Food eaten on a spring holiday: 2 wds.
4 Credit card material
5 Fu ____ (kind of mustache)
6 Section
7 Looks over
8 Meowing pet
9 Kind of poem
10 ____-down (this answer)
18 Simple beds
20 Food eaten on a winter holiday: 2 wds.
21 ____ vera (lotion ingredient)
22 8-down with no tail
23 Action word
24 Song for one, in an opera
25 Damage permanently
29 Wanted in on the poker hand: 2 wds.
32 Sped by, on the highway
34 Backyard structures
37 Small piece of land in the water
39 Jabba the ____ (villain in "Return of the Jedi")
40 Woodwind instrument
41 Tiny crawler
42 Catch a glimpse of
43 Hemingway book "The Old Man and the ____"

9

Across

1 "Chiquitita" quartet
5 Plead: 2 wds.
11 Woman's net cap, historically
12 One of two roughly equal parts
13 I.O.U.
14 White Rabbit's cry: 2 wds.
15 French crescent-shaped roll
17 Mushroom-cloud creator: abbr., 2 wds.
18 Pinafore letters?
21 Painkiller
23 "___ at the Table" (Solange album): 2 wds.
25 In, on a stamp: abbr.
26 "___ Little Tenderness": 2 wds.
27 Jacket part that is folded back
29 Coolidge's veep
30 ___ King, bearded giant or goblin of German myth
31 Bring out
33 Make English in character
37 German heavy tank of World War II: 2 wds.
39 Ending for teen or new
40 Problem-laden chores
41 World created by Jim Henson for "The Dark Crystal"
42 Quick court contest: 2 wds.
43 Platte River people

Down

1 Kind of adapter: hyph.
2 1935 loser to Braddock
3 Disease transmitted by rat fleas: 2 wds.
4 Height of an object from the ground
5 Out of whack
6 Bodies of organisms
7 Where clay cooks
8 Boxer who weighs no more than 126 pounds
9 Giants great Mel
10 Kvass ingredient
16 Place for a father-to-be: abbr.
19 Lee ___, Major League Baseball player (1959–71)
20 Railroad buildings, briefly
21 Shield border
22 Juicy, gritty-textured fruit
24 Detached, musically
28 Stowe character
29 Big cause of accidents on the highway, initially
32 Has beens, probably: hyph.
34 Capone's nemesis
35 Beetle Bailey boob
36 Important times
37 "___ Much" (Presley chart-topper of 1957)
38 Vacation spot

10

Across

1 Lack of war
6 Assistants
11 Edgar ___ Poe
12 Child's coughing
13 Coins often given away: 2 wds.
15 Professor's helpers: abbr.
16 West of Old Hollywood
17 Male doll
18 Inquire
19 State south of Mich.
20 Finale
21 Wetter than wet
23 Pro votes
24 Up to now: 2 wds.
26 "Hey, you!"
29 French port on the English Channel
33 Charged particle
34 Pet you may brush
35 Longtime NBC show
36 Gunk
37 Mono-
38 First word of countless book titles
39 Umpire's shout before "You're out!": 2 wds.
42 Not here
43 German WWI menace
44 Approving replies
45 Blog entries

Down

1 Tortellini, rigatoni, etc.
2 Texas city on the border with Mexico: 2 wds.
3 Anchorage's state
4 Jaguar or Jeep
5 Foes
6 Suffered from soreness
7 Tax shelter
8 Shrek's buddy
9 Oregon city, or a man's name
10 Throws around, as money
14 Christmas treat: 2 wds.
22 Kit ___ (candy bar)
23 Ocean that Portugal is on: abbr.
25 Accept flattery eagerly: 3 wds.
26 Where you'll hear oinks
27 Be calming
28 Sleeping sounds
30 Houston's baseball team
31 Ready to reproduce, like dogs: 2 wds.
32 Comes down hard from the sky
34 Green vegetables, casually
40 Wrath
41 "Entourage" channel

11

Across

1 Country karaoke came from
6 Astound
11 Cognizant
12 Sprite flavor
13 Brawl
14 Lend ___ (assist): 2 wds.
15 Respected lady
17 Hi-___ graphics
18 "I ___ you one"
20 Baggy
22 Toy company
24 Tiny particle
27 Chips in
28 Foreword, for short
29 Advertising sign gas
30 Negates
31 Begin
33 "Help!"
34 Butter amount
36 Old Oldsmobile
38 Broadcasting: 2 wds.
40 Dutch cheese
43 Back in style
44 Bucolic
45 Sixth-grader, maybe
46 Sailing: 2 wds.

Down

1 Improvise musically
2 Leave astonished
3 South Carolina's nickname: 2 wds.
4 Length times width, for a square
5 Pokes fun at
6 San Antone landmark
7 Just OK
8 Bar drinks: 2 wds.
9 Area
10 Ultimate goals
16 "You've got mail" co.
18 Arab League member
19 Decline
21 Beach grains
23 Camping gear
25 Cookie often eaten with milk
26 What a rolling stone doesn't gather
28 Acura model
30 Website address, for short
32 Hank with 755 home runs
34 After-dinner drink
35 Again
37 Beat badly
39 Anger
41 Actor Daniel ___ Kim
42 Miss. neighbor

12

Across

1 Poem set to music
5 "No problem": 2 wds.
10 "Hold it!"
11 Pollute
12 Indigenous Japanese people
13 Clasp lovingly in one's arms
14 Basis for comparison
16 Cicero, for one
17 ___ corpus (law)
19 Doctor's spoonful
23 That, in Spanish
24 Ferdinand, e.g.
25 Boxing location
27 Soapmaking compound
30 Pressing
32 Risk everything in an all-out effort: 3 wds.
36 Make quieter or less distinct
37 Bit of Kurdistan
38 Records
39 Ring: abbr.
40 Comes down in flakes
41 Sacred

Down

1 Smack, as at a fly
2 Buckeye State
3 Outside a town or city
4 Socially awkward
5 100, in Italy
6 Be able to spare
7 Midday
8 Hill of "The West Wing"
9 Long practiced
11 Conquers
15 "Hath ___ sister?" (Shakespeare's "Measure for Measure"): 2 wds.
17 Old what's-___-name
18 "Good ___ Been to You" (Dylan album): 2 wds.
20 Haydn's "The Creation," for one
21 Lay
22 Peeper
26 Loud and boisterous laugh
27 Brutish baddies
28 Isr. neighbor
29 Improve, in a way
31 Turns over and over
32 "Treasure Island" castaway Ben
33 "River ___ Return" movie starring Mitchum and Monroe: 2 wds.
34 Malone or Marx
35 Suffix with consist or depend
36 Family V.I.P.s

13

Across

1 Soak, old-style

4 Trophy

7 Producer: abbr.

10 Part of military addresses, initially

11 Queue after Q

12 Stellar altar

13 District under the care of a bishop

15 Deficiency

16 Misleading clues in a murder mystery: 2 wds.

18 But, to Brutus

19 Verne captain

20 High priest

23 Calif.-Fla. route: 2 wds.

24 Making someone feel ashamed and foolish

26 Turkish titles

27 Official decrees

28 Play the siren

29 Brit. fliers

30 Period for relaxation: 2 wds.

35 Mich. neighbor

36 Thin decorative layers of wood

37 "Epitaph ___ Dog" (Byron poem): 2 wds.

38 Writer LeShan

39 Say it's so when you know it's not

40 Place to get off: abbr.

41 Jewish org. founded in 1913

42 Welfare org.

Down

1 Baghdad's ___ City

2 Bee Taylor's grandnephew

3 Charitable person: 2 wds.

4 Relating to articles of religious belief

5 The Beatles' "Back in the ___"

6 Wing: prefix

7 Region around a moving electric charge: 2 wds.

8 Broken piece

9 Aminé's output: 2 wds.

14 Shifts

17 Launch

20 Small bulbs used for pickling

21 French Protestant of the 16th–17th centuries

22 Never, in Germany

25 Kind of gland

31 Iris's place

32 Funnyman Foxx

33 Certain hosp. scans

34 Spanish men, colloquially

14

Across

1. The Spartans, for short
4. Queen ___ (Madonna title): 2 wds.
9. Poetic time of day
10. Of a certain planet
13. Thin piece of wood used to light a fire: 2 wds.
15. Former Los Angeles KISS coach Smith
16. Makes a map of
17. Extent-wise: 2 wds.
19. Karel Capek robot play: inits.
21. Making a mistake
25. Shoe with rollers fixed to the sole: hyph., 2 wds.
28. Gland in the neck
29. Measure of conductance
30. Kind of house
33. Moves, in real estate jargon
36. Signs on for another term: hyph.
39. Without a sound
41. Obliterate
42. A, in Austria
43. Safe havens
44. Bishop's jurisdiction

Down

1. Middle: prefix
2. Ore deposit
3. In a biased way
4. Portuguese "other"
5. Sizzle in the heat
6. Babies
7. For the heck of it: 3 wds.
8. Edible pocket
11. Take effect
12. Brit. medical org.
14. Ending for north or northwest
18. Candy manufacturer Harry
19. Slowing, in mus.
20. Granite State sch.
22. Metrical feet: var.
23. Math degree
24. Prefix with thermal
26. Duties
27. Plant place
31. Norse goddess of love
32. 1950s political inits.
33. Wrestling match div.
34. Help wanted ad letters
35. Actress Bonet
37. Knee bend for Nijinsky
38. "Auld Lang ___"
40. Chat room chuckle

15

Across

1 Breakfast food

4 Small amount

7 Neither fish ___ fowl

8 Singer Grant or novelist Tan

9 Grocery store holder

12 Make neat: 2 wds.

14 Ending for Japan or Surinam

15 Way, way off

16 U-Haul rival

18 Allots, with "out"

20 Soul great Redding

21 Not post-

22 Baseball announcer's phrase when a home run is hit: 2 wds.

25 Hole in your car

27 Fun on a lake: 2 wds.

29 Santa ___, Calif.

32 Advil target

33 More competent

35 Arsenic, e.g.

38 Border

39 Little pest

40 Nature's "opponent"

42 Discouraging words

43 Hawaiian instrument, for short

44 Ruin

45 Prepared

46 Untrustworthy

Down

1 Set up tents, e.g.

2 Jack Nicklaus or Tiger Woods

3 Top tunes for a band: 2 wds.

4 Blackout

5 "It's my turn!": 2 wds.

6 Sort

9 Where 3-down often appear: 3 wds.

10 Invite to the house: 2 wds.

11 "Silly" birds

13 "___ we having fun yet?"

17 Canceled: 2 wds.

19 Make, as a putt

23 The first "T" of TNT

24 Sammy of baseball fame

26 Functions

27 Tokyo's country

28 ___ Lodge (motel chain)

30 Nerve-related

31 Blood route

34 Baseball equipment

36 Burden

37 Put in the microwave

41 Not working any longer: abbr.

16

Across

1 Emergency strategy: 2 wds.
6 Center of emotions
11 Cabinet department
12 Prefix for trendy or light
13 What fans do
14 Attach with string: 2 wds.
15 Guitarist Nugent
16 Sir John Gielgud, notably
18 Poem for the praiseworthy
19 Backgammon cube
20 Espectador's reaction
23 Show-offs
25 Brownish pigment
28 Stereotypical dog names
29 "Ooh la la!": 2 wds.
31 Desire to have Japanese money?
32 Cooped-up female
33 Grow weaker
36 Composer Edvard
38 Dessert
39 Westwood mascot
41 Sra. Perón
43 "Princess Mononoke" genre
44 Reduced to granules
45 Prides of lions
46 Like minxes

Down

1 "Republic" author
2 Packed the freight
3 Living quarters
4 Negative connector
5 Some people get a rise out of them: 2 wds.
6 Clumsy person
7 Gallimaufry
8 Olympic Games taboo
9 Spanish riches
10 "Holy smokes!"
17 It has moles: abbr.
21 Summer beast
22 It can turn one into many
23 Lucy, to Linus
24 Muscular twitch
25 Where pigs play
26 Poetic word for "before"
27 Bird in a "tuxedo"
30 Silly laugh sound
33 Heroic narratives
34 Stings like a bee
35 Small, round and glistening
37 Coleridge poem
39 A mah-jongg tile
40 Part of the gene pool
42 Rome's Appia or Veneto

17

Across

1 Not macho at all
6 Sailing on the ocean: 2 wds.
11 Italian for "love"
12 P.F. ___'s
13 Taboo acts
14 Dull photography finish
15 Finishes up
16 Go back
17 Day: Sp.
18 "For ___ a jolly good fellow..."
19 Traffic light color
20 Hits the keyboard
22 Conception
23 Tennis great Navratilova
25 "Glee" or "Mad Men"
27 Persuades
29 Cadillac or Porsche
30 Cattle call?
31 Quick sip, as of brandy
33 Indicate that you know the answer, on a game show: 2 wds.
35 One of Columbus's ships
36 Creature from outer space
37 Pup
38 Tube-shaped pasta
39 Without color
40 Defeats by a little
41 London measurement, a bit more than a yard

Down

1 Lessened
2 "The problem is being taken care of!": 3 wds.
3 Worst time of the week, in a 1966 Mamas & Papas #1 hit: 2 wds.
4 Experts
5 "What can I do for you?"
6 High points
7 "How is ___ my problem?"
8 Best time of the week, in a 1976 Bay City Rollers #1 hit: 2 wds.
9 Main course
10 Items to be discussed at a meeting
16 Uses for support: 2 wds.
18 Billy Joel's "Tell ___ About It"
21 Cat's foot
22 One ___ million chance: 2 wds.
24 ___ Jima (WWII battle site)
25 Use a spatula, sometimes
26 Flagged down, as a taxi
28 Madonna or Lady Gaga
30 Gold and silver sources
32 Last name that sounds hurtful
34 Trait carrier
35 Sniffer
37 River blocker

18

Across

1 Clever people
5 Attraction
11 "That's funny!" sound
12 Play a simple instrument
13 Actor Sharif of "Funny Girl"
14 Sweet and soothing, ironically
15 Dutch spy of WWI: 2 wds.
17 Cole ___ (picnic side dish)
18 Is in possession of
22 Summer workers, often unpaid
25 Cool
26 ___ and aahed
27 Earth-shaking event
29 Patriotic letters
30 Said "1, 2, 3..."
32 Becomes solid, like concrete
34 Friends
35 Refreshing item given in spas: 2 wds.
39 Italian sausage
42 Tea you can order at Starbucks
43 Not what you'd think
44 Model Moss or actress Winslet
45 Is the father of, in the Bible
46 Baseball great Musial

Down

1 "To ___ it may concern..."
2 "___ Man of Constant Sorrow": 3 wds.
3 Words to wind things up: 2 wds.
4 Pastry brand: 2 wds.
5 When the sun comes up: 2 wds.
6 Come down hard
7 FDR's affliction
8 And so forth
9 Kind of beer
10 Allow
16 First letter in "crosswords," e.g.: 2 wds.
19 The general situation: 2 wds.
20 "Swoosh" name
21 Went too fast
22 Notes for those in debt
23 It smells
24 Sit in a crouching position
28 Opens, as a door
31 Field of vision?
33 1953 Alan Ladd movie
36 Leave out
37 "I'm so hungry, I could ___ horse!": 2 wds.
38 Financial claim, as on a house
39 Bro or sis
40 "Just the Way You ___" (Bruno Mars song)
41 Fireplace piece

19

Across

1 Washington hockey team, casually

5 Medieval drinks

10 Find ___ for the common cold: 2 wds.

12 See eye to eye

13 Appetizer on Chinese menus: 2 wds.

15 "Rocky ___"

16 "Dig in!"

17 Small amount

18 Pioneering game console, for short

19 Four Monopoly properties: abbr.

20 Extreme anger

21 Nicaraguan leader Daniel

23 Computer brand...

24 ...and those who help people navigate them

26 French author Emile ___

29 "Very funny!": 3 wds.

33 Laundry detergent brand

34 Beer drinker's stomach

35 Mr. Flanders

36 Intent

37 Past tense of 16-across

38 Wander (about), looking for fun

39 Maine course?: 2 wds.

42 Time-tested tune

43 Binge

44 Drops of sadness

45 Earth neighbor

Down

1 Place to play poker

2 More sore

3 Not one to embrace the new

4 ___ Lanka (Asian island nation)

5 LeBlanc and Damon

6 Driving force

7 Language of the Koran

8 Wish

9 Irish ___ (breed of dog)

11 Come to the forefront

14 Skydiving need

22 Greek H

23 Tap one's cigar

25 Not fans at all

26 Ardent supporter

27 American League East bird

28 Four after 22-down

30 Kind of cat or sweater

31 Medicine man

32 Confuses

34 Microsoft's Bill

40 "Can I help you, ___?"

41 Car tire abbr.

20

Across

1. Arms and legs
6. "Beat it!"
11. Honda brand
12. Texas food
13. Have a temper tantrum, maybe: 2 wds.
15. Holed up
16. Prior to
17. Go-___ (1980s band)
18. "___ you serious?"
19. Faint
20. Anger
21. "Beetle Bailey" creator Walker
23. Hit with a baseball
25. Waken from slumber
27. Hidden
30. Janitor's tools
34. Valuable mineral
35. "Dig in!"
37. By way of
38. High card
39. ___ Lanka
40. Christmas present wrapper, maybe
41. XXXIII
44. Kind of dye
45. Doozies
46. ___ Allan Poe
47. Pharaoh's land

Down

1. English poet John
2. Suzuki of baseball
3. "___ on the Orient Express"
4. "My man!"
5. Did a lumberjack's job
6. Plans
7. Greek letter
8. Try to answer on "Jeopardy!": 2 wds.
9. Former vice president: 2 wds.
10. Didn't hit
14. Small river, often
22. Three: It.
24. Store convenience, for short
26. Lousy, like a movie
27. Hate
28. Tried to appear larger, as a cat
29. ___ up (preparing to drive a golf ball)
31. Too
32. Get larger, as a workload: 2 wds.
33. Least risky
36. Deed
42. Biology abbr.
43. Embrace

21

Across

1 Resort island off the coast of Italy

6 Ear cleaners: hyph.

11 Tim ___, "Santa Clause" actor

12 Of the city

13 Diamond alternative

14 Auto repair chain with two beeps in their ads, initially

15 They get angry quickly

17 Ending for Power or lemon

18 Unclear

22 They sacrifice for a cause

26 "Crouching Tiger, Hidden Dragon" director

27 Ginger drink

28 Alley ___

29 Greek H

30 Philosophically deep

31 Lemon, perhaps: 2 wds.

33 Former loves

35 In first place

36 Second thoughts before the event: 2 wds.

41 Force to fit: 2 wds.

44 Took care of: 2 wds.

45 In the air

46 Indian, for one

47 Music source

48 Sparrow houses

Down

1 Cold, hard money

2 Dog food brand

3 ___ du jour (dish of the day)

4 Software company named for a colorful piece of clothing: 2 wds.

5 Beatles song off "Help!": 3 wds.

6 College area surrounded by buildings

7 Rubbish

8 "Think" company

9 Ms. ___-Man

10 ___-Caps (candy brand)

16 Spray can

19 Mr. Guinness

20 Catherine ___-Jones

21 One trip around the sun

22 Puzzle with a "start"

23 "Jeopardy!" name

24 Russo of "Get Shorty"

25 Puts money into: 2 wds.

32 Spoil

34 Movie genre with aliens: hyph.

37 Not tricked by

38 Some sheep

39 Coup d'___

40 Oodles

41 Shock

42 In the style of: 2 wds.

43 "The ___ Squad"

22

Across

1 Restaurant requests

7 ___ spumante (Italian sparkling wine)

11 Not wide

12 Pig that's wild

13 Emphasize the similarities between

14 1970s group that sang "Waterloo"

15 Closest star to us

16 Poem often about a person

18 Peyton Manning's brother/rival

19 "Mice!!!"

20 Puts on a pedestal

22 Oyster's cousin

24 Undo

25 Girl of the house

27 Rejecting replies

28 "Alright with you?": 2 wds.

31 Backtalk

34 Fruit used to make tea and jelly: 2 wds.

36 One of the Brady kids

37 Just fine and dandy

38 Yoko born in Tokyo

39 Coll. founded by Thomas Jefferson

40 "___ and away!": 2 wds.

42 Tarantula, e.g.

44 Fix, like fences or clothes

45 Checkers demand: 2 wds.

46 Big boats

47 Poverty stricken: 2 wds.

Down

1 "Hold on": 2 wds.

2 Sex symbol Welch

3 Completely wasted: 4 wds.

4 Dishwasher detergent brand

5 Moving part of an engine

6 Neighbor of Norway

7 Lawyers' org.

8 Not wasted at all: 4 wds.

9 Small computer, like an iPad

10 Poker announcement: 2 wds.

17 All square

21 They might clash

23 Tiny bit

26 Trendy area of London

28 Major shock to the system

29 1978 Burt Reynolds comedy

30 Nastassja of "Tess"

32 "Help!": 2 wds.

33 Caught in a trap

35 Visit briefly and without warning: 2 wds.

41 There are three in a hockey game: abbr.

43 Roadside stopover

23

Across

1 In shape
4 "Yecch!"
7 Typing class statistic: abbr.
10 Poetic tribute
11 Experienced
12 Laugh syllable
13 Trophy wives, perhaps: 2 wds.
16 Aerial maneuver
17 Island rings
18 Furnace output
20 Add up
21 Unfavorably
22 Letter-shaped brace: hyph.
24 Classic Christmas song: 2 wds.
29 Listening devices
30 Word of support
31 True
34 Erupt
35 Actor Lugosi
36 Watch face
38 Military decorations for valor: 2 wds.
42 Android alternative for smartphones
43 Pledge of Allegiance ender
44 Unduly
45 Ogle
46 ___-eyed
47 Sum (up)

Down

1 Befuddle
2 Nuptial confirmation: 2 wds.
3 Revelatory: hyph.
4 Beehive, e.g.
5 Handshake
6 Monopolize
7 Cart part
8 Menace
9 Unpleasant
14 URL part
15 Driving hazard
18 ___ Master's Voice
19 Bulldog
20 Keep ___ on (watch)
22 Like Jack Sprat's diet
23 "Can we move this inside?"
25 Many a tofu eater
26 Capital of Buenos Aires Province: 2 wds.
27 Strong cleaner
28 Clinch, with "up"
31 "Steal This Book" writer Hoffman
32 Conductor Anderson
33 "You beat me": 2 wds.
34 Cal. col.
36 Sandwich shop
37 "Cast Away" setting
39 Microwave
40 Bacillus shape
41 Turf

24

Across

1 ___ pole (Native American icon)
6 Tries for a field goal
11 Humorous ending meaning "big amount of"
12 "I'm on ___" ("Saturday Night Live" song): 2 wds.
13 Offer a counterargument
14 Prefix with surgery or transmitter
15 "The Sopranos" role, or part of RSVP
16 Give it a whirl
18 Company boss, briefly
19 "___ to a Nightingale"
20 Weeding tool
21 Like cool cats, in 1960s-speak
22 Completely clueless: 2 wds.
24 Cash dispensers, initially
25 What does it cost?: 2 wds.
27 X-ray ___ (novelty eyeglasses)
29 Decided
31 Hawaiian necklace made of flowers
32 Painter's deg.
33 Danger in Iraq, for short (hidden in PIEDMONT)
35 Tax-collecting org.
36 Towards the back, on a ship
37 ___ Lanka (country off the coast of India)
38 Songs and such
40 Amber source
42 Charging too much interest
43 Give off, as confidence
44 Sneaks a look
45 Olympic swords

Down

1 Trunk of the body
2 Tater tots brand
3 Put off a decision for a while: 3 wds.
4 Meat source in Australia
5 One of the four Gospels
6 Rapper ___ West
7 "May ___ excused?": 2 wds.
8 Frame a decision in a certain way: 3 wds.
9 ___ Abdul-Jabbar (basketball legend)
10 Bends down
17 Wander away: 2 wds.
23 Chicago White ___
24 Pretend
26 Trapped, like kitty: 3 wds.
27 Get thinner: 2 wds.
28 Read through casually
30 Make fun of
32 Famous New York City department store
34 Eats out at a restaurant
39 Aggravate
41 Previous work: abbr.

25

Across

1 Paid athletes
5 Confession phrase: 3 wds.
11 The moon, in poetry
12 Secondhand transaction
13 "Family Ties" role: 3 wds.
15 Perfect score, often
16 Blue jeans hole
17 Actress Gardner of "Mogambo"
18 Make a 14-down
20 Affable Mr. Affleck
21 Hi-Q pieces
23 Quite drunk
24 Varieties
27 Helps in a criminal act
29 Santa ___ Winds (California weather phenomenon)
30 "Slaves of New York" author Janowitz
32 Fond du ___, Wisconsin
33 Revved up, as a motorcycle
37 Wonderment
38 Before, to bards
39 Valuable mineral deposit
40 Actor who played 13-across: 3 wds.
43 Texas hold 'em pronouncement: 2 wds.
44 Madam
45 Starts a tennis point
46 Small bills

Down

1 Greek philosopher who wrote "The Republic"
2 12-inch stick
3 Standing upright: 2 wds.
4 John Coltrane's musical instrument: abbr.
5 Irritating
6 Adele's "Rolling in the ___"
7 "There ___ way out": 2 wds.
8 OK to see romantically
9 "That was excellent!": 3 wds.
10 Lease signers
14 Catholic cleric
19 Fitting
22 Clemens or L. Jackson
24 Italian sausages
25 Where a bird may perch: 3 wds.
26 Palindromic vehicle: 2 wds.
28 Total embargo
31 Sees it the same way
34 ___ of (disliking): 2 wds.
35 Eat away
36 ___ Midnight Runners ("Come on, Eileen" band)
38 Facility
41 AIDS cause
42 She used to go out with 20-across, familiarly

26

Across

1 Under sedation
6 One way to stop: 3 wds.
9 Sample
12 Larch
13 Norris Dam's project, initially
14 Middle of Q.E.D.
15 Cosmetics company
17 Prefix with physical
19 Admits, with "up"
20 Muffle
22 Soda brand
23 Biblical suffix
24 Performance
26 Kind of skin
27 "The Godfather" actor James
29 Viral skin disease
31 PR people: abbr.
32 "The Wire" character Little
33 Micromanager's concern
35 "The Texas Troubador"
38 "___ tu" (Verdi aria)
39 Find money from (somewhere): 2 wds.
41 "Understand?"
42 Fried quickly in a little fat
43 Intermediate, at law

Down

1 Las ___ (12:00, in Spain)
2 "___ off?": 2 wds.
3 1940 Cole Porter musical: 2 wds.
4 Revised (text)
5 Subtraction amt.
7 Deep gloom
8 Canyon or haban suffix
9 Fruity breakfast option: 2 wds.
10 Historical novel by Sir Walter Scott
11 Affects with paralysis
16 Howard or Paul
18 Chamomile or Earl Grey
20 Periods of ten years
21 Bric-a-brac holder
25 Pro ___ (for now)
28 Hush-hush D.C. org.
30 Cassowary or moa, e.g.
34 Bouncers ask for them
36 Bingo call: 2 wds.
37 Foreshadow
40 Chewing ___

27

Across

1 Chichen Itza builders
6 Long, long time
10 Mexican brick
11 ___ Plus (shampoo brand)
12 Baseball feat: 2 wds.
14 Otherwise
15 Art class material
18 Store with a bull's-eye logo
23 Backstabber
24 Dentist's direction
25 "I had no ___!"
27 Forest growth
28 Gross dinner sound
30 Shook hands with
31 ___ tank
33 Alluring
34 Lady ___ (pop star)
36 Track and field sport: 2 wds.
42 "Take this!"
43 Newswoman Shriver
44 All tied up
45 Expertise

Down

1 "Spy vs. Spy" magazine
2 Fuss
3 "What did ___ say?"
4 "___ Road" (Beatles album)
5 Unload, as stock
6 Enter the picture
7 Come together
8 Historian's period
9 Oinker's place
13 Guess: abbr.
15 Magician ___ Angel
16 Soup server
17 Consumed quickly: 2 wds.
19 Hoop
20 Garden statue, sometime
21 County of England
22 Cantankerous
26 Paintings, photography, etc.
29 See 9-down
32 "Silent" prez
33 Pat of "Wheel of Fortune"
35 Nice rocks
36 Word in many movie titles
37 Show off, on a Harley
38 Wrath
39 Spoon-bender Geller
40 Dot follower, in some e-mail addresses
41 Amigo

28

Across

1 Talent
6 Italian fashion city
11 Bellybutton type
12 Not just fat
13 Direction this clue's answer reads: 3 wds.
15 Losing come-out roll in craps
16 Fasten
17 Kosher ___
18 The Battle of ___ Jima
21 Notre Dame niche
24 Fasten with a pop: 2 wds.
26 Shade of purple
28 Knot
29 Met productions
31 Small whirlpool
32 Poet laureat Hughes
33 Team's burden
35 "Cut it out!"
36 Chicken ___ king: 2 wds.
39 Direction this puzzle's answer reads: 3 wds.
43 Enjoy
44 Words of certainty: 2 wds.
45 Warms up
46 Checked things

Down

1 River deposit
2 Sensed
3 Scoop
4 On, as a lamp
5 Don't bother: 2 wds.
6 Start of the day
7 Bibliographical abbr.
8 Race unit
9 Shade of blond
10 Fishing equipment
14 Perfume ingredients
17 Sweet
18 Apple introduction of 2010
19 Promise
20 Sole
21 Gobs: 2 wds.
22 Snowman prop
23 Runner's place
25 Over again
27 Ransom seekers
30 Coin opening
34 Sight-related
35 Unappetizing food
36 Lago contents
37 "Schindler's ___"
38 Sciences' partner
39 Sugar amt.
40 Wide's partner
41 Race starter?
42 Med. plan

29

Across

1 ___ talk (encouraging words)
4 The Colonel's restaurant
7 Software program, briefly
10 Mine stuff
11 Rounded shape
13 She won the U.S. Open in 1979 and 1981: 2 wds.
15 Common flower
16 Possesses, in the Bible
19 Quickly
23 Role for Paul
24 Try it out: 3 wds.
27 "Bloom County" character: 2 wds.
29 Metal named for an animal: 2 wds.
30 Compete
31 Gets a look at
32 Cravings
33 "Who's there?" reply: 2 wds.
37 1980s show about a detective from Texas: 2 wds.
43 Pencil parts
44 Amaze
45 Fly catcher
46 Came into contact with
47 Drops in the morning meadow

Down

1 Daisy holder
2 Go wrong
3 Little green vegetable
4 Lock openers
5 Apartment
6 Game with Colonel Mustard
7 Appropriate
8 Greek consonant
9 Writing instrument
12 Tel Aviv's nation
14 Meowing pet
16 Lock parts
17 Bandleader Shaw
18 Military tactic
20 Medical application
21 "Encore!"
22 Mugs for the camera
24 Not his
25 "Without further ___..."
26 Delivery vehicle
28 Drops in on
32 "Absolutely!"
34 Not us
35 Achy
36 Has to
37 Kitty's sound
38 "You ___ so right!"
39 Bill at a bar
40 Tiny amount
41 Have to repay
42 "What's ___?"

30

Across

1 Treasury
6 Way up
11 Flexible
12 "You there?"
13 Singer John
14 Trojan War story
15 Imperfection
16 Actress Bonham Carter
17 Manifest
19 Hold opposing views
22 M.P.'s quarry
26 Elite: hyph.
27 Lawnmower part
28 "Sacre ___!"
29 Made to resemble nappy leather
30 Quilt part
32 Visit briefly: 2 wds.
35 Unaffectedness
39 "Goody!": 2 wds.
40 Former French First Lady ___ Bruni-Sarkozy
41 Retreats
42 Dismal
43 Fare reductions
44 Doesn't dash off

Down

1 Musical sign
2 Sledder's spot
3 Singer James
4 Donation, perhaps: 3 wds.
5 Mark of perfection
6 More likely to retire
7 Poe classic, with "The": 2 wds.
8 Medicine Nobelist Metchnikoff
9 Think ahead
10 Fizzy drink
16 Feminine pronoun
18 Dog doc
19 Smidgen
20 Hurting
21 Cry of disgust
23 Roll of bills
24 Wordsworth work
25 Fronted
27 Tampa Bay N.F.L.er
29 It's a mess
31 Depths
32 Gone
33 Asian cuisine choice
34 New York theater award
36 Locale
37 Destroy
38 Canal sites
40 Record store purchases

31

Across

1 Producer of "Cordon Rouge" champagne
5 "Morning's at Seven" playwright Paul
11 Forest ox
12 Cop
13 Ltr. directive
14 Croaky
15 Section of a car that is usually tinted
17 Bahaism, for one: abbr.
18 "Professor" ___ Corey, "World's Foremost Authority"
22 How some songs are sold: 2 wds.
24 Some Indian breads
25 Baltic or Aegean
26 Jeanne d'Arc, for one: abbr.
27 Hindu ascetic
30 Body of good conduct
32 Bread spreads
33 Ring org.
34 Inhabitant of the coast
38 One of the Brothers Karamazov
41 Former "Saturday Night Live" player Dunn
42 Possible response to "what happened to the last cookie?": 3 wds.
43 Largest Mariana Island
44 Rates of return
45 Late singer ___ James

Down

1 Palindromic title for a woman
2 "Once more ___ the breach…" ("Henry V" line)
3 Parade of cars
4 Having a crew
5 Roman emperor defeated by Vitellius
6 Person certain to succeed: hyph.
7 Nigerian civil war site, 1967–70
8 It precedes "the land of the free"
9 Campers, briefly
10 Born in France
16 "Treasure Island" author's initials
19 Pale and tired: 2 wds.
20 100 céntimos in Peru, once
21 Tiny fraction of a min.: 2 wds.
22 ___ buco
23 "The Subject Was Roses" star Patricia
28 Lodge
29 Cyber-handle: 2 wds.
30 "Gross!" sounds
31 Emotional pang
35 Isles
36 "In principio ___ Verbum" (biblical phrase)
37 Hindu deity
38 Handyman's letters
39 ___ tai (rum cocktail)
40 Resident's suffix

32

Across

1 Drink from a dish
4 Ruffle
7 Cow chow
10 C.S.A. state
11 Grayish brown
12 Uvea locale
13 Fish tales: 2 wds.
16 Jane Austen novel
17 Draft
18 Martini's partner in vermouth
20 Resistance units
23 Modern music holder
26 Sob syllable
27 Old Gothic soap: 2 wds.
31 Don't waste
32 Present opener?
33 Where Lima is
35 Wipe out, in surfing lingo: 2 wds.
39 Secluded valley
42 Companion of gramps
43 Big pile of cash: 2 wds.
46 Poetic paean
47 Samsung Galaxy, e.g.: abbr.
48 ___ Jong-un
49 Pan, e.g.
50 Surfing site
51 What a mess!

Down

1 Procrastinator's word
2 "Remember the ___"
3 Conceals sneakily
4 Fingers
5 Tracks
6 Comprehend
7 Cry of joy or boredom: hyph.
8 Word of support
9 Word of support
14 Corrective eye surgery
15 Guanabara Bay city
19 "___ facto"
21 Cut a swath
22 Letters of distress
24 Law man?
25 Tycho Brahe, for one
27 Twosome
28 Cigarette's end
29 Occupied the throne
30 Actress Keaton
34 Dated
36 Duties
37 Indigenous Canadian
38 "Stand by Your Man" singer Wynette
40 Sports cable channel
41 Orbital point
43 Monopolize
44 Excitement
45 Welcome ___

33

Across

1 Deep valley
6 Tennis star Rafael ___
11 Rent-a-truck company
12 Last name on the TV show "Dallas"
13 Make petty comments
14 Slacks
15 Beijing for 2008 and London for the 2012 Olympics, e.g.: 2 wds.
17 Visit a restaurant: 2 wds.
18 Do some math
20 Odd
24 People, places or things
27 Mrs. Archie Bunker
28 Train stations
30 North Carolina city: abbr.
31 It steeps in hot water: 2 wds.
34 Archaeologists often rediscover them, like Chichen Itza or Mohenjo Daro: 2 wds.
38 Boyfriends
39 Karan of DKNY
40 Nostalgia-evoking
41 One side in the Civil War
42 Pale-looking
43 "___ porridge hot..."

Down

1 Spew, like an oil well
2 "I shouldn't have done that!": 2 wds.
3 Lifted: 2 wds.
4 "Paging Dr. ___" (CNN show)
5 Put into office
6 Uranus neighbor
7 Looked forward to
8 Have a sumptuous meal
9 Insects that form colonies
10 T-shirt sizes: abbr.
16 Three vowels that mean "you'll get your money"
18 Additionally
19 Buck's mate
21 Staunton's state
22 Greek letter
23 The Los Angeles Kings, the Edmonton Oilers, etc.
25 Unwilling to bet on it: 2 wds.
26 Cowboy's hat
29 ___ fly (baseball play)
32 Cause to get higher, as a price at auction: 2 wds.
33 Make up (for)
34 Spike and Ang
35 Promising words
36 First son of Seth, in Genesis
37 Not nuts
38 Victoria's Secret product

34

Across

1 Like many a cellar
5 Syrian president
10 Israel's Golda
11 Affluent area in a city
12 Duncan appointed to the Obama cabinet
13 Having a stout body
14 "Lethal Weapon" star: 2 wds.
16 Unique
17 Attention-getters
21 Sounds some approval from a distance: 2 wds.
23 Printer's ink color
24 Convulsive movement
25 "À votre ___!"
26 Husband's partner
27 Incursion
28 Takes in
29 Word of honor
30 Certain court order
34 Jawaharlal's daughter
37 Suffix for abnormalities
38 ___ Brezhnev, former president of the USSR
39 Evening, in ads
40 Respiratory organs
41 Retired fleet, initially

Down

1 Key of Mozart's Violin Concerto No. 4: abbr., 2 wds.
2 Prefix with space
3 Vertical tunnel
4 Attractive, appealing
5 Bk. of Revelation

6 "Gasoline Alley" and "Blondie", e.g.: 2 wds.
7 Tippler
8 Hole maker
9 Letters after Charles Schumer's name
11 Thrown into a state of disarray
15 Broncos kicker Jason
18 Amalgamation, fusion
19 "Play Time" star Jacques
20 Snick's partner
21 "___ forgive those who…": 2 wds.
22 Western Samoa's capital
25 It's sold in bars
27 "Yer ___" (Tom Petty song): 2 wds.
31 "Battle Cry" author
32 What remains after deductions, British style
33 Enzymes' suffixes
34 Hostile
35 Original, in Osnabrück
36 Slip into

35

Across

1 Bug-eyed
5 Letter-shaped vise: hyph.
11 Way out
12 Concert tour employee
13 Resting place
14 Smoke out
15 Support provider
17 1982 Disney film
18 Good-luck symbol
22 Yellowfin tuna
23 Kind of breath
24 Alpine call
26 Remains
30 Beloved
32 Ring master?
33 Carriage driver's accessory: 2 wds.
35 Vast
37 "And I Love ___"
38 "___ Butterfly" (Puccini opera)
40 Rapscallions
44 The way things currently stand: 3 wds.
45 Poet Teasdale
46 Have the subsequent turn: 2 wds.
47 Hurry

Down

1 Commercials
2 Gloppy stuff
3 Gut reaction?
4 Gets the attention of
5 Fold
6 "Friends" actress Courteney
7 Portable PCs
8 Be nuts about
9 Soybean paste
10 Hammer part
16 Civil War guerrilla
18 Stable diet?
19 Cry of surprise
20 Free
21 Court announcement: 2 wds.
25 School
27 "A likely story!"
28 Wallach of "The Magnificent Seven"
29 Small intake
31 Shocked
33 Buy goods at one's own auction: 2 wds.
34 Slap target, sometimes
35 Online 'zine
36 ___ doble (Spanish dance)
39 Combine
41 Uglify
42 Old hand
43 Was idle

36

Across

1 Medieval weapon, or modern spray weapon
5 Different
10 Milky gemstones
12 "Hand over the money!": 2 wds.
13 "Be quiet!": 2 wds.
14 Kick out
15 Concealed
16 Sought office
18 Period of time
19 "Nevertheless..."
21 Will Smith musical genre
22 Moan and groan
24 Pacino and Capone
25 ___ cards (spooky deck)
27 First five of 26
29 Chicken ___ king: 2 wds.
30 Walk proudly
32 Little doggy
33 Part of a baseball game
36 Mischief maker
37 Big primate
38 "C'est la ___!"
39 Shaquille or Tatum
41 Piece of pizza
43 Some teachers grade on one
44 Lugs (around)
45 Obnoxious people
46 Funeral fire

Down

1 Kind of coffee
2 Be ___ in the neck: 2 wds.
3 You see a lot of them on November 1st: 2 wds.
4 Quarterback Manning
5 Ready for business
6 Money for the government
7 Behavior some kids may exhibit on November 1st
8 The ___ City (capital of the Land of Oz)
9 Fall back, as into a bad pattern of behavior
11 Narrow waterways
17 "The Fountainhead" novelist Rand
20 "Which person?"
23 Honest and sincere
25 Kind of pudding
26 Male graduate
28 Part of a hamburger
31 Waiter's money
34 More pleasant
35 Silly birds
37 Ginger ___ (some soft drinks)
40 Wide road: abbr.
42 Cut (off)

37

Across

1 "Seinfeld" uncle
4 Marvelous, like the Beatles
7 Tombstone letters
10 Christmas creature
11 Anger
12 "First..."
13 ___ sprouts
15 Attorney's field
16 Last name that sounds hurtful
17 Vulcan mind tricks
19 Mel who hit 511 home runs
20 "... happily ___ after"
21 "Hop on Pop" author
23 Had the nerve
25 Score for Tiger Woods
26 Rolls-Royce or Maserati
27 Cupid's projectile
30 Spacious
32 John Paul II, e.g.
33 Historical time
34 Jasmine and basmati
35 Fancy pool shot
38 "A rat!"
39 Overly formal
41 Highest heart
42 Control
43 ___ foo yung
44 The P in MPG
45 "Yes" indication
46 Funny Romano

Down

1 Ballet move
2 "___ Enchanted"
3 Nuts: 3 wds.
4 Choice cuts
5 Kennel sound
6 Broadcast
7 Amusement park fun: 2 wds.
8 Imagined: 3 wds.
9 Seats with kneelers
14 Aardvark food
18 Actress ___ Marie Saint
21 Health resort
22 Secret Service agent's wear
24 Arid
28 "Well done!"
29 Vegetable oil brand
30 Tell again
31 Face-to-face exam
34 Do farm work
36 Big name in computer games
37 Hip
40 One roll of the dice

38

Across

1 Taradiddle
4 Trendy
7 Steve Carell's "Despicable Me" character
10 Kind of trip
11 Farm mother
12 Alley ___
13 Prepare to use a rifle: 3 wds.
16 Property
17 Big do
18 "___ life!"
21 Tire filler
24 Peanut butter cup brand
28 National system of buying and selling securities: 2 wds.
31 Fancy party
32 Tina Turner's ex
33 Land of a billion
36 Lip
39 Had a shot?
43 Laugh riot: 3 wds.
46 Ring king
47 "Oysters ___ season": 2 wds.
48 Hoopla
49 In addition
50 To the point
51 Roman title

Down

1 Experienced
2 Dr. Frankenstein's assistant
3 ___ Grande, Fla.
4 Moor
5 Hold
6 Newscaster Koppel
7 Bobble
8 Surf sound
9 Beehive, e.g.
14 Word with mess or press
15 Surgery tool
19 Holding one's piece?
20 Kind of service
21 Fool
22 "How was ___ know?": 2 wds.
23 Louis XIV, e.g.
25 Word with bum or bunny
26 "A rat!"
27 ___-Foy, Que.
29 Town ___ (early newsman)
30 Writer Kesey
34 Runaway bride's response?: 2 wds.
35 Kennel sound
36 On-line auction venue
37 Depression
38 Sand
40 Winston Churchill's "___ Country": 2 wds.
41 In the raw
42 Fort ___ (gold site)
44 Victorian, for one
45 Sass

39

Across

1 Does one's fly
5 Canada's capital
11 Actor McGregor
12 Van Gogh painting of flowers
13 Former "Saturday Night Live" player Dunn
14 Nooks
15 Candy bar in a red wrapper: 2 wds.
17 iPhone company
19 Little bits
22 Mexican restaurant condiment
23 F. ___ Fitzgerald
25 Glass of NPR
26 "That's relaxing!"
27 Tree found in people's houses
30 North Dakota city that's also a movie
32 Video game brand name
33 Tell the waiter what you want
34 President Jackson
36 Items for a meeting
39 California valley known for its wine
42 On ___ knee (proposing marriage, perhaps)
43 Baldwin of "30 Rock"
44 Earns after expenses
45 Campfire entertainment

Down

1 Buddhist sect
2 "Sands of ___ Jima"
3 Expensive property in Monopoly: 2 wds.
4 Gourmet's dish
5 Pig's sound
6 Groups of three
7 Breath mint brand
8 Cigar detritus
9 Tiny
10 Rude person
16 Darjeeling or oolong
17 "Yeah, I'm so sure!": 2 wds.
18 The Eiffel Tower's city
20 Most expensive property in Monopoly
21 Part of a theater
24 Norse god played by Chris Hemsworth in a 2011 movie
28 African nation once run by Idi Amin
29 Machine that makes wood smooth
30 In favor of
31 Stadiums
35 Pops
36 "Dancing with the Stars" network
37 Alternative to shaving cream
38 Compass dir.
40 Architect I.M. ___
41 Pretend

40

Across

1 "Fat" farm
4 Inaccurate
7 Dash
8 "2001" computer
9 Actor Holm
12 Series entry
14 Couple
15 Fencing sword
16 Bugs: 2 wds.
18 Coffee that won't keep you up
20 "Present and accounted for"
21 Word after iron or lead
22 Progress, metaphorically
25 Captain ___ (person who proudly states something everyone already knows)
27 Where the shortstop and second baseman play
29 Be a chatterbox
32 ___ tape (powerful adhesive)
33 "We ___ Overcome"
35 Uses one end of a pencil
38 Actress Fisher of "Wedding Crashers"
39 Pose a question
40 Track and field event that uses a heavy ball: 2 wds.
42 General whose father was a general
43 Palindromic music genre
44 Great anger
45 Badminton barrier
46 Suffix with employ or induct

Down

1 Bathing suit brand
2 Salt's pal
3 "So simple!": 4 wds.
4 "I gotcha"
5 Grow dim
6 ___ market
9 "So simple!": 4 wds.
10 Emmy or Tony
11 Jottings
13 Baltic or Aegean
17 Old-school word for "you"
19 Number of fingers
23 Zero, in soccer scores
24 Fishing store selection
26 Tiny pieces
27 Perfect
28 Drink slowly, as a beer
30 Attraction
31 Kitchen cupboard items
34 Popular song
36 Cable channel that sometimes shows bowling
37 Sock cover
41 Decide

41

Across

1 Aria, e.g.
5 Was just kidding around
11 "___ Brockovich"
12 Strike caller
13 Fishing equipment
14 Put in order
15 "The lady ___ protest too much"
16 Finale
17 Kinks hit
19 Site for bidders
23 Look through a peephole: 2 wds.
26 Beer variety
27 Fencing swords
28 Fit for a queen
30 Second-century date
31 Make a misstep
33 Old Chrysler
35 "Can ___ serious for a moment?": 2 wds.
36 "It's no ___!"
38 Song and dance, e.g.
41 "Goodness!": 2 wds.
44 Increase, with "up"
45 Two dots over a vowel, in German
46 Former NYC stadium
47 Courtroom plea
48 Thanksgiving dish

Down

1 E-mail, e.g.
2 Cookie often twisted
3 "The Loco-Motion" singer: 2 wds.
4 Off the cruise ship for a while: 2 wds.
5 Alaska's capital
6 Sign of the future
7 Not a heart, club or diamond
8 Bestseller
9 Before
10 Room where work gets done
18 Red ink amount
20 Nickname for a W.W. I weapon: 2 wds.
21 "Come on, be ___!": 2 wds.
22 Ivy League school
23 Eat like a bird
24 Long saga
25 Not false
29 Government outpost
32 Cartoon bird
34 Of the country
37 Blue books?
39 Abound
40 Fitness centers
41 Used a shovel
42 Australian runner
43 Role for Will Smith

42

Across

1 "Who Can ___ To" (2014 musical movie): 2 wds.
5 Carried on
10 Stag
11 Extra Dry antiperspirant
12 Surpassing all others
14 Wide shoe specification
15 A hundred bucks: 2 wds.
16 Commercial property holder, often
18 Gp. of musicians
22 Andre who won Wimbledon in 1992
24 Greek winged goddess of the dawn
25 Pledge to wed
26 Explosive experiment: abbr., 2 wds.
28 N.L. city: abbr.
29 Passionate
31 Academic degs.
33 Suggest: 2 wds.
35 Prefix meaning bull
37 Time off, initially
38 Describe as worthy of disgrace
41 Poison oak, e.g.
42 Bering and Beaufort, e.g.
43 Words repeated at the start of the "Sailor's Song": 2 wds.
44 Automatic updates from favorite websites, initially

Down

1 Force
2 ___ elements (scandium, yttrium, et al.): 2 wds.
3 1997 movie about a beekeeper: 2 wds.
4 Harriet Stowe, ___ Beecher
5 Ella ___, actress with two stars on the Hollywood Walk of Fame
6 Barack Obama's Secretary of Education ___ Duncan
7 ___-Roman
8 "Ich bin ___ Berliner"
9 Banned insecticide, initially
13 Former UPN sitcom series
17 Did nothing
19 Returns of spacecraft to the Earth's atmosphere
20 Family on "Seinfeld"
21 President between F.D.R. and D.D.E.
23 Jawaharlal's daughter
25 Beer barrel poker
27 X in old Rome
30 Hip-swaying Cuban dance
32 Mixes up
34 Pigtail
36 Flu symptom
38 Mach 1 breaker, initially
39 In spite of, simplified
40 Battlesystem game co., initially

43

Across

1 Boozer
4 Blood-typing letters
7 Disbelief in God
9 French vineyard
12 Stripe in the shape of an inverted 'V'
13 Suffix with pont or plat
14 Held another session
15 "___ Little Prayer" (Dionne Warwick hit): 3 wds.
17 Family of northern European languages
19 Danube tributary
20 Packaged foods additive, initially
21 Horrible
23 Be left (money, etc.) from a predecessor
25 Thrilled
27 Annual Ashland event, initially
30 Coarse
31 Sharpener insertion
33 Like some olives: 2 wds.
35 Actress Kathleen (Ellen Dalton in "All My Children")
36 Sisters' org.
37 Scandalize
39 Finish up
40 Director's domain: 2 wds.
41 Mystery novel author Josephine
42 Change the position of words, letters, etc.: abbr.

Down

1 Pelvic bone
2 Everybody else
3 What an adult may ask a child to say before giving them something: 3 wds.
4 Having no weak points
5 Freq. performer at Tanglewood
6 Onetime science mag
8 First name in motorcycle jumping
9 Across the entire nation: 2 wds.
10 Fit for a king
11 Involving a single component (math)
16 No-no's opposite?: 2 wds.
18 Aviary sound
22 In an enthusiastic way
24 Spiders' nests
25 "Child's Play 2" costar Christine
26 Noble gas
28 Vocalist
29 Large groups of naval vessels
32 Test standard
34 Pigeon house
38 Quick turnaround, slangily

44

Across

1 Pork products

5 Checkers demand: 2 wds.

11 Fertilizer component

12 Lofty verse

13 Encircle

14 Has a traditional meal: 2 wds.

15 Casa grande

17 Annapolis inits.

18 Hit the brakes quickly

22 Drink with a twist

25 Columbus sch.

26 Worker nest-egg legis.

27 Charlotte Corday's 1793 victim

29 Peeples of pop

30 Having a reddish-brown color

32 "___ Have" (Jennifer Lopez song)

34 Type of air filter

35 Imaginary

39 Avid: hyph.

42 "When ___ one-and-twenty…": 2 wds.

43 Cool

44 Japanese capital (710–84)

45 African scourge

46 Weigh station allowance

Down

1 "Four Weddings and a Funeral" actor Grant

2 Number for one

3 Volatile, subject to sudden change

4 They love inflicting pain

5 "Dr. Strangelove" actor Wynn

6 Apple introduction of 2010

7 "___ a Stranger" (1955 Robert Mitchum movie): 2 wds.

8 Locating device, initially

9 "Kill Bill" tutor Pai ___

10 Dark time for poets

16 Military computer built under the codename "Project PX"

19 "M*A*S*H" conflict: 2 wds.

20 Danube feeder

21 Moral obligation

22 Actress Suvari

23 Seed cover

24 Louvre pyramid architect: 3 wds.

28 Decide on (a time or place)

31 "___ in England…": 3 wds.

33 Fort Knox bar

36 Some resistance units

37 Swiss river

38 Future J.D.'s hurdle

39 Narrow channel of water

40 Raises

41 Washington Nationals' div.

45

Across

1 Sheltered little bays
6 Easy victories
11 Popular printing font
12 Actor Hirsch of "Into the Wild"
13 Word before Christmas or Pranksters
14 Full of too much energy
15 Food that comes in a dozen
16 Flag
17 King, to the French
18 ___-Mex cuisine
19 Before, in poems
20 Occurring every year, as an event
22 "Hey, you!"
23 Inside the womb: 2 wds.
25 "See ya!" in Rome (or Hollywood)
27 "...that saved a ___ like me" ("Amazing Grace" line)
30 Extra pds. of a basketball game
31 Container for peanut butter
32 Exist
33 Silicon ___ (high-tech part of California)
35 In the distance
36 Cuban kid ___ Gonzalez in 2000 headlines
37 Escapee on the Underground Railroad
38 Shakespeare's "___ of Athens"
39 Greek letters
40 Fresh-mouthed
41 Irritable

Down

1 Picture taker
2 Portland's state
3 Cigarette brand: 2 wds.
4 Vincent van Gogh cut one of his off
5 Sneaky
6 Real estate company
7 Arabian sultanate
8 Famed pool player: 2 wds.
9 Toolbox tool
10 Something only a few people know
16 Road that runs around a big city
18 Another Greek letter
21 One, in Mexico
22 Not post-
24 Make a mistake
25 Is jealous of
26 Rome's country, to Romans
28 Necktie alternative
29 Speaking against the church's beliefs
31 Weight loss expert ___ Craig
34 Country that borders Vietnam and Thailand
35 Soothing plant
37 "Take a chair!"

46

Across

1 Actor Damon of "Rounders" and "The Bourne Ultimatum"
5 Hollywood awards
11 Burden
12 Perfect society
13 Restaurant list
14 City of Ohio or Spain
15 "Black ___" (Natalie Portman film)
16 Place for a manicure or a massage
17 "___ understand it...": 2 wds.
19 Hit with the hand
23 Atlantic island with a triangle named for it
27 "Nicely done!"
28 Journalist's information: 2 wds.
30 "Mazel ___!"
31 Underhanded plans
32 Sports channel
34 Female chicken
35 "Cat ___ Hot Tin Roof": 2 wds.
37 "And there we have it!"
41 Put down
44 Computer owner
45 Unexpected
46 It's thrown at a wedding
47 Thread holder
48 Talks incessantly

Down

1 Not dads
2 From the beginning
3 Fish in a salad or a can
4 Tidal wave, to the Japanese
5 Long shot possibility: 2 wds.
6 Grind to a halt
7 Pepsi, Coke and RC
8 Mimic
9 Cleansed (of)
10 ___ Paulo, Brazil
18 Beer, casually
20 Hang ominously on the horizon
21 ___ vera (lotion ingredient)
22 ___ up (invigorates)
23 Crunch down on
24 Deputy ___ Strate ("The Dukes of Hazzard" bumbler)
25 Say whether you're going to the party
26 Arthur who won the U.S. Open in 1968
29 100 years
33 Eternally: 2 wds.
36 Hammer's target
38 Where China and India are
39 52 cards
40 God of war
41 Noise
42 Prior to, palindromically
43 One of the Three Stooges

47

Across

1 1205, to the Romans
5 Hoi ___
11 Portico
12 "La Dolce Vita" actress
13 Dealer's nemesis
14 Rogue
15 Ugly and run-down (of a building)
17 Commenter's "If you ask me"
18 Rider
20 1957 Physics Nobelist Tsung-___ Lee
21 Division
23 China's Lao-___
24 Five-star 1950s monogram
25 Z preceder?: 2 wds.
28 ___ Valley
30 "2001" mainframe
33 Oscar-winning actress, ___ Leachman
34 It may be stroked
35 Actor Jones who starred in "Night of the Living Dead"
36 Kernel product: 2 wds.
38 Literary character whose first word is "'Sblood"
41 Neighborhood in the San Fernando Valley
42 Farmer's prefix
43 ___ Isaac Rabi, physicist and Nobel laureate
44 ___ tide

Down

1 AOL rival
2 Windy City rail system letters
3 Ropes in a ship's rigging
4 Appliance that cleans by suction
5 Vertical
6 Thumb-and-forefinger sign
7 Weightlifters' abbr.
8 Massenet opera: 2 wds.
9 Suffix for di or pan
10 Ice house
16 Certain teaching degs.
18 It's six hours behind UTC
19 Guitar great ___ Paul
22 ___ story: 2 wds.
25 Land
26 Parisian pronoun
27 Come-___ (advertising ploys)
29 Sea south of Italy
30 French painter Matisse
31 Shivering fits
32 Whole mess of, slangily
35 Aeneas left her
37 Ref. staple
39 Irish sweetheart
40 Alley-___

48

Across

1 Go well together

5 ___ sea (cruising): 2 wds.

10 Wings

11 Place in store, as green fodder

12 Neither fem. nor neut.

13 Former cager Bob

14 Refusing to work, as a protest: 2 wds.

16 Responses to fireworks

17 Baby

21 Depose from the priesthood

24 Jaguar of the 1960s

25 Read (over)

26 He drove the Moors from Spain: 2 wds.

28 Kate's role in "The Aviator"

29 On the shore

31 Mia Farrow's sister, familiarly

33 Caltech grad, maybe

34 Parent's demand: 4 wds.

38 Extreme fear

41 Motion picture

42 Like some old movies

43 Athletic shoe brand with an arrow in its logo

44 Hip scooter

45 Monocle part

Down

1 Hawaiian honeycreeper

2 Snap

3 Tree of the laurel family

4 European farm unit

5 Short footrace, maybe: 2 wds.

6 Spanish personal pronoun

7 Songbird

8 Big name in pugilism

9 New Year, in Hanoi

11 Protestant denom.

15 "The Mary Tyler Moore Show" spinoff

18 Deviating from the main point

19 Cut from the same cloth

20 Foxx of "Sanford and Son"

21 ___ dawn: 2 wds.

22 ___ Sad (capital of Vojvodina, Serbia)

23 Composer Jerome and others

27 Based on sound reasoning

30 Anthony of "General Hospital"

32 Leaking

35 Wife of "The Gold Rush" star

36 Have ___ (be connected): 2 wds.

37 Pros

38 France's 200 m.p.h. train, initially

39 Before, to Byron

40 ___ al-Khaimah (one of the United Arab Emirates)

49

Across

1 Marrying types: abbr.
4 Parts of finan. portfolios
7 Undertake
10 Take the cake
11 Gallery display
12 Peach or tangerine
13 Check cancellation: 2 wds.
16 Cultivate
17 Suds
18 French sister
20 Kind of blocks
23 Sled dog command
26 Finalize, with "up"
27 Fumble: 3 wds.
31 La-la preceder
32 Replaceable shoe part
33 Bodybuilding buildings
35 Duffer's dislodged dirt
39 Fresh talk
42 Nibble
43 Take one's turn, in board games: 3 wds.
46 HTC phone, e.g.
47 Hunky-dory: hyph.
48 Mouse catcher
49 Kitten's cry
50 Caviar
51 Historic period

Down

1 Kids
2 Place to lounge
3 Lifted
4 Limit
5 Blah
6 Eye problem
7 Russell of "Spider-Man 3"
8 Bleed
9 "Is it soup ___?"
14 Chubby
15 Funnyman Brooks
19 Obed's mother, in the Bible
21 Toothpaste type
22 Wise one
24 Any boat
25 Attention
27 Follow
28 Mr. Rogers
29 i = v/r: 2 wds.
30 Unable to see
34 Erie Canal mule
36 Express
37 Acting award
38 Letter before iota
40 Hollywood Boulevard sight
41 Send off
43 Engine speed, for short
44 Laudatory lines
45 ___ out a living

50

Across

1 Without warranty: 2 wds.
5 Nomad of the Sahara
11 One-time bathroom brand, ___-Flush
12 Put together, as pages in a book
13 Enclosed conduit for a fluid
14 Boneheads
15 Together: 2 wds.
17 One can be hailed
18 ___ wrack, common brown seaweed
22 Suit to ___: 2 wds.
24 Interminable time
25 Influenced by corruption: 2 wds.
27 Surmise
28 Where G.I.s get mail
29 High: prefix
30 Bond's bar order
32 Coins: abbr.
35 Visionary
37 Canonized Archbishop of Canterbury
40 Hard to catch
41 First stage of an operation: 2 wds.
42 "___out?" (tennis shot query): 2 wds.
43 Horny front wings of beetles
44 One-quintillionth: prefix

Down

1 Early form of sonar, initially
2 Spa feature
3 Apparatus for hatching eggs
4 ___ Spin (classic toy): 2 wds.
5 Go at it
6 ___ point (only so far): 3 wds.
7 Plentiful
8 Jeans' hole
9 Montreal to Quebec City dir.
10 Dept. store stuff
16 "Yeah, sure!": 2 wds.
19 Inadequate
20 Fair hirer's abbr.
21 Time off, initially
23 Having the most pleasant flavor
25 School of porpoises
26 ___-Locka, Florida
27 Hipbone areas
29 Deficiency of red blood cells
31 Goldbrick
33 Letter-shaped opening in some pistons: hyph.
34 Foam prefix
36 Sci-fi princess
37 Burlesque
38 Devils' org.
39 Utter

51

Across

1 Last name of Russian czars

8 "That's hilarious," when texting

11 Texas city

12 Columbus coll.

13 Black TV cartoon animal: 3 wds.

15 Side facing the street

16 Public perception

17 Hazy history

18 Symbol of Libra

19 Tight ___ (football position)

20 "___ of the Field" (Sidney Poitier movie)

21 Dot on a computer screen

22 Shipping boxes

24 Capture, like a crook

27 Containers sometimes made of cedar

28 Additional

29 It makes waste

30 Small string instrument

31 Academy Award recipient, like Julia Roberts or Matt Damon: 2 wds.

33 Man's name made of three consecutive letters

34 Section of London: 2 wds.

35 Wide shoe size

36 Prom outfits

Down

1 Contest with a drawing

2 "A Midsummer Night's Dream" role

3 Not milady

4 Draw ___ in the sand: 2 wds.

5 Immediately following

6 Toronto's province: abbr.

7 Cars, trucks, etc.

8 Site

9 Oklahoma Indians

10 Old stringed instruments

14 Letter, these days

18 Followers of fives

20 Threw trash on the ground

21 Spaghetti or tortellini

22 Pure

23 Save

24 Not belonging to anybody

25 Woman's name that rhymes with 11-across

26 They cover faces

27 Selected

28 Altoids or tic tacs

30 Holding tool in shop class

32 Armed conflict

52

Across

1 Hack
5 Rushing sound
11 Italy's currency, before the euro
12 "There was no choice for me!": 3 wds.
13 Not many: 2 wds.
14 All-___ (late study sessions, casually)
15 Settler
17 Walters of TV news
22 Where two peas go: 3 wds.
26 Kitchen appliance
27 Jay Leno rival: 2 wds.
29 Winds up
30 Birthday cake item
31 Obliterate
33 Not questions
38 Edge
42 "___ to the Chief"
43 Be that as it may: 2 wds.
44 Capital of Norway
45 Quickness to anger
46 Mishmash

Down

1 Applaud
2 LP player
3 Cookie with florets on it
4 Weakest piece, in chess
5 "Nothing Compares 2 U" singer: 2 wds.
6 Machine's sound
7 Horse's morsel
8 "___ to Billie Joe"
9 Narrow waterway: abbr.
10 Christmas sounds
16 Black, in poetry
18 Delivered, as a baby
19 Enthusiastic
20 Movie holder
21 "___ of Green Gables"
22 Decorated, as a cake
23 ___ of the above
24 "No ifs, ___ ..."
25 History
28 Hudson and Chesapeake
32 Bring up
34 "___ next?"
35 "___ of Eden"
36 Anger, with "up"
37 At a snail's pace
38 Came into contact with
39 Monopoly property, often: abbr.
40 Band from Athens, Ga.
41 Economics stat

53

Across

1 In the sky
6 Money substitute
11 Spice in curries
12 Scarlett of Tara
13 Take up space
14 Like some points
15 Clockmaker Thomas
16 Chucklehead
17 Be a pain
19 Ivory, e.g.
23 Bush veep
26 Up to snuff
27 Distiller Walker
28 Fairy tale figure
29 Pequod skipper
30 Ingratiate
31 Santa ___, California
32 Clear the tables
33 Josh
35 "Dancing Queen" pop group
39 Live's partner
42 Detective Pinkerton
43 Whimsical poet Nash
44 Astronaut's wear: hyph.
45 Hoes and hammers
46 Noblemen

Down

1 One-spots
2 Opulence
3 Pass over
4 Easy things to shoot: 4 wds.
5 Demolition ball alternative, briefly
6 Divan
7 Spicy Tex-Mex munchies: 3 wds.
8 Jogged
9 Wrath
10 When it's broken, that's good
16 Shade of blue
18 "The One I Love" group
20 Slender reed
21 Mrs. Alfred Hitchcock
22 Look closely
23 Blacken
24 Snack cracker brand: hyph.
25 History chapters
28 Serengeti grazer
30 Fade away
34 Places to overnight
36 Picture problem
37 Get-out-of-jail money
38 Myrmecologist's study
39 Good deal
40 It may be easily bruised
41 Commotion, to old poets
42 Cause of wrinkles

54

Across

1 President between Grant and Garfield

6 Much higher than before: 2 wds.

11 By oneself

12 White ___ (where 1-across lived)

13 Flying transportation, in mythical tales: 2 wds.

15 Stocking problem

16 Computer key that's usually next to the space bar

17 Leave town for good: 2 wds.

22 Demi Moore movie about the military: 3 wds.

25 Ginger ___ (soft drink)

26 Came up, as a topic of conversation

27 One of Columbus's ships

29 Pan used in Chinese cooking

30 Bird that's a symbol of the Andes Mountains

31 Volleyball players' equipment

34 Delivery vehicle

35 Take the peel off, as an apple

39 Where scandals may be "swept": 3 wds.

43 Brief

44 Stuff on a cake

45 Kills, in the Bible

46 RBI or ERA, e.g.

Down

1 Pork products

2 Alda or Arkin

3 Exercise from India

4 Puzzles

5 "Hold on a ___!"

6 Mammal of the sea

7 Largest artery

8 "Uh-huh!"

9 Purpose

10 Kitty or puppy

14 Bear's home

18 Dollar bill

19 Magician's stick

20 Palo ___, Calif.

21 365 days, usually

22 Stare

23 Press

24 It may start "knock-knock"

27 Like two peas in a ___

28 Look over closely

30 Lacks the ability to

32 Each

33 Roles

36 Opera song

37 Smallest of the litter

38 They're colored at Easter

39 Letters on navy boats

40 The Toronto Maple Leafs, the Los Angeles Kings, etc.

41 Classic 1950 film noir movie remade in 1988

42 Not hers

55

Across

1 Shrimp ___
7 Late humor writer Bombeck
11 Andy Warhol's field: 2 wds.
12 Continue: 2 wds.
13 Common compliment: 3 wds.
15 Black, to poets
16 Married woman
17 No longer in style
20 Computer company
22 Scary snake
23 Burning
26 "What an improvement!": 2 wds.
29 Like Superman's actions
30 Dark and depressing, as music
31 Frat party need
32 Jerks
34 ___ talk
36 Space shuttle org.
38 "Can't make any promises": 4 wds.
43 One of the primary colors
44 Herman of movies and TV
45 Word after trash or sandwich
46 River's little cousin

Down

1 Secret agent
2 Dove's sound
3 Mountain god in Incan mythology
4 Guys
5 Investigation
6 "Was ___ harsh?": 2 wds.
7 One of twelve
8 Rent sharers
9 Anchor
10 "No ifs, ___ or buts!"
14 Weapon in the game Clue
17 Route
18 1975 Wimbledon champ Arthur
19 Car part: 2 wds.
21 Diner sandwich
23 First three of 26
24 Idea
25 God of love
27 Foot "finger"
28 Prince album "___ the Times": 2 wds.
32 Up to now: 2 wds.
33 Scary sword
34 ___ Xtra (soft drink)
35 Singing great Fitzgerald
37 Band equipment
39 ___ Moines, Ia.
40 She's a sheep
41 The Red or the Med
42 President pro ___

56

Across

1 Country whose largest island is Honshu

6 Two-wheeled vehicles

11 Stadium

12 Country whose largest island is Sicily

13 Traditional healer: 2 wds.

15 Robe closer

16 Cigarette stub stuff

17 "That hurts!!!"

19 Place to work out

23 Nunnery

27 Internet company that merged with Time Warner in 2000

28 Does what one's told

29 To the left or right

31 Big snake that squeezes its prey

32 Takes down, in football

34 Wagers

36 "Little ol' me?!"

37 Family dog, for short

39 Big book

43 Traditional healer: 2 wds.

47 Dodge

48 Cousin of the guitar

49 John and Jane

50 Not quite right

Down

1 1975 movie about sharks

2 "Tosca" tune

3 Darlings

4 Pungent fish put on pizza

5 "I don't think so"

6 Life stories, for short

7 In need of scratching

8 Kit ____ (candy bar)

9 "Do Ya" rock grp.

10 Damascus is its cap.

14 When the sun comes up

18 Where the sun goes down

20 Letters, bills, flyers, etc.

21 Secret language

22 Bar orders

23 Famed baseball player Ty

24 Instrument in an orchestra

25 In good order

26 ____ Bell (Mexican fast-food chain)

30 They go downhill in a hurry: 2 wds.

33 Prefix with dextrous

35 Decline

38 High cards

40 Prefix meaning "all"

41 Army members below col.

42 Genesis name

43 Fellows

44 A Gabor

45 Hoover, for one

46 Hoops player's org.

57

Across

1 Don't come, e.g.
4 Ask for
7 "I knew it!"
10 Unreturnable serve
11 Gene material, briefly
12 Sharp left or right
13 He wrote for the Globe
16 Split country
17 Skating jump
18 Skillful
21 Near Eastern honorific
24 Key employee?
28 Side winder
31 Divine
32 Sack
33 Fragrant oil
36 Stem
39 Lecterns
43 Writing station with a pull-down cover: 2 wds.
46 Kick in
47 Sinuous swimmer
48 Will Smith title role
49 "You bet!"
50 It may follow you
51 Bog

Down

1 Soak up the sun
2 Canyon effect
3 Fly
4 Scratch
5 U.S.N.A. graduate
6 Mind the ___
7 Sophocles tragedy
8 Jumper
9 Cain's brother
14 Mauna ___ Observatory
15 Kind of kitchen: 2 wds.
19 Bounce
20 Mas' mates
21 Line made with a compass
22 Guy's date
23 Took a course?
25 Big pooch
26 Squeeze (out)
27 Checkers color
29 Dragged fishing net
30 Bombed
34 Big name in computers
35 Towel holder
36 Beseech
37 Was a passenger
38 Cutlass or Delta 88
40 Like Beethoven
41 Archipelago part
42 Related
44 Tetley product
45 Poet's contraction

58

Across

1. They make up stuff
6. Dirties
11. Miserable dwelling
12. "Calvin and Hobbes" girl
13. Over: 3 wds.
15. No longer green
16. Brit. decorations
17. 1960s campus org.
19. S. Amer. country
21. ___ Legend (rock band fronted by Schuylar Croom): 2 wds.
23. Bait
27. Teenage years
29. Exceptional creative ability
30. Actor Van Dyke
31. Map overlay
33. Decorates with bathroom tissue, for short
34. Rainfall unit
37. Animal doctors
39. Mattresses filled with down: 2 wds.
43. Give extreme unction, once
44. Of the cheekbone
45. Country singer Tucker
46. Gluck's "___ ed Euridice"

Down

1. Killer of J.F.K.
2. Physicist's study
3. Distaste
4. Fa precursors: 2 wds.
5. Skiing locale
6. Wind dir.
7. Obsolete
8. Egyptian fertility goddess
9. VIP's vehicle
10. Makes out
14. Tending to withdraw
17. Lively old dance
18. 2000s Bengals running back Dorsey
20. The Tar Heels, initially
22. To a small degree
24. Essentially: 2 wds.
25. Soyuz rocket letters
26. Cries of surprise
28. Where Lux. is
32. Prefix with -plasty
34. "___ first you...": 2 wds.
35. Singer of the 1983 New German Wave song "99 Luftballons"
36. French city near the English Channel
38. Tahoe transport: hyph.
40. "Isn't ___ bit like you and me?" (Beatles lyric): 2 wds.
41. Actor Daniel ___ Kim
42. Sign for a packed theater, initially

59

Across

1 Adorable animal that's a symbol of China

6 Beauty queen's crown

11 Expend, as resources: 2 wds.

12 Did some math, maybe

13 Multi-purpose living room furniture: 2 wds.

15 Owned

16 California's largest newspaper, for short

17 Fix, like an election

18 Make bigger, as a photo: abbr.

19 Juan Peron's wife

20 180 degrees from WSW

21 Part of a process

23 Undoes, as pencil marks

25 Last name of twin actresses Ashley and Mary-Kate

27 Swapped

30 Show no respect for

34 Lipstick color, often

35 Pablo Picasso's field

37 Eat well

38 Part of speech like "happy" or "wonderful": abbr.

39 Overly

40 Brazilian city, briefly

41 Expert with the remote control: 2 wds.

44 Come after

45 12-year-old, say

46 Put off

47 Embraces

Down

1 Shoves

2 Leaning

3 Sewing item

4 Deserving

5 Fruit that's also a computer

6 Steak ____ (raw dish)

7 Passports, driver's licenses, etc.

8 Loves to pieces

9 Process sugar

10 Wise sayings

14 Listen in

22 Place for peas

24 "What else?"

26 Moccasin material

27 Didn't draw freehand

28 Renovated

29 Tweak

31 Neighbor of Lebanon and Egypt

32 Both having hearts or diamonds, like a pair of cards

33 Silverware drawer slot

36 Canine or molar

42 Signal for an actor

43 Possible roll of the die

60

Across

1 Some desktops
4 Arena where the Knicks play, for short
7 "Now I understand!"
8 Every last bit
9 Place for a pea
12 Nameless man, in court: 2 wds.
14 Comic Gasteyer
15 Middle Easterner, often
16 Warning signal
18 Painting on a wall
20 Raise
21 Nutty ___ fruitcake: 2 wds.
22 Georgia known for painting flowers
25 Mona Lisa painter
27 Make believe
29 "Survivor" network
32 Show set on an island
33 Reproductive structure, in biology
35 Makes changes to, as a piece of legislation
38 Financial field, for short
39 ___ and feather
40 Stock analyst's arrow, in good times
42 Critter found in a messy kitchen
43 Ruin
44 High card, in many games
45 Ask nosy questions
46 Neither here ___ there

Down

1 Word before party or bottoms
2 Singing group
3 Big hot place: 2 wds.
4 Magazine with Alfred E. Neuman
5 No neat freak
6 Singing show set in Ohio
9 Big wet place: 2 wds.
10 Light switch choices: 2 wds.
11 "The Divine Comedy" author
13 Heat, Nuggets, etc.
17 Actor Guinness
19 Adore
23 Relatives
24 Winds up
26 Letters on business envelopes
27 Silver: Sp.
28 Like Julius Caesar
30 Untamed horse
31 "Return to ___"
34 Each
36 Pour (out)
37 Practice boxing
41 Attempt

61

Across

1 Dust remover
4 Bill
7 Automobile
10 Singer Yoko ___
11 Peyton's brother
12 "I ___ you one"
13 Cats and dogs
15 Club ___
16 Big house
17 Prefix meaning "three"
19 African antelope
20 Sought help from: 2 wds.
23 Jazz genre
25 Weary cry: 2 wds.
26 Juan Peron's wife
27 Gave chow to
28 Fiesta food
31 Go to the other side of the street
33 Bracelet site, sometimes
34 Balloon filler
35 Marry
36 "Forget it!": 2 wds.
39 Health resort
41 Make all riled up
43 Not just him
44 Brown shade
45 Howard of "Happy Days"
46 Finale
47 Keep watch on
48 Two-out plays, in baseball stats

Down

1 Be itinerant
2 Palindromic woman's name
3 Regressing: 2 wds.
4 Get weepy: 2 wds.
5 100%
6 Casual eatery
7 Volunteering: 2 wds.
8 Leave in wonder
9 Traffic light color
14 Uni-
18 "Go team!"
21 Little piggies, so to speak
22 Chances
23 ___ carotene
24 Twitter co-founder Williams
29 "Bravo!"
30 Calm
31 Dog
32 Brawl
37 Above
38 Cravings
39 That lady
40 Be the author
42 Happy

62

Across

1 Applies lightly
5 TV interviewer who praised Donald Trump for being a "genuine gangsta": 2 wds.
9 Apple Inc. products
11 Style
13 Subject of debate
14 Sammy Kaye's "___ Tomorrow"
15 Kind of computer monitor, for short
16 ___ way (kind of): 2 wds.
18 Chinese philosopher Chu ___
19 Former speed-skater Eric
21 Double curve in a road
22 Tendon
24 "We're sinking!" letters
25 Copycat
27 One of the Old Testament "Cities of the Plain"
29 Punk offshoot
30 Conductor Kurtz
32 Lotion letters
33 Homeowner's concern
36 TV title alien
37 Pitching number
38 Alt. spelling
39 Spring release sound
41 "...to hold, as ___, the mirror up to nature..." (Hamlet)
43 Like some vbs.
44 Salutes
45 Slippery and serpentine
46 Chemical suffixes

Down

1 Get rid of
2 Dean Martin's "That's ___"
3 Difficult undertaking: 3 wds.
4 Kind of fair: abbr.
5 Water in Seville
6 Deighton or Dykstra
7 Similar: 4 wds.
8 Astronaut Gus
10 "She Blinded Me With ___"
12 H. Ryder Haggard novel
17 Helmsman's heading letters
20 502, to Caesar
23 On the ___, angry and ready for confrontation
25 Minnesota's ___ Range
26 Beg earnestly
28 Prefix meaning "ten": var.
31 Cat's coat
34 Alt-country singer Steve
35 Squeeze
37 Like flan
40 Classical pianist Anton
42 Like a Burnsian mouse

63

Across

1. "Very funny!"
5. Las Vegas business
11. Actor Sharif
12. Lessened
13. 40-day period
14. Didn't just throw away
15. Doesn't leave any hard feelings: 2 wds.
17. Be the father
18. "Take ___ Train": 2 wds.
22. Essentially: 2 wds.
25. Golfer Ernie
26. Not dull
27. Wanders far and wide
29. Fine and dandy
30. Use, as a ladder: 2 wds.
32. LBJ or JFK
34. Untouched serves, in tennis
35. Carpenter's place
39. At the dinner table
42. "And there you have it!"
43. Quick look
44. Related (to)
45. Gizmo
46. Monthly bill

Down

1. Golfer's target
2. "I agree completely!"
3. Act of agreement
4. More pretentious, as a painting
5. Life's work
6. Cain's brother
7. ___ Ste. Marie, Mich.
8. "___ just what I wanted!"
9. French word before a maiden name
10. Like the numbers 3, 5 and 7
16. Alternatives to sandwiches
19. Act of disagreement
20. "St. ___'s Fire"
21. Org.
22. Letters that mean "very fast"
23. Norse god, son of 37-down
24. Train's path
28. Low-rated, as a movie or a hotel
31. Wal-Mart rival
33. Try to hit a baseball
36. Just a single time
37. Norse god, father of 23-down
38. Gasp for air
39. ___ McMuffin
40. Pie ___ mode
41. Tiny bit

64

Across

1 "I will sing ___ the Lord…": Exodus

5 Further down

10 Bury

11 Cat ___ tails: 2 wds.

12 Adverse results of some medication: 2 wds.

14 Monogram for the 18th pres.

15 Dockworkers' gp.

16 Korean make of car

17 Pulitzer playwright Akins

18 Musical dir.

19 Suffix with mock

20 Free (a sink) from obstruction

22 Salt Lake City collegians

23 Reason (from)

25 Riffle (through)

28 Craziness

32 Ending for web or video

33 Bronx, e.g.: abbr.

34 World view

35 "___ you being served?"

36 River that forms part of the Paraguay-Brazil border

37 Gold: prefix

38 Cultural rebirth from the 14th to 17th centuries

41 ___ de Cuéllar, former secretary general of the U.N.

42 Pakistani river

43 "Life is not ___, it is a gift": 2 wds.

44 Hutchinson and Candler

Down

1 In ___ (all together)

2 Elbows

3 Amount past due?

4 Club not often seen: 2 wds.

5 Diet food term: hyph.

6 Inseparable

7 Wire hoop on a croquet course

8 From A to Z

9 Puts another way

10 Trooper automaker

13 Backward handsprings: hyph.

21 Element in a "Wizard of Oz" character's name

22 Kind of vase

24 One of the three superpowers in "Nineteen Eighty-Four"

25 Shoe: It.

26 Life's work

27 Supreme Egyptian god: hyph.

29 Blake or Bynes

30 Closed political meeting

31 Town destroyed during W.W. I

33 Billiard table material

39 Truman's nuclear agcy.

40 Opposite of a ques.

65

Across

1 Reindeer's relative
4 Two-out plays, in baseball stats.
7 Club ___
10 Pause in verse
12 Pro
13 Brief peek: 2 wds.
14 300-3,000 MHz, initially
15 Prefix with suction
16 Spirited
18 Loose long-sleeved shirt
20 "Let me handle the situation": 3 wds.
22 Tachometer readings, initially
26 Controller of corp. purse strings
27 "Wheel of Fortune" channel, initially
29 German compass point
30 Math subj.
32 Gap
34 African nation once run by Idi Amin
36 One-dimensional
39 Oklahoma tribe
42 Soccer's Freddy or Fro
43 Get rid of by throwing away
45 Lowest two-digit number
46 Lab diagnosis of genetic makeup: inits, 2 wds.
47 QVC rival
48 Some time ___
49 Carrier to Sweden, initially

Down

1 Biol. branch
2 Legal scholar Guinier
3 "Don't panic!": 2 wds.
4 The Judds, for example
5 Scheme that incentivizes employees: hyph.
6 "___ alive!"
7 Art Spiegelman's comic rodent
8 Real: Ger.
9 Beard
11 "Backyards, Greenwich Village" artist
17 Suffix with front
19 Enemies in "Top Gun"
20 Old trucking watchdog gp.
21 Degree from RISD
23 Idaho's crop
24 Spartan's college, for short
25 Holy ones: abbr.
28 Trent Reznor's band, initially
31 Pool tool
33 Take in
35 Italian Modernist poet Carlo Emilio
36 Plaster backing
37 Days of old
38 Former Georgia senator Sam
40 Mountain in Thessaly
41 Gets hard
44 ___ Paulo (Brazilian city)

66

Across

1 Call on

6 Fruit that's also a computer

11 Dress type: hyph.

12 Goddess of agriculture

13 Athletic events

14 Pioneering 1940s computer

15 Exciting book, so to speak: 2 wds.

17 Beatles' "Eleanor ___"

18 What flamingos often stand on: 2 wds.

21 Actress West and others

25 Enjoy

26 "___ Theme" (song from "Gone With the Wind")

27 Kind of sheet: abbr.

28 Goofs

29 "___ directed" (RX instruction): 2 wds.

31 Stupid person

36 California-Nevada resort

37 ___-loading (pre-athletics activity)

38 Town in Tennessee

39 "___ Gantry"

40 Word on old gas pumps

41 Schedule

Down

1 Frequent Marlene Dietrich character

2 Police officer training school in Plainfield, initially

3 Victory: Ger.

4 Provisional decree before a final decision

5 More snappy

6 Sour-tasting

7 "Awakenings" director: 2 wds.

8 ___ blanc (Italian wine grape variety)

9 Regan's father

10 PC user's bailout key

16 Fashionable boot brand

18 W.W. II intelligence org.

19 Drop off

20 Gloaming

22 Nigerian native

23 Piercing locale

24 Lottery-running org., once

26 Stupefied states

28 Fair-hiring inits.

30 Crib

31 Beer component

32 "That could mean trouble!": hyph.

33 "Piece of My Heart" singer Franklin

34 Aid in criminal activity

35 French illustrator Gustave

36 Kickoff tool, in football

67

Across

1 Big mess
6 Put down
11 Creator of many talking animals
12 Yellow shade
13 Kleptomaniac
14 Tortilla sandwiches
15 Christian ___
16 Confess (to): 2 wds.
18 Center of the solar system
19 Teller
20 Teacup handle
23 Parting word
25 Sing softly
28 Brownish gray
29 Two-paneled paintings
31 Fishy eggs
32 Summer wear
33 Garden of Eden woman
36 Not at all
38 Novelist Deighton
39 Disney deer
41 "Impossible!": 2 wds.
43 Table part
44 Chopper blade
45 "Peer Gynt" composer
46 Opposition

Down

1 Fills
2 Kind of jacket
3 ___ flu
4 Other side
5 Game: 3 wds.
6 Exciting, as a finish: 4 wds.
7 Hosiery shade
8 Mademoiselle's hat
9 Gym round, briefly
10 Jr. and sr.
17 Avenue
21 Dadaism founder
22 Actress Charlotte
23 W. C. Fields persona
24 ___ in "November": 2 wds.
25 Burnable data-holder, for short
26 Océano feeder
27 Uncovered exam at some hospitals: 2 wds.
30 Corporate V.I.P.
33 Carry away, in a way
34 Snake poison
35 Door
37 Mitch Miller's instrument
39 Breathalyzer attachment
40 Mar. follower
42 Pro's opposite

68

Across

1 Blows up, initially

5 Son of Odin in Norse mythology

11 Alpine stream

12 "Nets to Catch the Wind" poet Wylie

13 Gp. that gives out PG-13s and NC-17s

14 First name of a 1994 Peace Nobelist

15 Cook with little or no fat: hyph.

17 Actor Connery

18 Donkey's years

22 First day of the month in Ancient Rome

25 Coll. basketball tourney

26 She played Cecile in "Dangerous Liaisons"

27 AAU member, briefly

28 Teacher's deg.

29 Well-worn path, like at work

30 Cry of inspiration: 2 wds.

32 "Desperate Housewives" character Van de Kamp

34 Writer Wiesel

35 Make it big: 2 wds.

39 1998 winner of the Masters and British Open

42 Caramel-and-chocolate candy brand

43 Jewish campus group

44 Extremity of Saturn's ring system

45 Britney Spears song: 2 wds.

46 Badlands Natl. Park locale: 2 wds.

Down

1 Pound (down)

2 Wine area

3 Interpret

4 Navy constructor

5 Outside the bounds of acceptable behavior: 3 wds.

6 Jai ___ (game similar to pelota)

7 Hosiery material

8 Internet protocol inits.

9 Letters in a help wanted ad

10 Grammar school basics, for short

16 Rushed, as to attack: 2 wds.

19 "I'll be right there!": 2 wds.

20 Insect nests

21 Bank acct. report

22 Rein in

23 River the Chinese call Heilong

24 Will

31 Beauty queens' crowns

33 The same, in Saint-Malo

36 Self-styled "Family City U.S.A."

37 Wagner soprano

38 Juicehead

39 Volt ÷ ampere result

40 ___ Wallace, "Pulp Fiction" character

41 Hunter's quarry

69

Across

1 One on a dollar
5 Effluvia
10 Short-billed rail
11 Twaddle
12 Detailed account, for short
13 "The Singularity ___" (2010 movie): 2 wds.
14 Russian Revolution victim
15 Zoom like an eagle
16 Junior high subj.
18 Chinese dynasty established by Yu the Great: var.
21 Idle fancy
25 Logo letters
26 Forest animals: 2 wds.
28 PC key
29 Follow: 2 wds.
30 Suffix with gang
32 Twisty curve
33 Massage deeply
35 Thompson of "Family"
39 "___ Please Crawl Out Your Window" (Bob Dylan song): 2 wds.
41 Ancient Greek coin
42 Constituent base of RNA
43 Vehicle pulled by a horse
44 Mayberry's Goober and Gomer
45 Drop for the count

Down

1 DOT, alternatively
2 Refusals
3 "Superman II" villainess
4 Technique with knots
5 Guesstimate words: 2 wds.
6 Alice's cat in "Alice's Adventures in Wonderland"
7 Go beyond the bounds
8 Country-lighting org.
9 Camera type, briefly
11 Causing shame
17 Golfer who won the 1964 British Open
19 "___ Angel" (Mae West movie): 2 wds.
20 Part of Y.W.C.A.
21 Tax pros, briefly
22 Sword handle
23 Occurring within an institution
24 Cultural interests
27 Bunchy clump of grass
31 Rolls-___ (luxury car)
34 Superman lover Lane
36 Four-line rhyme scheme
37 Small rowboat
38 Choir role
39 Container used for drinking
40 Ending for station or second

70

Across

1 Mexican food, sometimes

6 Elevator's home

11 Video game company that made Asteroids

12 Sarah from Alaska

13 Jovial O'Brien

14 Fail to be

15 Souvenir, often

17 Green vegetables used in potato soup

18 Business with rolling pins

21 Hide and go ___

25 Boxer known for verbal jabs with Howard Cosell

26 Assistant for Santa

27 Send a message to, over the phone

29 Unexpected

32 Academy Award

34 Kind of joke

39 Look into

40 Bird on the U.S. Great Seal

41 Colossus

42 "___ its course": 2 wds.

43 For later use

44 Requirements

Down

1 Pushpin alternative

2 Plenty: 2 wds.

3 "Would you allow me to do that?": 2 wds.

4 Source of wisdom

5 Tricky baseball pitch

6 Defeat soundly, in slang

7 Bother continuously

8 Baldwin of "Malice"

9 He rats people out to the fuzz

10 Explosive palindrome

16 Lock unlocker

18 Piece of baseball equipment

19 Bar order

20 Cereal that's "Kid-Tested, Mother-Approved"

22 Ending for velvet

23 QB Manning

24 McDonald's rival

28 "So sorry to hear that!": 2 wds.

29 "Gross!"

30 Earn, as a large sum of money: 2 wds.

31 Finely decorated

33 Part of a movie

34 Singer/actor Kristofferson

35 Phrase of denial: 2 wds.

36 Shrek is one

37 Dressed (in)

38 Jennings and Burns

39 Elementary school group, for short

71

Across

1 Predatory birds
6 Album parts
11 To no ___ (pointlessly)
12 Crown
13 Inflammation suffered by athletes: 2 wds.
15 Finish
16 ___ talk (inspiring speech)
17 Man of the future?
18 Regret
19 Roads: abbr.
20 Christmas ___
21 Worker with few rights
23 Join two pieces of metal
25 Lee or Levi's, for jeans
27 ___ of water (lakes, rivers, etc.)
30 Impromptu singing style
34 Bauxite, e.g.
35 Gillman in the Pro Football Hall of Fame
37 Genetic matter
38 Come out on top
39 Wedding day phrase: 2 wds.
40 Its T stands for "teller"
41 South Dakota creek where Crazy Horse was killed: 2 wds.
44 Tune from the past
45 Biological classification
46 "While My Guitar Gently ___"
47 Cairo's country

Down

1 Not fanboys
2 Means of access
3 Roam
4 Relatives
5 Falls on a banana peel
6 Family member by marriage
7 Peanut or grapeseed
8 Caught, like a criminal
9 Vinyl record feature
10 Twain's Tom
14 Saves for later: 2 wds.
22 J. Edgar Hoover once led it
24 The Mormon church, for short
26 Lives
27 Dog's sound
28 Yankee's rival, in the American League East
29 Remove clothing from
31 Small pocket, as in an English muffin
32 Get the poker pot started: 2 wds.
33 Least wild
36 Get out of the way of
42 ___ in the bud (catch a problem early)
43 Beer holder, at a fraternity house

72

Across

1 King, queen or jack
5 Watchdog org.?
10 Genus to which celery belongs
12 Reform Party presidential candidate of 1996
13 Comaneci with five Olympic gold medals
14 Capital with the airports Incheon and Gimpo
15 Here, in Hainaut
16 Duchess in "Il Trovatore"
18 Lack of acknowledgement
20 PM times: abbr.
21 Brothers' name in children's literature
23 "___-wee's Big Adventure"
24 Conceals
26 Cherubs
28 Ordinal suffix
29 Operatic bass-baritone singer Simon
31 From ___ (the gamut): 3 wds.
33 More smooth
36 Japanese mats
38 Menlo Park monogram
39 Crowd together in dirty conditions: 2 wds.
40 Goat-like antelope of central Eurasia
42 Entomb
43 Like many roofs
44 Old laborers
45 Half a matched set?

Down

1 Fox, e.g.
2 On the double
3 Occupying the front passenger seat: 2 wds.
4 Its U stands for "under"
5 Lhasa ___
6 "I've Just ___ Face" (Beatles song): 2 wds.
7 Evidence that is incontrovertible: 2 wds.
8 Wooing one
9 Library section
11 Sick-and-tired feeling
17 Slippery ___
19 Bother
22 "Woman Reading" artist Henri
24 British dish: 2 wds.
25 Realizes
27 Funnyman Brooks
30 "___ Married an Axe Murderer": 2 wds.
32 100 makuta in the Democratic Republic of Congo, once
34 Like a beaver
35 Peruses
37 K2 and Matterhorn, briefly
41 "What a relief!"

73

Across

1 Narrow-minded
6 Steinbeck characters
11 Après-ski drink
12 Actress Zellweger
13 It shows the way
14 Passed out
15 General in gray
16 Some guard dogs, for short
18 Two-time U.S. Open champ Ernie
19 One for the road
20 Nave bench
23 Swimming pool additive
25 Prohibited thing
28 Wards (off)
29 Dulles and Orly
31 Mahmoud Abbas's grp.
32 "Well, ___-di-dah!"
33 S. & L. offerings
36 Trivial Pursuit piece
38 Raft
39 Fake jewelry
41 Part of L.E.D.
43 Combat zone
44 "Time is money," e.g.
45 Showed over
46 Hayseed

Down

1 Bathroom item
2 Fashionable mushroom
3 Farm size measure
4 W.C.
5 Overseer of a specific post-graduate studies department: 3 wds.
6 Group agenda: 4 wds.
7 Castle part
8 Spiraling: 3 wds.
9 Wriggly fish
10 Put in rollers
17 Computer in "2001"
21 Wipe out
22 Director Craven or Anderson
23 Bluecoat
24 Low-___
25 Kind of dance
26 Be bedridden
27 One who's "just looking"
30 Maid's cloth
33 Hide
34 Artful move
35 Brace
37 European erupter
39 Standard
40 Metric measure
42 Rite answer?: 2 wds.

74

Across

1 Servilius ___, one of Caesar's assassins
6 Bowl-shaped part of a digging machine
11 Some grad school exams
12 African antelope
13 "A Song Flung Up to Heaven" writer: 2 wds.
15 Blood part
16 Navy replies
17 Order to a guard dog: 2 wds.
19 Cries of disgust
22 Model train maker
26 Apple desktops
28 Mature: 2 wds.
29 Redeem, as poker chips: 2 wds.
31 Try
32 Bonus
34 Dry as dust
37 Composer Prokofiev
41 Extended urban area
43 Alfalfa's sweetie
44 "Sock it to me" Judy of "Laugh-In"
45 Angler's basket
46 Reform Party founder Perot: 2 wds.

Down

1 Freebie
2 Shrinking Asian sea
3 ___ little prayer: 2 wds.
4 Student's week: 2 wds.
5 "Me, too": 3 wds.
6 Saturate, in dialect
7 Active ingredient in baking powder: 3 wds.
8 Too smooth
9 Instrument in an orchestra
10 Papal name
14 Salt, to a chemist
18 Letters that end a kids' song
19 Fan-___ (literary genre): 2 wds.
20 "___ Believer": 2 wds.
21 Federal warning system, initially
23 Scottish refusal
24 Latin examples, briefly
25 Serve to be re-served
27 High roll on a die
30 Govt. investigative org.
33 Stretch an arm to touch something
34 Multimodal letters, electrically: hyph.
35 Loud laugh
36 As regards: 2 wds.
38 Aircraft type, for short
39 Years on end
40 Chemical suffixes
42 North Carolina city, briefly

75

Across

1 "Dancing Queen" band from Sweden

5 Spa treatment

11 Easy victory

12 Makes into law

13 Addition, subtraction and such

14 "I see it the same way!"

15 Guinea pig

17 Say it never happened

18 Some turns on the road

22 Showed over again

23 Set aside (for)

24 Going

25 Put ___ fight: 2 wds.

26 Songs for one person

29 Tennessee football player

31 The Sphinx's country

32 1998 movie with Jennifer Lopez and Sylvester Stallone's voices

33 Get there

35 One of a kind

38 "Alice's Restaurant" singer Guthrie

41 Argues against

42 "Yeah, sure!": 2 wds.

43 Least believable

44 No, to Russians

Down

1 What a shoulder holds

2 Constricting snake

3 Caterpillar of the future

4 Goddess for whom Greece's capital is named

5 Accomplishment

6 Actress Bassett

7 Library desk

8 Cold cubes

9 Devoured

10 Drug also called "acid"

16 Dictionary entry: abbr.

17 Clear up, as a cold windshield

19 What a 3-down may do: 2 wds.

20 November birthstone

21 Laurel or Mikita

22 Valentine's Day flower

27 Not translucent

28 Walks sassily

29 ___ chi (Chinese exercise)

30 Fruitlessly: 2 wds.

34 Relax

35 Web address, for short

36 Teacher's union

37 Computer company

39 "I Hope You Dance" singer ___ Ann Womack

40 Mel of baseball fame

76

Across

1 Circus performers
7 Once around the track
10 Lasso
11 Woman of the house
12 Marcos with a lot of shoes
13 Sign of the future
14 "The Da Vinci Code" author: 2 wds.
16 Gush (forth)
19 Actor Mineo of "Rebel Without a Cause"
20 Scientist Marie
22 Badge with a photo on it, for short: 2 wds.
26 Walk ___ in someone else's shoes: 2 wds.
27 It's tougher than string
28 Time away from work, for short: 3 wds.
29 ___ & Garfunkel
30 Fake hair
32 Fender-bender result
33 One of five "Great" bodies of water: 2 wds.
37 Allies' foes, in WWII
38 "___ and upward!"
42 40-day period
43 Music system
44 Append
45 "Amen!": 3 wds.

Down

1 151, in Roman numerals
2 On the ___ (fleeing the police)
3 Valuable mineral deposit
4 1999 Will Smith/ Kevin Kline movie: 3 wds.
5 Zippo
6 Musial and Laurel
7 Big car for a celeb
8 Several: 2 wds.
9 Sean of "Mystic River"
11 Internet: 3 wds.
15 Puts worms on a hook, e.g.
16 Damage permanently
17 Mountain lion
18 "___ Brockovich"
21 Creepy
23 Magazine that chooses a Person of the Year
24 With an unknown author: abbr.
25 Fellow
31 Disgusting
33 Random chorus syllables
34 Fired, in slang
35 Gentle
36 "___ the Groove" (Madonna hit)
39 "Where ___ we?"
40 Outdoor sports chain
41 Period

77

Across

1 Minnelli of "Cabaret"

5 Get a closer shot with your camera: 2 wds.

11 Clapton who sang "Change the World"

12 Introduce by force, as laws

13 Cried

14 Mortar and ___

15 Lady

17 Williams or Turner

18 Teamed (up with)

20 Pig's home

21 Make a mistake

22 New member of society, for short

24 Tiny

25 Ending for cloth or bombard

26 Put in the microwave

29 Oklahoma city

30 Kind of beer

31 ___-tac-toe

34 Productivity

36 Yoko who loved John Lennon

37 Gin and ___

38 No longer edible, as butter

40 ___ Lisa (famed painting)

43 Portuguese-speaking African nation

44 Garden of ___ (Biblical paradise)

45 Physical well-being

46 Covered in morning moisture, as a meadow

Down

1 Alcindor or Ayres

2 Wrath

3 Fun way down from a tree: 2 wds.

4 Tom Cruise or John Travolta

5 Song with the line "Mr. Bluebird's on my shoulder"

6 Sign of the future

7 Photo-___ (politician's engagements)

8 Apple juice brand

9 Small dot in the ocean

10 Impoverished

16 Newspapers, magazines, etc.

18 Church bench

19 "___ you kidding me?"

23 Coffee maker brand

26 Part of a mailing address: 2 wds.

27 Mountain god in Incan mythology

28 Butter amount

31 Jewish holy book

32 Nonsensical

33 Cuban dance

35 Against the clock

37 Pinball infraction

39 Rank below gen.

41 ___ Hampshire

42 "Did you have ___ luck?"

78

Across

1 Big handfuls, as of cash
5 Rat out, as to Mom or Dad: 2 wds.
11 Bring on at the company
12 Black, white and orange bird
13 Father of Thor
14 Told a lie
15 "___ the Fockers"
16 Tina of "30 Rock"
17 "Okey-___!"
19 Tall hairstyle
23 Java and Kona, for two
26 Totally cool
27 Bring together
28 Express a viewpoint
30 Ask for charity
31 U2's "Where the ___ Have No Name"
33 Helper: abbr.
35 Robert of "The Brady Bunch"
36 Have bills
38 One of Jacob's wives
41 Kind of soup on Chinese menus: 2 wds.
44 Stare
45 "All ___!" (conductor's shout)
46 Jamaican fruit
47 "Thelma & Louise" director ___ Scott
48 Bygone autocrat

Down

1 "To ___ It May Concern:"
2 Helper
3 Snack from the Middle East: 2 wds.
4 Dispatched, as an envoy: 2 wds.
5 Candy type
6 Cleveland's lake
7 North African nation whose capital is Tripoli
8 Tennis shot that should have topspin
9 "Nicely done!"
10 Actor Beatty
18 Florida archipelago
20 They may be ordered sunny side-up: 2 wds.
21 Carry on
22 Some poetry
23 Caribbean island that gave us mojitos and mambo music
24 Small bills
25 Achy
29 Drive away in a hurry: 2 wds.
32 All the rage
34 Breakfast cereal in a blue box
37 Had on
39 Teatro ___ Scala
40 Person mentioned in a will
41 Armed conflict
42 ___-Wan Kenobi (Alec Guinness role)
43 Indicate that you agree

79

Across

1. Delay
4. Mel of baseball fame
7. "___ Maria"
8. Bank offering
9. In good shape
12. Scary snake
14. Solid ___ rock: 2 wds.
15. Otherwise
16. "Welcome Back, Kotter" star
18. Was sweet (on)
20. Oil of ___
21. Lennon's lady
22. "West Side Story" song
25. Exact revenge: 2 wds.
27. Like some country roads
29. "Scram!"
32. Miles per hour, e.g.
33. Prepared
35. Stick (to)
38. Each
39. Even score
40. Unthankful person
42. "To ___ is human ..."
43. Coloring fluid
44. "Winnie-the-Pooh" baby
45. "Casablanca" pianist
46. 2,000 lb.

Down

1. Texas city on the Rio Grande
2. Toyota model
3. Meets up: 2 wds.
4. Black gold
5. Arduous journey
6. "Gone With the Wind" plantation
9. Not doing well emotionally: 2 wds.
10. Bartender on "The Love Boat"
11. Roberts of "That '70s Show"
13. Golf peg
17. Small hole
19. Computer info
23. Guys
24. "... lived happily ___ after"
26. Robert ___: 2 wds.
27. Give a speech
28. Low point
30. "Same here!": 3 wds.
31. Use, as a computer: 2 wds.
34. Listening organ
36. Clears
37. Irish singing great
41. Beauty

80

Across

1. "I'm impressed!"
4. "The Wizard of Oz" studio
7. "So there you are!"
10. "___ Blue?": 2 wds.
11. Son of a son
12. Get-up-and-go
13. Like some clothing: 3 wds.
16. Side by side?
17. In a melancholy manner
18. Accord
21. Brunch fare
24. Org. for golfers
27. Washing machine modes: 2 wds.
30. Even's opposite
31. Saintly circles
32. 2003 OutKast chart-topper: 2 wds.
34. Drivel
37. "Finding ___"
41. Echo: 2 wds.
44. Marge's father-in-law on "The Simpsons"
45. Christmas list item
46. Boo-hoo
47. Peaked
48. Flock member
49. Curse

Down

1. Trumpet sound
2. Actor/bridge expert Sharif
3. Solomonlike
4. Italian pronoun
5. Martini ingredient
6. Thick
7. Newspaper page: hyph.
8. Make well
9. Grand Ole ___
14. Does a trucker's work
15. Kind of station
19. Born, in France
20. In need of scratch?
21. Gold in Barcelona
22. Central prefix
23. Halt
24. Mideast grp.
25. "Oh, my!"
26. Equine critter
28. "I'm thrilled!"
29. Bell sound
32. Weeder's tool
33. Cheer up
34. No-win situation
35. Singer McEntire
36. Frank
38. A head
39. Entangle
40. Cameo stone
42. Service station offering
43. Affirmative vote

81

Across

1   "Funny!": hyph.
5   Mezzo Berganza
11 Opposite of good
12 Finally finish: 2 wds.
13 Fixes, like an election
14 Complete
15 ___ Wednesday
16 "Aladdin" prince
17 109, in Roman
    numerals
18 Fidgety person's
    problem
21 Immediately: 2 wds.
23 See 25-down
27 Golf great Tiger
28 Snippy, as remarks
29 Half of Mork's sign-off,
    on "Mork & Mindy"
30 Bested
31 1980s video game
    with a little yellow
    guy eating dots
33 Hesitant syllables
36 "Alice" waitress
37 "May ___
    excused?": 2 wds.
40 Mr. ___ Head
    (kid's toy)
42 A long, long time
43 "Hold on!": 2 wds.
44 Fellow
45 New Jersey city
46 Shock

Down

1   Zeus's wife and sister
2   Rival rent-a-car
    company of Dollar
    and Enterprise
3   Classic Gary Cooper
    western: 2 wds.
4   Green and Franken
5   With 30-down,
    another term for
    the two times
    in this puzzle
6   Bert's puppet pal
7   Animal that carries
    the plague
8   ___ fail (big
    blunder)
9   Tom and Katie's kid
10 Peak point
16 Semicircles
19 Finish: 2 wds.
20 Christmas guy
21 Wheat covering
22 Come ___
    standstill: 2 wds.
24 When the day
    begins
25 With 23-across,
    former dictator
    of Uganda
26 Mr. Flanders, on
    "The Simpsons"
28 Japanese wrestling
30 See 5-down
32 Not before
33 "Once ___ a time..."
34 Sharpen
35 Hungarian
    goulash, e.g.
38 Male companion
39 Sports channel
41 Solid ___
    rock: 2 wds.
42 Summertime
    coolers, for short

82

Across

1 Go down in defeat
5 Chocolate substitute
10 Lobbing Lendl
11 Crescent-shaped fruit
12 Bridge play
13 Part of 28-across
14 Hillside, in Scotland
15 QB Tebow
16 It's thrown in a bar
18 Nile snakes
22 Get out of jail: 2 wds.
24 Theater magnate Marcus
25 "Now I see!"
26 "___ Robinson"
28 1994 World Cup host
29 Swallow or hawk
31 Continue: 2 wds.
33 John Lennon's "Dear ___"
34 The latest
35 "That's more than I needed to hear!"
37 Popular tablet
40 Greatest hits: 2 wds.
43 Zero
44 "Where are you?" response: 2 wds.
45 Vanished
46 Bonnie's partner in crime
47 Keep the beat, maybe

Down

1 Arm or leg
2 Finito
3 What to eat greens with: 2 wds.
4 Make liked
5 "Would you allow me...?": 2 wds.
6 Raccoon or racehorse
7 Critter on the Chinese calendar
8 "First..."
9 Awful
11 What to cut pats with: 2 wds.
17 "Stand" band
19 What to eat bouillabaisse with: 2 wds.
20 Mexican money
21 "Black ___" (Natalie Portman movie)
22 Elapse, as time: 2 wds.
23 Cincy's state
27 Get a look at
30 Like lowercase i's and j's
32 "Dallas" family
36 Extra
38 "___ Karenina"
39 Like the pool beneath a diving board
40 Pen or lighter brand
41 Make bigger, like a photo: abbr.
42 Like wallflowers

83

Across

1. Leap in the air
5. Have big goals
11. Bills with George Washington on them
12. Exactly right
13. Sicilian mountain an insurance company is named for
14. Texas city, or a TV show
15. African-American woman, in 1970's slang: 2 wds.
17. Person under 18
18. Engage in a Renaissance Fair sport
21. Synthetic material for stockings
25. Strong tree
26. Lamb's mom
27. Say hi to
30. Complete and total
32. ___ Cheesier! (Doritos flavor)
34. Overly large government, in George Orwell's phrase: 2 wds.
39. Easy to control
40. Use a swimming pool, sometimes
41. Worker bees
42. Some poems
43. Deeply held beliefs
44. Fellow, for short

Down

1. Montana, Pesci and Frazier
2. "Do ___ others..."
3. Bill of fare
4. Book of the Bible
5. Recipe phrase: 2 wds.
6. Spring or summer
7. Hardly worth mentioning
8. Not being productive
9. Lion's "meow"
10. Printing measures
16. Take a chair
18. Do a few laps around the track
19. Rower's need
20. Hawaiian "guitar," for short
22. "Titanic" name
23. Barn bird
24. French word before a maiden name
28. Motor
29. iPad, for example
30. "___ am I kidding?"
31. Picnic food in a bun: 2 wds.
33. Winter ___ (flowering plant)
34. Uninteresting type
35. Person everyone has heard of
36. ___ and seek
37. Like 2, 22 or 2,000,000
38. Take it easy
39. Pesticide banned in the 1970s

84

Across

1 Arthur ___ Stadium (NYC tennis locale)
5 Entered: 2 wds.
11 "Black diamonds"
12 Immediately: 2 wds.
13 Pet food brand
14 Held (over someone's head)
15 Overthrowing, like a dictator
17 Vote in favor
18 "The ___ Has Landed"
22 President Roosevelt
24 Go looking in other people's stuff
25 Baseball stat
26 "First off..."
27 Country the Nile flows through
30 Econo ___ (motel chain)
32 Army reply to a superior officer: 2 wds.
33 Frequently, in poems
34 Fuel for a Ford
38 Misbehave for attention: 2 wds.
41 Part of USA
42 Start back up again
43 Eye drop?
44 Beat-keeping movement
45 Guesses: abbr.

Down

1 "There's more than one way to skin ___": 2 wds.
2 Song for one voice
3 1970s-80s sitcom with Ron Howard: 2 wds.
4 Ran off to get married
5 San Diego's state, casually
6 Makes up (for)
7 "The Shawshank Redemption" actor Freeman
8 Last part
9 Surface for Wayne Gretzky
10 Mr. Flanders, on "The Simpsons"
16 Produce eggs
19 1970s sitcom with Esther Rolle
20 Taking up a lot of time, like a speech
21 Sword used in an Olympic event
22 High school student, usually
23 Therefore
28 Eat way more than you should: 2 wds.
29 Shock to the system
30 Lavatory, in London
31 Recently: 2 wds.
35 "___ right up!"
36 Not messy
37 Goes astray
38 Music, paintings, etc.
39 Company head, for short
40 Mao ___-tung

85

Across

1 Quick-spreading ideas
6 Brazilian dance, or its music
11 "That's ___ excuse!": 2 wds.
12 Characteristic
13 Copy machine company
14 Corrosive liquids
15 Wall-climbing vine
16 Make a mistake
18 Born, in wedding announcements
19 Bad: Fr.
20 Performed
21 Airport guess: abbr.
22 One of the Four Corners states
24 Pre-election survey
26 Servers hand them out
28 Demi or Dudley
31 God: Lat.
33 Microsoft game console
34 "Lord of the Rings" bad guy
36 4.0 is a perfect one
38 Dallas sch.
39 Golf course score
40 Talk and talk
41 World Chess Champion of the 1960s Mikhail ___
42 Keep away from
44 Spy
46 Picture puzzle
47 Radium discoverer
48 Plus
49 Blue statement: 2 wds.

Down

1 Largest possible amount
2 Raise up
3 Seafood pulled from the Chesapeake Bay: 2 wds.
4 Depressing, like music
5 Junior high class: 2 wds.
6 Celebrity's reality
7 Three-point line in basketball, for example
8 Seafood from Casco Bay: 2 wds.
9 Giggle-evoking bathroom fixture
10 Far from the coast: 2 wds.
17 Gravestone letters
23 Tint
25 Smoked salmon
27 Hint at
29 European country
30 Rejoiced
32 Where to get a facial
34 Bizet's "Carmen" is one
35 Very positive reviews
37 Ancient counting devices
43 Word on bills
45 Doublemint, e.g.

86

Across

1 Zines
5 Burning
10 Biol. subject
11 Travel book
12 "Young Frankenstein" woman
13 Not pen
14 Scary knives
16 Finale
17 ___ Mujeres, Mexico
18 Amiss
20 Motel
22 President before LBJ
25 Soaked
26 Go downhill
27 Portland's st.
28 Norton and Wood
29 "The Name of the Rose" author Umberto ___
30 Relatives
31 ___-bodied
33 Play on words
36 Run-down hotel
39 Sloth or panda
41 Forbidden act
42 Egyptian peninsula
43 Inflict upon: 2 wds.
44 Ringo of the Beatles
45 By the ___ of one's teeth

Down

1 Domestic
2 Late model ___ Nicole Smith
3 Funny presents: 2 wds.
4 Bucks
5 Long, long time
6 Pistol, e.g.
7 Hair critters
8 Norse god
9 Fuse
13 Bart Simpson specialty: 2 wds.
15 "Fur ___" (Beethoven work)
18 Have debts to
19 Gave grub to
21 Mythical weeper
22 It's full of funny things: 2 wds.
23 Thu. follower
24 Barbie's guy
32 Comes down to Earth
33 Quarterback's throw
34 Apartment
35 One of Columbus's ships
36 Just OK
37 Not pro-
38 Continue: 2 wds.
40 Ruin

87

Across

1. "Now I see!"
4. Gift of ___ (ability to talk to people)
7. Pose a question
10. Fish often batter-dipped
11. "Bravissimo!"
12. School org.
13. With 40-across, hit CBS sitcom that debuted in 2003: 5 wds.
15. Politician's "no" vote
16. Super-cool
17. Period of history
18. Zsa Zsa or Eva
21. What you look for on a first date
23. Inch or foot
24. ABC morning show, for short
25. Hit ABC and then CBS sitcom that debuted in 1960: 3 wds.
30. "Electric" creature
31. Take to the seas
32. Japanese car
35. How some things are contested
36. Took off quickly
37. Restaurant big shot
39. "___ and Nancy"
40. See 13-across
44. Mineral deposit
45. All Hallow's ___ (another name for Halloween)
46. Sailor's agreement
47. Neither this ___ that
48. Cave
49. Tree that doesn't sound like me

Down

1. Make believe
2. "In what way?"
3. Shakespearean fuss
4. Doomed individual
5. Alan of "Sweet Liberty"
6. "I have no idea!": 2 wds.
7. Sleeping condition
8. Oldest of the Beatles
9. Quick little watercraft
14. One more
18. Chewing ___
19. "Is it ___ wonder?"
20. Chomped
22. Falsely present (something as): 2 wds.
24. Some shaving cream
26. Attained
27. Little piece in a feedbag
28. Zero
29. Sneaky
32. Starting a destructive fire on purpose
33. Capital city on the Nile
34. Beneath
35. Keller or Hunt
38. Own
41. Fifth month
42. It blinks and winks
43. ___ Mexico

88

Across

1 Talk casually
4 Psychic Geller
7 Hem and ___ (be indecisive)
10 Unfeeling
11 Brown of renown
12 Blogger's viewpoint intro
13 Dustin Hoffman movie of 1976: 2 wds.
16 Shoe brand
17 ___ cloud (comet-filled region of space)
18 Diana Ross song of 1970: 2 wds.
21 "Exodus" hero
22 Nile vipers
23 Central position
25 "What did ___ do to you?": 2 wds.
29 Diving birds
31 Motorist's org.
32 Pasta made in long slender threads
35 Like some threats
36 WKRP's Jennifer
37 Arena of commercial dealings
41 Canyon or ranch ending
42 PBS supporter
43 "No sirree"
44 Division of a week
45 ___ King, bearded giant of German myth
46 Three: It.

Down

1 Edge
2 Code breakers' org.
3 Ancient Egyptian tomb
4 Action just before a war
5 Detox centers, briefly
6 Equal: prefix
7 Shout by someone only on TV for a few seconds: 2 wds.
8 To love, Italian style
9 Custom
14 Wide road: abbr.
15 Like Odin
18 Aries animal
19 Verdi's "___ tu"
20 Pertaining to bishops
24 ___ of Vulcan ("Star Trek" character)
26 Showing courage
27 Suffix with rep or rev
28 Style of music, a fusion of Arabic and Western elements
30 Out of ___ (awry)
32 Las Vegas hotel and spa
33 Young Jetson
34 Big picture: abbr.
35 Sent a brief note online, for short
38 NYC to Boston dir.
39 Rolls-Royce or Maserati
40 Woolly female

89

Across

1. "Schindler's List" extras
6. Accidentally walks (into)
11. "What was ___ wanted?": 2 wds.
12. Make ___ of the tongue: 2 wds.
13. Put into cardboard containers: 2 wds.
14. George of "Star Trek"
15. German automaker known by three initials
16. Cheer from the stands
18. "The Lord of the Rings" author ___ Tolkien
19. Actress Tyler or actress Ullmann
20. Museum stuff
21. Wrath
22. Old French coins
24. Is in a hurry
26. Over-the-shoulder carrier: 2 wds.
28. Clears tables
30. Trade-___ (pluses and minuses)
33. Make a blunder
34. Peaks: abbr.
36. Before, in poetry
37. Lawyer's abbr.
38. Greek letter after chi
39. Room in the house to get work done
40. Student
42. Shoe attachments
44. Flying solo
45. Walk casually
46. Armored vehicles
47. Fixes kitty

Down

1. Tiny bit of food
2. Nuclear
3. Start of a reversed sequence
4. Letters that mean "you'll get paid back"
5. Toyota model until 2002
6. Place for a warm soak
7. USSR rival, during the Cold War
8. End of the reversed sequence
9. South Dakota's capital
10. Church high points
17. Hauls down to the station
23. "Mayday!"
25. ___ Paulo (Brazilian city)
27. Places of worship
28. Alert another car with a honk: 2 wds.
29. Actress Andress or novelist Le Guin
31. Without coercion
32. Sight, hearing, etc.
35. "___ Marner"
41. Pen fluid
43. Concert equipment that makes the music louder, briefly

90

Across

1 Painting holder
6 Throws, as a stone
11 ___ noodles (cheap instant meal)
12 Ask (for a loan): 2 wds.
13 Not acceptable: 3 wds.
15 Popular wine, for short
16 ___ room (place to play in the house)
17 "Fancy that!"
18 Final part, as of a movie
19 Animal whose name also means "to talk nonstop"
20 Dirt plus water
21 Empty ___ syndrome (when the kids leave home)
23 Summarizes
25 The Jetsons' dog
27 "That's fine!": abbr., 2 wds.
30 City on the water, like New Orleans or Los Angeles
34 Antipollution grp.
35 Word after spelling or quilting
37 Each
38 Color on the Canadian flag
39 Polish off, like pancakes
40 Take advantage of
41 Song from "The Little Mermaid": 3 wds.
44 John ___ tractors
45 "___ you the one who said..."
46 Tacked on
47 More than mean

Down

1 Glacial
2 Gully
3 Makes right
4 Mal de ___ (seasickness)
5 Diary bit
6 Piece in the game where you say "king me!"
7 Be sick
8 Societal disapproval
9 Auto garage service
10 Goes too fast on the highway
14 Sound heard by a stethoscope
22 ___ and feather
24 Policeman
26 ___ up (let the liquor wear off)
27 Poet Pablo ___
28 Took the wrapping paper off
29 Put questionable expenses on, like a report
31 Masterworks
32 Find offensive, as someone's words
33 Agreement between nations
36 Patriot ___ Allen
42 Before
43 Historical time

91

Across

1 "The Heat ___," Glenn Frey song: 2 wds.
5 Glove material
10 Second beginning?
11 Cause of hereditary variation
13 Insincere sort
15 Lacto-___ vegetarian
16 Vietnam War Memorial designer
17 "Hometown proud" supermarket chain: inits.
18 "___ not amused!": 2 wds.
20 Joe and Jane, briefly
21 Chew the fat
24 Poster site
27 Milk source
28 Without a definite shape
30 Rapper who has feuded with Jay-Z
31 Bone: prefix
34 Shine, in product names
35 Florida city, briefly
36 FAA and IATA code for John Wayne Airport
38 Set of bandages and medicines: hyph., 2 wds.
41 Frees
42 Metric prefix
43 "Cómo ___?"
44 Orchard unit

Down

1 Poop
2 Sudden outburst
3 Ring source
4 ___ de plume (pen name)
5 British Columbian Indian
6 ___-Ude (Trans-Siberian Railroad city)
7 Popular street name
8 Minor deity
9 Write mournfully about someone
12 Writing remover
14 Online video hosting site
19 "The sign of extra service" sloganeer
22 Breakfast cereal
23 They're often played
24 Chinese martial art: 2 wds.
25 One behind the other: 3 wds.
26 In some respects: 2 wds.
29 Entanglement
32 Gravelly ridge
33 In abeyance: 2 wds.
35 Traditional dance from Tahiti
37 End in ___ (be even): 2 wds.
39 Use a chair
40 "Silent Spring" subject

92

Across

1 Iranian money
5 Garage job
9 Goodbye
11 Bar selection
12 Fertility goddess: 2 wds.
14 Top of the heap
15 Inflatable sleeping surface: 2 wds.
21 French vineyard
22 Modern: pref.
23 Cattle call
24 Flight
25 Chapel vow: 2 wds.
26 Record producer Brian
27 Shooter pellet
30 Animal house
31 1970 James Taylor hit: 3 wds.
34 Part of LED
35 Reservoir: 2 wds.
41 Courses of action
42 Break down
43 Kind of room
44 Part of BYO

Down

1 Sally Field's "Norma ___"
2 State whose cap. is Boise: abbr.
3 Put on
4 "___ Eat Cake" (Gershwin musical): 2 wds.
5 "Ciao!"
6 "That's disgusting!"
7 Buzzer
8 Stray
10 Prussian cavalryman
11 Numbers game
13 Bit
15 Roman ___ (novel genre): 2 wds.
16 Shiraz native
17 Buzz
18 "My Fair Lady" character
19 "Same here!": 3 wds.
20 Pass out
27 Skating event
28 1961 chimp in space
29 Make sense: 2 wds.
32 Idyllic places
33 Indemnify
35 Secretary's speed: abbr.
36 Beer's heavier relative
37 Lick
38 Favoring
39 Baton Rouge campus: abbr.
40 "___ durn tootin'!"

93

Across

1 Inclined (to)

4 It's spotted in casinos

7 Racehorse, slangily

10 ___ into (be nosy about)

11 Border-crossing necessities

12 Bush ___

13 Small person: 4 wds.

16 Alpine animal

17 Palooka

18 Made into hands

20 Source of possible harm

23 Island north of Santorini

25 Without further conclusion

26 Popular sing-along folk song: 4 wds.

31 Epitome of lightness

32 Afternoon break

33 Fairy-tale creature

36 Signs of close calls

40 Lioness in "The Lion King"

42 Home of Interstate H1

43 Severely scold (someone): 3 wds.

46 Start of a long-odds phrase

47 2-2 or 3-3

48 Wolf or conger

49 Coal carrier

50 Snack, say

51 Like a three-card monte player

Down

1 Greenhouse louse

2 Deep-space mission

3 Like some personalities: 2 wds.

4 About to go out, as a light bulb

5 Pastoral music

6 Bar

7 Renault gear

8 Shirt-sleeve filler

9 Trivial words

14 Primrose

15 Ecru, e.g.

19 Preschool attendee

21 Wedding day agreement: 2 wds.

22 Musical Reed

24 Heavy drinker

26 Show signs of age, as a roof

27 Family folk

28 Triathletes

29 Tabby's plaint

30 Google alternative

34 Street finder

35 Overjoy

37 Icicle-forming spots

38 Roulette spinner

39 Grumpy

41 Inter ___ (among others)

43 Robbery

44 Single at the beginning?

45 U.S. Open judge's shout

94

Across

1 50% there

8 Bat wood

11 The U.S.

12 Cow's sound

13 Gather, as a ground ball: 2 wds.

14 Play on words

15 "___ the ramparts..."

16 In addition

17 Left, on a liner

20 Show up

22 Ice skating maneuver

23 Little bit of a drink

24 Hot chocolate

26 Drink holder

30 Ancient

32 Actor Estrada of "CHiPs"

33 Not that complicated

36 "Return of the ___" ("Star Wars" sequel)

37 ___ Spunkmeyer cookies

38 Court org.

40 "Angels & Demons" author ___ Brown

41 Guacamole ingredient

45 Pale ___ (kind of beer)

46 Becomes more alert, as from coffee: 2 wds.

47 Part of DOS

48 Locks of hair

Down

1 Holds

2 Cable choice, for short

3 Only three-letter zodiac sign

4 Circular kids' cereal: 2 wds.

5 Use a napkin on

6 Popular Hondas

7 Talk non-stop

8 Sufficient

9 "El Capitan" composer

10 Sing the praises of

16 Circular kids' cereal: 2 wds.

17 ___-Man (1980s video game)

18 Grater maker

19 Word before room or center

21 Animal that makes bacon

25 Every bit

27 "___ you kidding?"

28 Old school comedian ___ Caesar

29 Go down the mountain

31 Colorado's biggest city

33 Pops

34 Country that completely surrounds Vatican City

35 Where people find gold

39 Uninteresting person

41 Fitting

42 Jerk

43 Word on bills

44 Photo-___ (politician's events)

95

Across

1 Where Adam and Eve were
5 Bobby Fischer's game
10 Block for kids
11 Part of a TV feed
12 Young wedding participant: 2 wds.
14 Plus
15 Speaks with the higher power
18 October birthstone
22 Chair part
23 Garden-variety
26 Mobile's state: abbr.
27 Sweet potato cousin
28 Novelist Levin
29 "Peace," in yoga class
31 Cabernet, for one
32 Board member, for short
33 Valentine's Day dozen
35 Difficult
38 Young wedding participant: 2 wds.
43 Love to pieces
44 Wander far and wide
45 Authority
46 Rival of NYSE

Down

1 One of Santa's little helpers
2 Md. neighbor
3 "I" problem?
4 "Forget it!": 2 wds.
5 Cadillacs and Chevrolets
6 Bigger than big
7 Newspaper worker
8 Respectful title
9 The sun
13 Some magazine pieces
15 Boeing 747, e.g.
16 "Calm down!"
17 "It's only ___!": 2 wds.
19 Couples
20 See eye to eye
21 Sporting advantages
24 Big wine holder
25 Arise
30 TV ad phrase: 2 wds.
34 "Gone With the Wind" last name
36 Shrek, e.g.
37 Coolest of the cool
38 Urban music style
39 Altar words: 2 wds.
40 CD-___
41 "The Three Faces of ___"
42 Man's name that means "king" in Latin

96

Across

1 Fat flier
6 ___ stick (incense)
10 Stage item
11 One's partner
12 Time not long past
14 Egg head?
15 Bad: prefix
16 Native of Abuja, e.g.
20 Establishment that makes and sells beer
23 Blood-group letters
24 Hawaiian veranda
25 "Groundhog Day" director
27 Ending for north, south, east or west
28 "You missed it": 2 wds.
30 Political movement launched in 2009: 2 wds.
32 Bryce Canyon's site
33 Cantonese dish
36 Cultured elegance in behavior
39 Facts sought, briefly
40 Underground network
41 Merchant vessel officer, briefly
42 Spread out

Down

1 Moss: pref.
2 "Scream" actor Schreiber
3 "And what ___ rare as a day…" (Lowell): 2 wds.
4 Satisfied
5 Rain that falls to the ground
6 Psychologist who was a frequent guest of Johnny Carson: 2 wds.
7 ___ more (several): 2 wds.
8 Patty Hearst kidnap grp.
9 Neighbor of Turk.
13 Old World Style pasta sauce brand
16 Early gangsta rap collective inits.
17 "___ Man of Constant Sorrow": 3 wds.
18 Rather: 2 wds.
19 Sniffer
20 Overripe fruit problem
21 Seldom seen
22 Sicilian resort
26 ___ Khan
29 Port of Algeria
31 Breathes hard
33 Earth sci.
34 Architectural pier
35 ___-bitsy
36 Thorax protector
37 Composer with the album "Music for Airports"
38 Unruly head of hair

97

Across

1 Wise bird
4 Absorbed, as a cost
7 Chair part
10 "___ won't be afraid" ("Stand by Me" line): 2 wds.
11 Toni Morrison novel "___ Baby"
12 "___ got it!"
13 "Seinfeld" role: 2 wds.
16 Another "Seinfeld" role
17 Dermatologist's hole
18 Helmsley of hotels
20 Away and in trouble
23 Everyday
27 Jeans name
29 Gawk
30 Old counter
32 Graze
33 "Come in!"
35 Play "Wheel of Fortune"
38 Hawaiian welcomes
42 Snide comment: 2 wds.
44 "Tarzan" extra
45 And so on
46 Confederate general
47 Battering device
48 "C'___ la vie!"
49 "___ & Order"

Down

1 "___ bitten, twice shy"
2 Cashmere, e.g.
3 Mona ___ (famous painting)
4 Make up (for)
5 Assume, as a role: 2 wds.
6 Go astray
7 Fancy wheels
8 For always
9 "Pretty Woman" star Richard
14 Old-fashioned woman's name
15 Besides: 2 wds.
19 Discouraging words
20 Pie ___ mode: 2 wds.
21 Spider's home
22 Eggs
24 Wild West?
25 "___ we alone?"
26 Was on the road to victory
28 Closest star to Earth, with "the"
31 Begins
34 Bumper sticker word
35 Wound reminder
36 ___ John's (pizza chain)
37 Thingy
39 Campus building
40 Part of town
41 Throw off, as poll results
43 "___-haw!"

98

Across

1 Taverns
5 Mock, maybe
10 "Everything's fine!": 2 wds.
11 Last letters in Greece
13 It's put on pasta: 2 wds.
15 Time of the past
16 Wedding day agreement: 2 wds.
17 Devoured
18 Goes off on a tirade
20 Take one's responsibilities seriously: 2 wds.
22 Not quick
23 Bother repeatedly
24 Eat away
26 Meryl of "Julie & Julia"
29 Feeling ill
33 Follower of eta
34 Coffee flavor
35 Ending for north, south, east or west
36 Cassette successors
38 Charged particle
39 Picnickers run races in them: 2 wds.
42 "Way down upon the ___ River..."
43 Bug that bugs cats
44 Has fun in the wintertime
45 Knight and Danson

Down

1 Dangerous dogs
2 Not knowing right from wrong
3 Sharp cheese
4 Musical genre from Jamaica
5 General feeling
6 Words said with steam coming out of your ears: 3 wds.
7 "Give ___ break!": 2 wds.
8 Lizard some keep as a pet
9 Prickly plant in Arizona
12 Accesses slowly
14 "___ the season..."
19 Canary's call
21 "You ___ Beautiful": 2 wds.
23 Move on one leg
25 Responded to a stimulus
26 Puts one foot in front of the other
27 Tosses
28 Car from Avis or Hertz
30 Roof growth in winter
31 Performed poorly when it counted, in sports
32 State whose largest city is Wichita
34 Submissions to an editor: abbr.
37 Performs
40 Chemistry suffix
41 Toward the back of the boat

99

Across

1 100 lbs.

4 Football positions: abbr.

7 Visa statement letters

10 Egypt and Syria, from 1958 to 1961: inits.

11 Really big shoe?

12 Actress ___ Dawn Chong

13 Draw air in and out of the lungs

15 Standard time letters

16 ___ Swedenborg, Swedish theologian and mystic

17 News org.

18 Male executive

20 Foam found on waves

21 "___ Rebel" (1962 hit): 2 wds.

22 Dorm overseers, for short

23 Negative in Normandy

24 Leave in, as text

26 Four Holy Roman emperors

29 Source of copra and coir: 2 wds.

32 German's outburst

33 One who has lost a limb

34 Lobster eggs

35 Like some relationships

36 Lifesaving squad, initially

37 French possessive

38 Giant teammate of Mize

39 Police rank, briefly

40 Multiples of three feet: abbr.

41 Wii ancestor

Down

1 Indonesian climbing pepper shrubs

2 Prepare leftovers: 2 wds.

3 Where one might expect to find valuables: 2 wds.

4 Alters the pitch of a musical instrument

5 A little laughter: var., hyph.

6 Makes blind, as a falcon

7 Line of reasoning

8 Grassy plains of Argentina

9 Eyeball layer

14 Lively, in music

19 Track and field event that uses a heavy ball: 2 wds.

23 Fail: 2 wds.

24 Very frightened

25 In the offing: 2 wds.

27 Fatty acid salt

28 Refines

30 Highly unpleasant

31 Called balls and strikes, casually

100

Across

1 Cooper cars
6 Be born, like a chick
11 Illogical
12 Mr. T & pals
13 Drink insertion
14 Kingdom
15 Get it in the goal!: 2 wds.
17 "Hasta la vista, baby"
18 Rotate
21 Light wind
25 Baseball number
26 Top
27 "Who's the Boss?" role
31 Goes down temporarily
32 Perhaps
34 Get it in the goal!: 2 wds.
39 Fracas
40 Claw
41 Tell the server what you want
42 Els of golf
43 Prom purchase
44 Not fresh

Down

1 Loretta Lynn's "___ Being Mrs."
2 Liking
3 Rat (on)
4 One way Coke comes: 3 wds.
5 Mended clothing
6 Safe place
7 "Relax," in the military: 2 wds.
8 Blue shade
9 "Safe!" or "Strike two!"
10 "Makes you wonder..."
16 Spare part?
18 English breakfast, e.g.
19 Kind of vase
20 Cloth for cleaning
22 Mr. Manning
23 24401 or 29340
24 NYT workers
28 Hosts
29 L.A. squad
30 Sailor's "sure"
31 Leave
33 Data units
34 No Frau
35 Time-tested, in cheesy store names
36 Arm bone
37 Cobra's configuration
38 Body part with a cap
39 Forum administrator, for short

101

Across

1 Small flute

5 Word before "party" or "bottoms"

11 Spoken

12 Tooth covering

13 Musical genre with its Hall of Fame in Cleveland: 3 wds.

15 Tiny crawler

16 "____ not the end of the world!"

17 Sports org. that includes the Houston Rockets

18 Gunk

19 Twosome

20 Like people who are "out"

21 Makes a blunder

23 Weasel's sound, in a song

25 Put back to zero

27 Slithery lizards

31 "A mouse!"

33 Too sweet

34 Stuff tapped off a cigarette

37 Marked a ballot, maybe

39 Not a "nay" vote

40 Highest card in the deck

41 Prefix meaning "three"

42 Cigarette additive

43 Beer that comes in a green bottle: 2 wds.

46 Black, white and orange bird

47 Stare

48 Cell phone giant bought by Sprint in 2005

49 Active person

Down

1 Someone who scours for food

2 Its mined in Minnesota's Mesabi Range: 2 wds.

3 Things to consider

4 Animal with antlers

5 Kept inside, as rage

6 Et cetera: 3 wds.

7 Peanut butter container

8 Surrounded by

9 Peach ____ (kind of dessert)

10 Soothe, as fears

14 Band-____ (scrape cover)

22 Get a look at

24 Puppy or kitten

26 Fabric

28 "Nice job!": 3 wds.

29 Sweet syrup served in England

30 More unadorned

32 Piece of unpopped popcorn

34 First name in the Bible, alphabetically

35 Make a goal or a basket

36 Curving line, like of DNA strands

38 Like, to a hippie

44 Parking place

45 Fishing pole

102

Across

1 Singing great ___ Horne

5 1980s pop singer ___ E.

11 Innovative Apple computer

12 ___ beef and cabbage (Irish dish)

13 Lion's hair

14 Changes for the better

15 Pedaled vehicle

17 Sneaky

18 Chocolate tycoon Milton

23 Action

25 Birthday dessert

26 Cylinder to suck a drink through

28 Opens (one's soul)

29 God of war

30 Brain

31 Albany's state: 2 wds.

33 More than months: abbr.

36 Fruity alternative to ice cream

38 Confusing

42 Obama 2008 campaign word

43 Take off a pickup truck

44 "Jane ___"

45 In abundance

46 "Unto us ___ is given": 2 wds.

Down

1 Arms and legs

2 Click "send"

3 Fictional female detective: 2 wds.

4 ___-deucey (backgammon variant)

5 ___ back (downsized)

6 Bart Simpson's dad

7 Before, for Burns

8 Motel

9 Quarterbacked

10 Magazines run them

16 Munch (on)

19 Look over quickly

20 Fictional male detectives, with "The": 2 wds.

21 Squeeze (out a living)

22 Not no

24 Simple

26 ___ Francisco

27 Three: It.

28 Short form of 15-across

30 Dr. Jekyll's counterpart: 2 wds.

32 Schindler of "Schindler's List"

34 Copy, for short

35 Dutch painter Jan ___

37 Perlman of "Cheers"

38 Yank

39 Genetic material

40 "___ tell you what..."

41 Make a dove's sound

103

Across

1 Deaden

5 Scratches

10 Native Nebraskan

11 Kept inside, as rage: 2 wds.

12 Change for a ten

13 Too

14 Large mass of land projecting into the sea

16 Give out

19 Monk of yore

22 Started, in poetry

23 "Midnight Cowboy" character Rizzo's nickname

24 Nail file mineral

26 Pilot's announcement, for short

27 Hank who voices Chief Wiggum

28 It can reverse a ball's forward motion

31 Feature in the console of a car

35 Phrase of inclusion: 2 wds.

37 "Yes, it's clear now": 2 wds.

38 Oldster

39 German name for Cologne

40 Pig in ___: 2 wds.

41 Italian pronoun

Down

1 Colloquial denial

2 Quarterly magazine founded in 1984, ___ Reader

3 Travis of the NHL

4 As well

5 Gun, as a motor, slangily: 2 wds.

6 Give extreme unction, once

7 More weird

8 Afghan monetary unit

9 Acquire intelligence

11 Oater group

15 El ___ (weather phenomenon)

17 Kolkata coverup

18 Irish singer of "Only Time"

19 Jewish holiday eve

20 ___ spell (rested briefly): 2 wds.

21 Detached, musically

24 1950 Tony winner Pinza

25 Resembling a human being

27 Greenhouse louse

29 Prosperous peasant farmer in Russia

30 Cathedral topper

32 Brit. awards

33 Sinuous shockers

34 Actress Sofer

35 "When Your Child Drives You Crazy" author LeShan

36 Exceed

104

Across

1 Tie with a clasp
5 "Such a pity": 2 wds.
10 "___, U of K" (college fight song): 2 wds.
11 Volunteer's statement: 2 wds.
12 Frame with netting panels: 2 wds.
14 Woman's light dressing gown
15 Political cartoonist Thomas
16 ___/Volt (Otis Redding label)
20 After all that has happened: 2 wds.
23 New age chant
24 Cosmetics maker Lauder
25 Sleep phenomenon
27 Landed
28 Leaves (a job) voluntarily
30 Final club at Harvard University
32 Half of Mork's sign-off, on "Mork & Mindy"
33 Dribbles at the mouth
37 Connected with something else
39 Circus sight
40 Director Wertmüller
41 "___ directed" (medicine alert): 2 wds.
42 Onion's cousin

Down

1 Cap'n's mate
2 Aforetime
3 Spectacles with a handle
4 Like some country roads: 2 wds.
5 Serenade: 2 wds.
6 Shoppe adjective
7 Tart fruits
8 Years ___
9 Palme ___ (Cannes Film Festival prize)
13 Disney head until 2005
17 Deprive of speech: hyph.
18 "Indeed!"
19 Present time?
20 Instruments used to examine the brain, initially
21 Letters on a brandy bottle
22 Sushi condiment
26 Arcade game
29 Passes
31 "The Devil's Disciple" girl
34 "Copacabana" showgirl
35 Québec's Levesque
36 Mt. Rushmore's state: 2 wds.
37 Sun Devils' campus letters
38 Blvds.

105

Across

1 Submachine gun
4 Cartoon "devil"
7 Golf course score
8 ___ code (5- or 9-digit number)
11 Bird: prefix
12 One of four in a deck
13 ___ Lanka
14 Before ninth
16 Camp water
17 Get older
18 From ___ (completely): 3 wds.
20 Charon's river
21 Stirred up
24 Little dog, for short
25 "Ciao!"
26 "___ Maria"
27 Mt. ___ (where Noah landed)
29 Worker's weekend shout
30 "Lovely" Beatles girl
31 "2001" computer
32 Canine cry
34 "Absolutely!": 2 wds.
37 "___ you there?"
38 100 percent
39 Olive ___ (Popeye's love)
40 Lock opener
41 Ground cover
42 ___ center
43 Apr. addressee

Down

1 ___ the crack of dawn: 2 wds.
2 12th president: 2 wds.
3 Anger
4 ___ Bo (exercise system)
5 Flying ace
6 Son of reggae star Bob, who sang "Tomorrow People": 2 wds.
8 Hungarian who slapped a cop in L.A.: 3 wds.
9 Aggravate
10 Apple or cherry
15 Bewitch
16 Singer Rawls
19 One of five on a foot
20 Day ___ (place for a pedicure)
22 Curse: 2 wds.
23 Dict. entry
25 Louisville Slugger, e.g.
28 Tear
29 Thanksgiving, e.g.: abbr.
32 Talk and talk
33 Before
35 Former GM car
36 Special attention, for short
38 "___ Lay Me Down": 2 wds.

106

Across

1 Catholic service
5 Common exercise
11 Soon, to a poet
12 Heir's concern
13 Data
14 President, say
15 After expenses
16 Lion's share
17 Movie actors with no lines
19 ___ butter
23 Sit in on, as a class
25 Actress Gardner
26 Aspect
28 TV host with a role in "The Color Purple"
30 Narcissist's problem
31 Took part in a democracy
33 ___ Virginia
35 Writing utensil
38 "Beware the ___ of March"
40 Man's name that reverses to another man's name
41 Swindler: 2 wds.
44 Promising words
45 Gentle wind
46 Department store section
47 Grow irate: 2 wds.
48 Approximately: 2 wds.

Down

1 Acadia National Park's state
2 Take by force, as a territory
3 Mexican entree: 2 wds.
4 ___-Caps
5 First female House Speaker
6 Functions
7 Sports figures
8 Owned
9 Western tribe for whom a U.S. state is named
10 Apiece
16 Fox comedy show
18 Wish you could take back
20 Alcoholic beverage: 2 wds.
21 ___ Marie Saint
22 "I see!"
24 Carries
26 Not many
27 Number of years
29 Fountain or ink
32 Began
34 It rings in the kitchen
36 "Reversal of Fortune" star Jeremy
37 Catch with a rope
39 Leave stunned
41 ABC rival
42 Miner's find
43 French word in wedding announcements
44 "What I think," when texting

107

Across

1 D.C.'s nation: abbr.
4 "Send help!," in Morse Code
7 Lulu
10 Holiday drink
11 Place to buy prints: 2 wds.
13 Spring outlook: 2 wds.
15 Iris holder
16 Actor Brynner
17 Groups of four
20 Muhammad ___
23 Maidenform product
24 Heater
25 Tidy Lotto prize: 2 wds.
29 In this place
30 Sorry
31 Bank offering, for short
32 Indirect routes
36 Kind of service
38 Target
39 In a self-possessed manner
43 Second wife's boy
44 Drink in a mug
45 "___ time"
46 Rug rat
47 "___ out!"

Down

1 Full-length
2 Italian wine
3 Lace tip
4 Woodshop tool
5 Kind of deposit
6 Collar inserts
7 Iranian shah's name
8 Paris' ___ de la Cité
9 Part of w.p.m.
12 "Rugrats" dad
14 Venus de Milo material
18 Pitcher's asset
19 Symbol of freshness
21 Sign before Virgo
22 Hostel
24 Senescence: 2 wds.
25 Phi follower
26 Anthem preposition
27 Medium settings?
28 Race unit
32 City of Brittany
33 Now
34 Oscar-winning Berry
35 More cunning
37 Matterhorn, e.g.
39 Forensic drama on CBS
40 Giant slugger Mel
41 Gentle sound
42 Discharge letters?

108

Across

1 Polishes, as a car
6 June 6th, 1944
10 Dark, as a passageway
11 Rich cake
12 Hit hard
13 Largest city in Nebraska
14 Spinning toy
15 First ___ kit
17 World ___ I
18 Cut (off)
19 Genetic material
20 Quality ___ (hotel chain)
21 Actor Estrada
23 Gets on one's feet
25 Money saved for retirement: 2 wds.
27 Laughing a lot
29 Sports channel
32 More genetic material
33 North African nation: abbr.
35 One of a foot's five
36 "Lost" network
37 Drink with scones
38 Aisle
39 Bullwinkle, e.g.
41 Duane ___ (drugstore chain)
43 Asked nosy questions
44 Tries to make a strike or a spare
45 "___ Karenina"
46 Beginning

Down

1 Hustle and ___
2 Bring up anchor
3 Way to randomly choose between two things: 3 wds.
4 In good shape
5 Word with farm or home
6 ___ Perignon champagne
7 Way to randomly choose a person for an unpleasant task: 2 wds.
8 Readily available: 2 wds.
9 Has a longing (for)
11 So far: 2 wds.
16 Fashionable: 2 wds.
22 Fraternity party container
24 Number of years
26 Scheduled
27 Nana's man
28 Not learned after birth
30 Dog that might be named Fifi
31 Most recent
34 Great Greta
40 Baltic or Irish
42 Long period of time

109

Across

1 Mighty trees
5 Purity units, to goldsmiths
11 Made a picture of
12 Roma's country
13 Eat well
14 Silver, tin, etc.
15 "For Pete's ___!"
16 Not just hugs
17 Hawke of Hollywood
19 "Absolutely, general!": 2 wds.
21 Mauna ___ (Hawaiian volcano)
24 Exist
25 iPhone, e.g.
27 Fluid in a pen
28 Be nosy
29 Actress Bynes of "What a Girl Wants"
31 "___ a Song of Bethlehem": 2 wds.
32 Like a mischievous child
36 ___ out a living (barely gets by)
39 Polynesian cocktail: 2 wds.
40 Long-term spy
41 Nicaraguan leader Daniel
42 Part of MIT
43 Male tennis players, sometimes
44 Long period of time

Down

1 Vegas calculations
2 Song for one
3 "One Flew Over the Cuckoo's Nest" author: 2 wds.
4 Candy and such
5 Member of a California reality TV family: 2 wds.
6 Had food at home: 2 wds.
7 "Darn it!"
8 "Woe is me!"
9 Scrabble piece
10 Backtalk
18 Cool and edgy, like Brooklyn kids
19 Talk and talk and talk
20 Make a blunder
21 Movie ape: 2 wds.
22 Wind up
23 Letters before a crook's alias
26 "What ___ going to do?": 2 wds.
30 Blood condition
31 Indian tribe
32 "It's my turn!": 2 wds.
33 Adult female horse
34 Brad of "Thelma & Louise"
35 Thingy
37 Different
38 Becomes hard, as concrete

110

Across

1 Resting place
6 Bundle of twigs bound together as fuel
11 Old liquid heaters
12 Heavenly prefix
13 Dish with parmesan cheese and croutons: 2 wds.
15 Cathedral city of England
16 Delicacy
17 Nod, maybe
18 "___ Around" (Beachboys song): 2 wds.
20 Like the eyes of the sleep-deprived
22 Place to listen to music and enjoy a cocktail: 2 wds.
24 Diviner's deck
25 One who mocks
29 Humdrum
31 "The ___ the Velvet Claws" (Perry Mason movie): 2 wds.
34 "More's the pity"
35 "Son ___ gun!": 2 wds.
36 Lady's man
38 Pose
39 In a self-assured way
42 ___ the elbows (poor): 2 wds.
43 Angler's basket
44 Relating to a wing
45 Afternoon in Alicante

Down

1 Proof of ownership
2 Earache
3 Twelve months: 2 wds.
4 European carrier letters
5 Autocrat until 1917
6 Central body of a plane
7 Constellation near Scorpius
8 Roman emperor 68–9 A.D.
9 TV studio sign: 2 wds.
10 Some like it hot
14 Former Virginia governor Chuck
19 Issuance from Uncle Sam: hyph.
21 IRA-establishing legislation
23 Purposelessness
26 Long thick pillow
27 Sent a modern message: hyph.
28 Give a makeover
30 Chip in passports, initially
31 Après-ski quaff
32 Entangled
33 Father Christmas
37 Geom. shape
40 Extreme
41 Gun gp.

111

Across

1. Another name for the buffalo
6. Tennis great Rod
11. Right as expected: 2 wds.
12. Singer Cara or Actress Dunne
13. "I've never seen its like before!": 3 wds.
15. ___ and feather
16. Letters on exploding crates, in Angry Birds
17. Designer Anna ___ (hidden in PURSUING)
18. "Excellent!"
19. "Help!"
20. Before, to bards
21. Kid's room, often
23. Checkers of vital signs
25. Online call service
27. Self-___
30. Big containers at a winery
34. Only three-letter zodiac sign
35. Negative replies
37. Use a needle and thread
38. Driver's licenses, e.g.
39. "Tastes good!"
40. Bruce or Spike
41. "Hold on!": 3 wds.
44. ___ the hole: 2 wds.
45. Failure
46. Receive a ___ welcome
47. 3s, in cards

Down

1. Underside
2. Absorb oxygen
3. Terrifies
4. Umpire's shout
5. Eagles' homes
6. Raises: 2 wds.
7. Former Bush spokesman Fleischer
8. Poetry divisions
9. Make certain
10. Tries the laces again
14. Unsigned by the author
22. Compass pt.
24. Show off, as a motorcycle's engine
26. Nairobi residents
27. Actor Wood of "The Lord of the Rings"
28. Tempt successfully
29. Person who throws something
31. Not level
32. Itty-bitty
33. People of Stockholm
36. Work with iron
42. Uncle: Sp.
43. Ride

112

Across

1 1940s–50s All-Star Johnny
5 Turner's 1986 rock autobiography: 2 wds.
10 Janis's hubby in the comics
11 Beneficial
12 Blockhead
13 Tokyo air hub
14 Supports, as a team: 2 wds.
16 Leon Uris's "___ 18"
17 Sumo wrestling move
21 Alphabetic sequence
23 Binge on food
25 French department and river
26 2007 World Series winner, for short
27 "___ for the way you look at me" (line from a song): 2 wds.
28 Translucent, informally: hyph.
30 Calendar abbr.
31 African antelope
32 Fruitless
34 Winner of seven Gold Gloves: 2 wds.
38 Regular
41 One before Hump Day: abbr.
42 US Congress assembly
43 Have ___ in one's bonnet: 2 wds.
44 Trite and mawkish
45 Benchmarks: abbr.

Down

1 Baghdad's ___ City
2 Slangy suffix for "buck"
3 Unlucky: hyph.
4 Nights, in Italy
5 Aoki of the PGA
6 Holy ___
7 "___ only had a...": 2 wds.
8 Filbert or cashew
9 ___ maison (indoors): Fr.: 2 wds.
11 Not encouraging or pleasing
15 Move with a splashing sound
18 Lack of confidence in one's abilities: hyph.
19 It'll grow on you
20 "Me here!," more grammatically: 2 wds.
21 Wine holder
22 God in Grenoble
24 Outermost community
29 Underground Railroad leader Harriet
33 Scintillas
35 Like some high-fiber cereal
36 Exigency
37 Suffixes of origin
38 White House advisory group, initially
39 Fair-hiring agcy.
40 Genre of popular music, initially

113

Across

1 Flip response?
6 Come to pass
11 Object
12 Frontiersman Daniel
13 Great-___
14 Get around
15 Education station
16 Refines
17 Gulf state
19 "___ and the Beast"
22 Bailiwick
26 Square (with)
27 Thoroughly botched
28 Dads' counterparts
29 Soprano Farrell
30 Beat
32 Not as certain
35 Church part
39 Flies alone
40 The ___ suspects
41 Desktop pictures
42 Thrills
43 Nearby things
44 A first name in cosmetics

Down

1 Full house, e.g.
2 Old railroad name
3 Awfully long time
4 Avoid answering things: 2 wds.
5 Envision
6 The 44th president
7 Deal with something thoroughly: 3 wds.
8 Not hot
9 Troop group
10 Cold war side
16 Hog haven
18 Had a bite
19 "Pow!"
20 It may be easily bruised
21 Shirt part
23 Lobster eggs
24 Farm female
25 New England's Cape ___
27 High school class, for short
29 Muff
31 "Siddhartha" writer
32 "What ___ now?": 2 wds.
33 Nina of "An American in Paris"
34 Sheet of ice
36 Boat with a kick
37 Marquis de ___
38 Choice word
40 Exploit

114

Across

1 Stylish
5 Capital of France
10 Zeus's wife
11 ___ in (overflowing with)
12 1992 Edward James Olmos movie: 2 wds.
14 Completed
15 One way to fall in love
18 Legislate
23 Individual
24 "Hey there!"
25 What parents may "put up" with their kids: 2 wds.
28 Detroit baseball team
29 "Do the Right Thing" director
30 Therefore
31 Salad green
33 Train's sound
35 Mississippi music: 2 wds.
41 Wedding
42 Biblical birthright seller
43 Brewskis
44 Belgrade native

Down

1 When doubled, a dance
2 ___ and haw (stall)
3 Anger
4 Christmas ___
5 Rate
6 Not in the dark about: 2 wds.
7 Took off quickly
8 School of thought
9 "___-Devil" (Meryl Streep movie)
13 Climbing plant
15 Tooth's home
16 "Tomorrow" musical
17 Condescend
19 Swed. neighbor
20 "Fixing ___" (Beatles song): 2 wds.
21 Ice cream holders
22 Carries
24 Running backs gain them: abbr.
26 P.I., in old slang
27 ___ Set (kid's toy)
31 Corn holder
32 Cameos, e.g.
34 ___ Christian Andersen
35 Do a voice-over
36 One way to go: abbr.
37 Deception
38 "It's no ___!"
39 Swimmer's ___
40 Big sandwich

115

Across

1 Siesta
6 Adrien ___ makeup brand
11 "Card" or "bard" sound: 2 wds.
12 Prefix with comic
13 At the height of activity: 3 wds.
15 Actress Donovan of "Clueless"
16 Start of Massachusetts' motto
17 Electrical units now called siemens
18 Badgers' burrow
20 Berne's river
21 Wild or frenzied
24 Opposite SSW
25 "Are you a man ___ mouse?": 2 wds.
26 "Le Coq ___"
27 Gathers on the surface, chemically
29 One-time AT&T rival
30 Cr. transaction
31 Gabs non-stop
32 March day
34 Encourages
36 Effusively or insincerely emotional
39 Big name in foil
40 Inscribed pillar
41 Prefix for stealing
42 Brand in the bedroom

Down

1 F.I.C.A. benefit
2 Play a ___ (act without help): 2 wds.
3 Powdery deposit on a surface
4 Needle holders
5 Buds
6 Palm Sunday transportation
7 Keeps from drying out
8 Books, magazines, etc.: 2 wds.
9 One, to a German
10 Stadium section
14 Light ray that stays narrow over great distances: 2 wds.
17 "Give that ___ medal!": 2 wds.
19 Long stretches
21 Swedish tennis player Björn
22 Halite: 2 wds.
23 ___ Kringle
28 "All right, I get it!": 2 wds.
31 Buttinsky
32 Writer Dinesen
33 Computer brand
35 Porgy's love
37 "Can ___ least sit down?": 2 wds.
38 When doubled, a yellow Teletubby

116

Across

1. "___, humbug!"
4. Narc's org.
7. "Mogambo" actress Gardner
8. Bobby of hockey fame
9. "Exodus" character
12. Singer Valens
14. Gen-___
15. "Goldberg Variations" composer
16. Nikon or Konica
18. Old anesthetic
20. Share a border with
21. Sandra ___ of "Gidget"
22. Every last thing: 2 wds.
25. Kind of newspaper
27. Halftime encouragement from the coach: 2 wds.
29. Football measurements: abbr.
32. Double-___ (kind of tournament, for short)
33. 1950's Ford flop
35. Binds: 2 wds.
38. Grand Ole ___
39. "Yada, yada, yada"
40. Diet number
42. "Understand?"
43. Deception
44. Infomercials, e.g.
45. "Go on ..."
46. "Are we there ___?"

Down

1. ___ wire (stuff on a fence)
2. Fly a plane
3. Unfair article by a journalist: 2 wds.
4. "Stupid me!"
5. Clapton who sang "Layla"
6. Section
9. Product with sexy TV ads: 3 wds.
10. Show shown again on TV
11. Really mad
13. "Evita" role
17. When repeated, a fish
19. Country great McEntire
23. Every bit
24. Pepsi rival
26. 24-hr. conveniences
27. "For ___ sake!"
28. A-list
30. Talk bad about
31. Most sneaky
34. Scooby-___ (cartoon dog)
36. The Bruins' sch.
37. Hurt
41. Was winning

117

Across

1 State in NE India
6 Decoy or siren, essentially
11 Hokkaido port
12 Island (Italian)
13 French government stock
14 Myopia remedy
15 RN's specialty
16 When doubled, sister of Magda
18 Versailles to Paris dir.
19 ___-rock (music genre)
20 Efron of "The Lucky One"
21 Skier Tommy
22 Kept aside for future use: 2 wds.
24 "No ___ done"
25 Pops, for example
26 Place for a drink
27 Breakfast-all-day chain, for short
29 Madonna song of 2007: 2 wds.
32 Boy child
33 Jim Bakker's club letters
34 Kind of camera, initially
35 You, in Toulouse
36 Tempe inst.
37 Plead
38 Crucial moment, militarily: hyph.
40 Toil
42 Manhandles
43 Hymn writer Reginald
44 Put out
45 Rustic poems

Down

1 Of the largest artery
2 Classic Brando utterance
3 Self-righteous
4 Verb in a famous Juliet line
5 He calls Muslims to prayer
6 Pale reddish purple
7 Olympics chant letters
8 Horror movie of 1968: 2 wds.
9 "Father Knows Best" actress Donahue
10 Rapper Prince ___
17 ___ Gabriel
23 Second-in-command, shortly
24 Stable staple
26 Comic with the Samurai Futaba character
27 Panama and others
28 Uproars: hyph.
29 Citrus ___, California: abbr.
30 British secondary school exam: 2 wds.
31 Prodding sorts
33 Break down
39 "The Deep End of the Ocean" director Grosbard
41 Managed

118

Across

1 Basic Halloween costume
6 Kind of committee: 2 wds.
11 Buzz
12 Spa feature
13 Kind of column
14 Type of ear or tube
15 Former Oriole slugger Powell
16 Take on
17 Kind of layer
19 Decide on: 2 wds
22 Waldorf salad ingredient
26 Whatever person, old style
27 Shot the breeze
28 Boy, to his madre
29 Collected
30 "Whole ___ Love" (Led Zeppelin song)
32 Shade provider
35 Radiohead's Yorke
39 Something in the air
40 Collapse under pressure
41 Taste
42 Actor Mandel
43 Bias
44 Arm

Down

1 Take the wrong way?
2 Boss of the fashion world
3 "Typee" sequel
4 1977 Toni Morrison novel: 3 wds.
5 Assay
6 One of 3.5 billion
7 Exhausting ballroom contest: 2 wds.
8 Stud muffin
9 First-year J.D. student
10 Worry
16 Windswept spot
18 Menagerie
19 Hold title to
20 Key letter
21 Large amount
23 Leave widemouthed
24 Craving
25 Flowery verse
27 Spout
29 Sloppy digs
31 Eyeball benders: 2 wds.
32 Elliot of the Mamas and the Papas
33 Asian sea name
34 Astronomer's sighting
36 Wolf's sound
37 Tom Joad, e.g.
38 Face up to
40 Fraternity letter

119

Across

1 Actress Gilpin of "Frasier"

5 Pocket breads

10 Small intestine section

11 "It's only ___!": 2 wds.

12 Shipping hazards

13 Not urban

14 It can aid a patient's breathing: 2 wds.

16 Some collars

17 Apple debut of 2010

20 Minnesota iron ore range

24 Ending with infer or inter

25 Russian space station

26 Suffix with man or habit

27 Wine holder

29 Some business card nos.

30 Diamond status: 2 wds.

32 Taking charge

37 "The Jeffersons" actress Gibbs

38 ___ León, Mexican state bordering the U.S.

39 Sell online: hyph.

40 Heraldic filets

41 View for a further time

42 Turner and others

Down

1 Suffix with googol

2 Strange and frightening: var.

3 Rough and sturdy

4 "That's enough for me": 2 wds.

5 Associate

6 "Dunno": 2 wds.

7 Small mountain lake

8 Amo, amas, ___

9 French seasoning

10 Nigerian native

15 Candidate for office

17 Like Brahms's Cello Sonata no. 2: 2 wds.

18 Intimate

19 Chef's phrase: 2 wds.

21 Back-up: abbr.

22 Swing

23 They, in France

25 Vice president 1977–81

28 Masked man with a stick

29 Make 100% positive

31 "Ready ___...": 2 wds.

32 Missing a deadline

33 Memorable periods

34 Believed

35 "Blue Tail Fly" singer

36 +: abbr.

37 Sea, to Debussy

120

Across

1 Without a weapon
8 Game console with a movement-sensing controller
11 Long Island town
12 Walk-___ (cameo parts)
13 Cutting tool used by two people
14 Matterhorn, e.g.
15 East: Ger.
16 Common vetch
17 Reagan's "Evil Empire" letters
20 Before the present: 2 wds.
22 Lug
23 Deep-___ pizza
24 Actress Albertson of "Bewitched"
26 Make things right
29 Citrus slakers
31 Pâté de ___ gras
32 Ball
34 Cholesterol varieties, initially
35 ___-bitty (small)
36 Baseball stat.
38 Calendar abbr.
39 ___ Fairbanks Jr.
43 Naval off.
44 To the heavens: hyph.
45 Egg layer
46 Groups of six

Down

1 Labor grp. founded in 1890
2 U.S. medical research agcy.
3 DiFranco of pop
4 According to what some say
5 It doesn't gather on rolling stones
6 On a high
7 Margery of rhyme
8 Certain adult status
9 Emcee's lines
10 "So what else ___?": 2 wds.
16 First airplane voyage, likely: 2 wds.
17 Einstein's birthplace
18 Risk assessors' group, initially
19 Army officer below the rank of captain
21 Inlet
25 Majors in acting
27 Nothing
28 Suffix meaning "recipients of an action"
30 Brush mark
32 High-pressure talk
33 Composition by Chopin
37 Acquires
39 Sheet music markings: abbr.
40 Rest
41 Realtor, e.g.: abbr.
42 "Quiet down!" sounds

121

Across

1 "___ Rich Pageant" (R.E.M. album)
6 About: 2 wds.
10 James Bond, for one
11 Practice boxing
12 "Golden Girls" actress: 2 wds.
14 Celebrity
15 Female lobster
16 "This ___ travesty!": 2 wds.
18 Epic tale
22 Takes willingly
26 Common container
27 Not better
28 Sharp, as a pain
30 Time of the past
31 The ___ (upper Great Plains region)
33 Audition tape
35 Each
36 Chop (off)
38 Cookie since 1912
42 Country music great: 2 wds.
45 Be the owner of
46 First Greek letter
47 Bad day for Caesar
48 Dapper

Down

1 Friendly dogs, for short
2 "___ it now!": 2 wds.
3 Greek cheese
4 Contest submissions
5 Pig's home
6 Arthur of tennis fame
7 Whirls
8 Piece of body art
9 Taconite, e.g.
13 "Come again?"
17 Went fast
19 Be next to
20 "I've ___ Secret": 2 wds.
21 Cancels
22 Blown away
23 Apple center
24 Shove (in)
25 Benefit
29 Popular Toyota
32 Datebook abbr.
34 Mediterranean food
37 Small bills
39 Totally engrossed (by)
40 Real: Ger.
41 Just fine
42 Greek letter
43 Young fella
44 Forbid

122

Across

1 Carpenters' grooves
7 Cylindrical metal container
10 Frozen spike of water
11 La ___: Mexican-American culture
12 Item opened at the pump: 2 wds.
13 "Where did ___ my keys?": 2 wds.
14 "Way to go!"
16 Antiquated
19 Rockford IceHogs' org.
20 Clear
21 Book with legends
24 Other, to Ortega
25 Ending for silver or glass
26 Ned ___ ("Henry IV Part 2" character)
28 About
29 "Fiddlesticks!"
30 "Drunk ___" Luke Bryan single: 2 wds.
31 Remote
34 Month before Tishri
35 Sylphlike
39 Not even
40 Less wordy
41 It's next to nothing
42 Marine mollusk

Down

1 Use a shovel
2 Here, in Mexico
3 Trash, slangily
4 Not very often
5 On cloud nine
6 Fall mo.
7 Minute blood vessel
8 Cote d'___
9 Coast-to-coast: abbr.
11 Conservatives: hyph.
15 Wall St. rating
16 Alka-Seltzer sound
17 Buick or Ford
18 Sacred writings of a religion
22 "Giovanna d'___" (Verdi opera)
23 Former Dolphins/Patriots linebacker Junior
27 Not an extrovert
28 Pass on
31 Prefix with -phile
32 Bator's leader, in outdated Anglicized form
33 Analogy words: 2 wds.
36 Mil. transport
37 Tie-dyed garment
38 Be at fault

123

Across

1 "Over There" composer George M. ____

6 Hate intensely

11 Make a speech

12 Keaton of "Annie Hall"

13 More ready for plucking

14 "____ of God" (Jane Fonda movie)

15 Bursting balloon's sound

16 High-ranking person

18 Function

19 Sneaky

20 Ending for insist

21 People related to you

22 Canadian sentence-enders

24 Was very stinky

26 North African nation bordering Libya

28 State of Mexico

30 Chicago Blackhawks, Toronto Maple Leafs, etc.

32 Shiba ____ (cute dog breed)

33 Part of a play

35 Santa's shouts

37 Animal with antlers

38 The woman over there

39 ____ de Triomphe

40 "Zorba the Greek" author ____ Kazantzakis

42 See it the same way

44 Author Zora ____ Hurston

45 Showed again

46 Campfire remains

47 Flair

Down

1 Peace ____

2 Baltimore ____ (state bird of Maryland)

3 Greeting for Jews, beginning tonight: 2 wds.

4 Chowed down on

5 Gumption

6 Electrical device

7 Ginormous

8 Jon Lovitz character from "Saturday Night Live"

9 Baby's garment

10 Try again, as to deliver an e-mail

17 Attainable

23 ____-mo cameras

25 "Ich bin ____ Berliner"

27 Green growths

28 Burnt ____ (Crayola color)

29 Kids with no siblings, in slang

31 Makeup company

34 Drops on your face?

36 Public fight

41 "Wonderful job!"

43 Comprehend

124

Across

1 Automobile pioneer
5 Relatively cool sun: 2 wds.
10 Maintain
11 Tennis doubles player
12 Hubs
13 Dog Star
14 Having a strong dislike of: 2 wds.
16 Completely without light: hyph.
20 LeBlanc and Damon
22 ___ appointment (fix a date): 2 wds.
23 Physics, for one: abbr.
24 Medical plan, briefly
25 Area between the abdomen and the thigh
28 "The Planets" composer
30 Make (meat) less tough
32 Defeated at the ballot box
35 River past Fremont, Nebraska
38 Spiders' nests
39 Vagrants
40 Critical hosp. areas, initially
41 ___ more (several): 2 wds.
42 Function used in arrays

Down

1 Neighbor of Mo.
2 10th-century pope: 2 wds.
3 Misleading falsehood
4 Apparition
5 Pianist Jarrett and others
6 Walked with a purpose
7 "That's more than I needed to know": inits.
8 Nonpro. sports org.
9 E.R. workers
11 Tiny time unit: abbr., 2 wds.
15 John and Paul: abbr.
17 Diversion requiring physical exertion
18 Joe Namath's last pro team
19 Granny ___
20 N.C.O. rank
21 Farmland measurement
26 Copycat's words: 3 wds.
27 Fix, like a kitten
28 AIDS cause
29 Like fresh air
31 Short ways to go?
33 P.T.A. concern: abbr.
34 Good-looker
35 Vietnamese beef broth soup
36 First name in horror
37 Globetrotters founder Saperstein

125

Across

1 Annoyingly self-confident

5 Military overthrow

9 Places to live

11 Had possession of

13 Russian unit of currency

14 Pitching great Martinez

15 He beat Frazier in "The Thrilla in Manila"

16 Sales agent, for short

18 Flightless bird from Down Under

19 Zero, in soccer scores

20 Sis's sibling

21 Fix, as an election

22 Make a sweater, maybe

24 Votes into office

26 Third-largest city in the U.S.

28 Show off, as wealth

30 Shape of the president's office

33 "You've got mail" company

34 Traffic lane you need passengers to use

36 Actress ___ Marie Saint

37 Director Jean-___ Godard

38 Semicircle

39 Tombstone letters

40 They're too good for you

42 Summary

44 Everglades bird

45 Killed, in the Bible

46 Border

47 Persuasive piece in the newspaper, for short

Down

1 Got smaller

2 "___ Rouge!" (2001 Nicole Kidman movie)

3 Source of a fetus's food: 2 wds.

4 Shaving option

5 "The Godfather" director

6 Have debts

7 Agent with an assumed name: 2 wds.

8 Allow

10 Belgrade resident

12 Flutie and Llewellyn

17 ___ Set (kid's building toy)

23 Day after Wed.

25 Self-importance

27 Too quickly: 2 wds.

28 Not true

29 One of the rooms in the board game Clue

31 Fly

32 Passed on the track

35 Old-school movie players

41 Ask for alms

43 Comedian Philips

126

Across

1 Biblical shepherd
5 Ali and Frazier, e.g.
11 Brazilian soccer legend
12 Outfit for baby
13 "___ on Down the Road"
14 Malicious
15 "A Is for Alibi" author: 2 wds.
17 Actress Russo
18 Break down
21 Humpback, e.g.
26 "Pumping ___"
27 "Here comes trouble!"
28 Dancer's boss?
30 Big tests
31 What ice does if you leave it out
33 Largest city in South Dakota: 2 wds.
39 Fight back against
40 Extremely tired
41 "Catch-22" author Joseph
42 Peru's capital
43 Seaport of the Ukraine
44 "Baseball Tonight" channel

Down

1 Copies
2 Boyfriend
3 Different
4 Oscar winner for "Shampoo": 2 wds.
5 Martin's "Laugh-In" partner
6 Soon: 3 wds.
7 Blow off steam
8 About: 2 wds.
9 Big cat
10 One of 100 in D.C.
16 King: Sp.
18 Criticize, slangily
19 Victorian, for one
20 Not a pro
22 Family last name on "The Cosby Show"
23 "Bingo!"
24 "Pink Panther" films actor
25 Hesitant syllables
29 Makes laugh
30 Will Ferrell comedy about Christmas
32 Additional
33 Future flower
34 Speck in the Pacific, e.g.
35 Peanut and vegetable
36 Hawaiian necklaces
37 Light
38 "South Park" boy
39 Greek letter

127

Across

1 Aide in the Army, initially
4 Old English letter
7 "Gross!" sounds
10 Ground-dwelling game bird of tropical America
12 Novel in Nuremberg
13 "___ was a merry old soul": 3 wds.
15 Flock of wild fowl
16 Shrub with prickly leaves
17 1962 hit for The Tornados
19 Carnivorous fish: var.
22 Bavarian river
24 Tucked away
25 Six-pointers, for short
27 "___ in alpha": 2 wds.
28 Cleveland basketball team, for short
30 Big name in insurance
32 Keep: 2 wds.
34 Sweet-singing bird
35 Wharves
39 Former name of Muhammad Ali: 2 wds.
41 Part of the gene pool, initially
42 Makes aware: 2 wds.
43 100 centavos in Peru
44 Nero's title, briefly
45 "Happy Days" diner

Down

1 1960s muscle cars, initially
2 Almond milk brand
3 Parisian wave
4 August
5 "Mad Men" protagonist Draper
6 Downs and Grant
7 Popular exhibit at the National Air and Space Museum: 2 wds.
8 Highly educated: hyph.
9 Chop ___ (Chinese dish)
11 Muscular dog
14 Bird shelter
18 Soup kitchen implement
19 D.C. fundraiser
20 1:1 espresso to hot water coffee drink
21 Complete change of direction
23 Automatic update from a favorite website, initially
26 Makes a mistake: 2 wds.
29 Manuscript encs.
31 Getting chilled: 2 wds.
33 Express
34 Old-school movie players, initially
36 Socialite Maxwell
37 Epitome of thinness
38 Dict. entries
40 City on the Danube

128

Across

1 Homecoming visitor, briefly

5 Big Apple pro

10 Response to a playground challenge: 2 wds.

12 First word of a counting rhyme

13 Corp. homebase

14 Military chaplain

15 Illuminated from below

17 Anion or cation

18 "Chances ___"

20 Siouan speakers

22 Rigging pro

24 Evening meal

27 Religious rite site

29 Late R&B singer ___ Marie

30 Winter aid: hyph.

32 Tolkien's Quickbeam and Treebeard, e.g.

33 Warner ___, Charlie Chan actor

35 Mme., in Mexico

36 Dude

38 "Our Gang" girl

40 Codeine source

42 Jazz pianist Blake

45 Song by hip hop recording artist Yung L.A.: 2 wds.

46 ___ of Langerhans

47 Father

48 Prefix with byte

Down

1 "___ du lieber Gott!"

2 Young 'un

3 Accepting without dissent or doubt

4 Letters on a car sticker

5 Barred: 2 wds.

6 Teacher's union letters

7 Absolutely necessary

8 Famous wine of Calabria, Italy

9 Eager

11 Nobel Peace Prize city

16 "___ not the end of the world!"

18 Having ___ hair day: 2 wds.

19 Part in a play

21 One-on-one sport

23 Salt, briefly

25 ___'acte: intermission

26 Tabula ___ (blank slate)

28 Let back in

31 Genetic messenger, briefly

34 Zwei plus eins

36 Ancient kingdom east of the Dead Sea

37 "...blackbirds baked in ___": 2 wds.

39 One of the deadly sins

41 Tribe for which Salt Lake City's state is named

43 Suffix with catch or cash

44 Greek H

129

Across

1. Computer key for emergencies
4. Friend of the French
7. Scholastic org.
10. Zero, to soccer players
11. Shortest room in the house?
12. "What can I do for you?"
13. Drink that may be black
14. Magazine pages, often
15. Congressperson: abbr.
16. Ninny
17. Harvard rival
18. Copy
19. "___ Too Late"
20. ___-fi movies
21. Dudes
22. Girl of Glasgow
24. Confederates
26. How to serve white wine
28. Capital city named for a Greek goddess
30. Scandinavian city
33. Guevara on T-shirts
34. Precursor to the DVD player
36. Not pro
37. Series of talks, or a man's name
38. "I knew it all along!"
39. Tool with a long handle
40. Hosp. section
41. Actor Chaney, Jr.
42. Finish
43. Kilmer of "The Doors"
44. Part of many German surnames
45. Ryan of Hollywood
46. Compass pt.
47. Ron who played Tarzan
48. Peeper

Down

1. Consist of
2. Nap
3. Student's week: 2 wds.
4. Second president
5. Where doctors went: 2 wds.
6. Firmly establish, as values
7. Unsustainable swindle: 2 wds.
8. Cone-shaped home
9. Trees that may grow at high altitudes
23. Not he
25. Only three-letter zodiac sign
27. Make a part of
28. Participating
29. Prison, in slang: 2 wds.
31. "___ Tunes"
32. Not relaxed: 2 wds.
35. Actor Cox

130

Across

1 Admiral's org.
4 Spleen
7 Very small quantity of something
9 "...made ___ woman" (Genesis 2:22): 2 wds.
12 Move rapidly: 2 wds.
14 Window ledge
15 Word on a dollar bill
16 Nest part
18 Pushes: 2 wds.
20 Early night, in an ode
21 Let go
22 Arena where the Knicks play, for short
23 Disorder in which someone feels obliged to do things repeatedly: inits.
24 Ending for pay or Cray
27 Greeting for a brave person: ___ welcome
29 Baseball Hall-of-Famer Roush
30 Mr. Magoo's trait
32 Old, in Edinburgh
33 Hemispherical roof
34 1976–81 skit show with John Candy and Martin Short
36 "The basis of optimism is..." (Oscar Wilde): 2 wds.
40 Sister of Helios in Greek mythology
41 Take over from, as shift duties
42 Pennsylvania and Reading, in Monopoly, briefly
43 Implant

Down

1 PC port
2 "___ man walks into a bar...": 2 wds.
3 Residental institutions for the elderly: 2 wds.
4 Country just south of the Arctic Circle: abbr.
5 Amusement park ride: 2 wds.
6 Old Spanish queen
8 Goody two shoes
9 Savory dishes served as an appetizer: 2 wds.
10 Inner prefix
11 Stravinsky ballet
13 The good seats
16 Pro ___ (for the time being)
17 "Rushmore" director Anderson
19 H.S. diploma alternatives
21 "Bless me, Father, ___ have sinned": 2 wds.
25 "Bad" checkup letters
26 Include
28 Sport involving touchés
30 Gds.: abbr.
31 Start of a pirate's cry: hyph.
32 "The Bell of ___" (Longfellow)
35 Collectible frames
37 Grammar-school trio, initially
38 Ab ___ (from day one)
39 RC button

131

Across

1 Monies owed
6 Reid and Lipinski
11 Nebraska city
12 Scent
13 Acknowledged
14 Shish ___
15 "A Nightmare on ___ Street"
16 Leave amazed
18 Ending for rational or lion
19 Vardalos of "My Big Fat Greek Wedding"
20 "___ bad!"
21 Neither here ___ there
22 Plenty
24 Agreed-upon facts
26 Off in the distance
28 "___ Stone"
29 April rain
32 Other
35 One of two on the head
36 Soaking
38 Soap brand
39 The E in NYE
40 "Much ___ About Nothing"
41 Mischievous type
42 Word after time or money
44 San Antonio building
46 Put ___ to (stop): 2 wds.
47 18-wheelers
48 Goods
49 Sip

Down

1 Museum guide
2 Estevez of "The Breakfast Club"
3 1995 Val Kilmer movie: 2 wds.
4 Definite article
5 1978 Peace Nobelist Anwar ___
6 Sign on a tray of samples: 2 wds.
7 "Who ___ you?"
8 "Mrs. Doubtfire" actor: 2 wds.
9 Online bookstore
10 Scary swords
17 Pan used in Beijing
23 Tool with teeth
25 "Bravo!"
27 Money for finding lost pets
29 Go up and down
30 Cuba's capital
31 Wine color
33 Peak
34 Smoke out
37 Breakfast bread that may get burnt
43 Compass dir.
45 Grassland

132

Across

1 Sticker on a windshield
6 Clearly surprised
11 Clear, as a disk
12 Far from fresh
13 Be off-target: 3 wds.
15 Chemical suffix
16 Long-term spy
17 Valuable stone
18 Couch
22 Groups of words
26 Brooks of "The Producers"
27 TV doctor
28 "Don't get any funny ___!"
30 "___ say!"
31 Corrode: 2 wds.
33 Onion's cousin
35 Carpet
36 Swedish retailer
38 Dove's sound
41 Country singer from Canada: 2 wds.
45 Groups of cattle
46 Symbol of the US
47 Live
48 Prom wear

Down

1 Moore of "G.I. Jane"
2 Andrews or Brockovich
3 Beer amount
4 Fool
5 "Hmmmm...": 3 wds.
6 Cain's brother
7 Chess and checkers
8 Santa ___ Winds
9 Golf score
10 Animal found in Finland
14 "Where the heart is"
17 Neon or argon
19 Sign of the future
20 Accomplishment
21 "Not to mention ..."
22 TV's Dr. ___
23 One of 18 on a golf course
24 Be a monarch
25 Placed
29 Archaeological site
32 Part of town
34 Varieties
37 Star___ (tuna brand)
38 Hamster's home
39 Sesame and olive
40 Mind ___ manners
41 That woman
42 Put a spell on
43 "Entourage" role
44 Armed conflict

133

Across

1 1970s music style
6 Ill-suited
11 Different
12 "___ the Greek"
13 Throws up a red flag
14 Poker announcement: 2 wds.
15 Reveal (that you know something): 2 wds.
17 Sailing on the ocean
18 eBay attempts
19 Inch, foot or yard
21 Young fella
22 Big fans
25 Between zero and two
26 Central
27 Scooby-___ (TV dog)
28 Aphrodite or Artemis
30 The latest craze
31 Towards the sunset
32 Alan of "M*A*S*H"
33 "That's so funny!"
35 Of the sun
37 Use, as influence
39 Senegal's capital city
41 Animal that starts with a double consonant
42 Last Greek letter
43 Director Jackson or singer Gabriel
44 Valentine's Day flowers

Down

1 ___ Jones Industrial Average
2 From Rome or Florence, to someone from Rome or Florence
3 Classic breakfast cereal: 2 wds.
4 Pennies
5 About: 2 wds.
6 Machine gun type
7 "That's cheating!": 2 wds.
8 Classic breakfast cereal: 2 wds.
9 Ending for convert or digest
10 "There!": hyph.
16 People who like to walk around naked
18 Online journal
20 Indicates "yes"
22 City where Iowa's straw poll is
23 Angry's driver's "condition": 2 wds.
24 Pop
29 "Oh goodness!": 2 wds.
32 San Antonio building, with "The"
33 Assistance
34 Rod in a car
36 Unpleasant smell
38 Cigarette additive
40 Dormitory heads, for short

134

Across

1 Jet ___
4 FedEx delivery, briefly
7 Sporty Pontiac letters
10 U.S./Eur. divider
11 "Weetzie Bat" author Francesca ___ Block
12 Big ISP
13 Unit of conductance
14 Freeway access points: hyph.
16 "The ___" (Peter Sellers movie of 1967)
18 White-tailed birds
19 Go after a mosquito, in a way: 2 wds.
21 Koh-i- ___ (famed diamond)
23 Director Riefenstahl
24 "What do you make ___?": 2 wds.
25 Cows reared for their milk: 2 wds.
28 Chichén ___ (Mayan city)
29 "Well, Did You ___!" (Porter classic)
30 Well-struck ball
31 Mineral salt found in dried lake beds
34 Answer
36 Almost forever
37 Chinese dish: hyph.
39 Marshal under Napoleon
40 Antipoverty agcy.
41 "T" size: abbr.
42 Suffix with Salvador
43 Former pro wrestler Anderson
44 Prefix meaning "bad"
45 Western metropolis, initially

Down

1 Ewes' kids
2 South African playwright Fugard
3 Growth to a worldwide scale
4 Ramallah grp.
5 Power a body has when in motion: 2 wds.
6 "Tootsie" actress
7 Fantasy TV show that takes place on Westeros and Essos: 3 wds.
8 Layer of earth on the surface
9 Certain football players, initially
15 Make comments on (a text, e.g.)
17 Switchboard worker
20 Some
22 Abbr. usually followed by a number
25 Prefix with respect or associate
26 Former Republican National Committee chairman Lee
27 Movie girl's name
32 Shaquille of the N.B.A.
33 Group that performed at Super Bowl XXXV
35 Can. island
37 Risk assessors' group, initially
38 "Uh-huh!"

135

Across

1 Donkey Kong or King Kong
4 Adept
7 "No great shakes"
10 Bowler's target
11 ___ Jones
12 Gardner of "On the Beach"
13 Arboreal rodent: 2 wds.
16 Big-ticket ___
17 Durable wood
18 Put aboard
20 Big tippler
23 Bart Simpson sister
26 Kindergarten break
27 Damsel's rescuer: 2 wds.
31 Long stretch
32 Opinion
33 Give a hand
35 Garlicky mayonnaise
39 Country for which a cat was named
42 Arabian sultanate
43 2013 Cate Blanchett movie: 2 wds.
46 "Certainement!"
47 Affirmative vote
48 Designate
49 Contract negotiator: abbr.
50 Donnybrook
51 Command to Fido

Down

1 It follows a long March
2 Michelangelo masterpiece
3 Closed
4 Immediately, initially
5 Drubbing
6 Boo-boo, to tots
7 Word before time or territory
8 Joanne Woodward Oscar-winning role
9 "2001" mainframe
14 Refine
15 Unvarnished
19 Per ___ (daily)
21 Slangy refusal
22 Decide to leave, with "out"
24 Hit the slopes
25 Kournikova of tennis
27 Made one
28 Weed killer
29 Formally dressed: 3 wds.
30 Manner of speaking
34 Fabrication
36 Misses
37 Hawaiian veranda
38 All thumbs
40 Not quite shut
41 ___ Clinic
43 ___ constrictor
44 Kind of nut
45 Use a Singer

136

Across

1 Clerical robe
6 Big initials in fashion
9 Bextra manufacturer, now part of Pfizer
10 Antipoverty agcy. created by LBJ
11 Los Angeles suburb: 2 wds.
13 5:50, vis-à-vis 6:00: 2 wds.
14 Neighbor of Minn.: 2 wds.
15 Parisian ones
16 Catlike mammals that secrete musk
18 Type of internet connection, briefly
19 "Dr. Strangelove," e.g.
20 Place for a corsage
21 Key of Mozart's Symphony No. 25: 2 wds.
23 When doubled, a Teletubby
26 Daniel Suarez novel
27 Bull: prefix
28 Wings
29 The Muffin Man's Lane
30 Granted on certain terms
33 F.D.R.'s successor
34 "Forget it!": 2 wds.
35 "Now I see!"
36 1976 Stevie Wonder chart-topper: 2 wds.

Down

1 Herb that tastes like licorice
2 Simple water vessels
3 Golden ___ (Nabisco cookie)
4 Jelmar product, initially
5 Half a math puzzle
6 Out there
7 Drug
8 Takes a peep
9 Composer Saint-___
11 Ear-piercer
12 Blacksmith's block
16 Fixed chicken
17 Anatomical passage
19 Healthy, in Spain
20 Treated a lawn, perhaps
21 Waterproof overshoe
22 "It ___ lot to me": 2 wds.
23 Send into orbit
24 Psychic glows
25 Chemical group
26 Russian country house
27 French three
29 Stu's wife on "Rugrats"
31 Config. file for computer applications
32 Pull along

137

Across

1 Dictionary entries, for short
5 Did another version of, as an old movie
11 Rapper who stars in "Law & Order: SVU"
12 In a fair way
13 Old stadium for the New York Mets
14 One under par on a hole in golf
15 "My goodness!": 2 wds.
17 Paddle's cousin
18 Similar to
22 Shimmering beads on a dress
26 Become droopy
27 Clumsy person
28 Noted caravel
30 "...then ___ monkey's uncle!": 2 wds.
31 Kicked out
33 Extinct bird
35 High card in the deck
36 Cute and chubby: 2 wds.
41 Black belt's specialty
44 Atlas section
45 "Understood!": 3 wds.
46 Cat's weapon
47 Equally: 2 wds.
48 Rock group that sounds like a vegetable

Down

1 Plate
2 Audio effect
3 Touch
4 "Don't come in here!": 2 wds.
5 Given a new life
6 Just plain bad
7 Streep of "It's Complicated"
8 "What else?"
9 551, in Ancient Rome
10 It may be blue or hazel
16 Native American crop
19 "___ that funny?"
20 Actress Winslet
21 "Oh my!"
22 Hit the brakes quickly
23 Red puppet on "Sesame Street"
24 Area of a college campus surrounded by buildings
25 Hot
29 You put it on an injury to stop the swelling: 2 wds.
32 Car parkers
34 Give a speech
37 Milo's dog buddy, in a movie title
38 Capital city on a fjord
39 "That's not true and you know it!"
40 Sign that someone's tired or bored
41 Relatives
42 Long ___ (way back when)
43 Catholicism or Hinduism: abbr.

138

Across

1 Parking ___
4 Relief: abbr.
7 Bar for beers
10 "I ___ Man of Constant Sorrow": 2 wds.
11 America, initially
12 Pollution-fighting branch of govt.
13 Medical procedure named for a Greek physician: 2 wds.
15 Fork over the cash
16 "Whoops!"
17 Butler of "Gone With the Wind"
19 Testifying group of experts
21 Beatle Ringo
23 Page in an atlas
25 1963 role for Liz
26 Urban music genre
29 Come out on top
31 Lock opener
32 Soothing plant
34 Master Mind game piece
36 Nation of ninjas
38 Put pen to paper
42 Take it all off
44 Supercelebrity, like Oprah or Madonna
45 Alias, initially
46 Small camping shelter: 2 wds.
48 Wheels
49 In favor of
50 Devoured
51 Explosive, initially
52 Up to this point
53 ___'easter

Down

1 Take in with relish: 2 wds.
2 Nebraska's largest city
3 Hit lightly, as glass: 2 wds.
4 Take to court
5 "Back in the ___"
6 Tubs
7 Words to encourage the team: 2 wds.
8 Cornered, like a cat: 3 wds.
9 Dark horse
14 Not us
18 And so forth
20 "___ & Order"
22 Mr. Rogers
24 Spot on a die
26 British rule in India
27 Sarah Palin, e.g.
28 Kellogg's breakfast food
30 "What's ___?"
33 Head attachment
35 "True ___" (1969 movie remade in 2010)
37 A little cold outside
39 Arctic or Atlantic
40 The Lone Ranger's kemo sabe
41 Oversized computer key
43 100%
45 Memorize lines and hit the stage

139

Across

1 High-cal
6 Take off
11 Video game pioneer
12 Demagnetize, as a tape
13 Venom
14 Checks
15 Vast
16 Popular theater name
17 Velveeta maker
19 Rotation-producing force
22 1993 standoff site
26 Hatred
27 Prime-time time
28 Internet ___ (viral phenomenon)
29 Wisconsin city or its college
30 Motionless
32 Kind of artist
35 Contents of some cartridges
39 Outfit
40 Angel
41 Continental currency
42 Person with a mike
43 Actor DeVito
44 Not even

Down

1 Lot
2 Resting on
3 Picker-upper
4 Sly inquiry: 2 wds.
5 Yang's counterpart
6 Printing flourish
7 "Prince of the City" actor: 2 wds.
8 Epitome of thinness
9 Fails to be
10 Baja bread
16 Singer Carly ___ Jepsen
18 Piña colada ingredient
19 Turkey's name
20 Poem of praise
21 Slam-dunk circle
23 Past
24 "The Sweetheart of Sigma ___"
25 Giant of note
27 Migratory fish
29 High school class, for short
31 ___-turvy
32 Got ready to drive, with "up"
33 Light greenish-blue
34 Go sour
36 Cutlet?
37 Joint with a cap
38 Hot pot
40 Where the buoys are

140

Across

1 Madras dresses
6 Pentagon quintet
11 Said, like Poe's raven
12 Director Kurosawa
13 Court org. 1920–75: 2 wds.
14 Israeli desert
15 Deaf person's communication letters
16 Victor's letters?
18 ___ manner of speaking: 2 wds.
19 You, in Berlin
20 Vintage touring car
22 Rupture
24 Verb used by Tweety Pie
25 Method of reproduction
27 Nordstrom rival
29 Goal-oriented activity
32 Suddenly, by a single action: 3 wds.
34 Fifth, e.g.: abbr.
35 More than warm
36 Canadian sch. with campuses in Fredericton and Saint John
37 Flag carrier of Lebanon, initially
38 Negatively charged particle
40 Better
42 "Children of a Lesser God" director Haines
43 Rose (up), oater-style
44 "Ragged Dick" author
45 Draws nigh

Down

1 Flatten
2 Down Under dweller
3 Gliding about on wheels: 2 wds.
4 Addamses' hairy cousin
5 New England sailboat
6 Yemen's capital
7 Mike and ___ candies
8 Canon PowerShot ELPH 160, e.g.: 2 wds.
9 Heretofore: 2 wds.
10 Learned scholar
17 French song
21 Suffix with phon or path
23 Aircraft accident investigators, initially
26 House for cattle: 2 wds.
27 Much of Niger
28 Discordant
30 More level
31 Checks the sums again
33 Like some calendars
39 Parabasis
41 West of "My Little Chickadee"

141

Across

1 Gross growth, but not from toads

5 Walk with confidence

11 Fleshy plant

12 Tempt

13 Votes against

14 Sounds

15 Embarrassing info, to the tabloids

16 Quality ___ (hotel chain)

17 Approximately: 2 wds.

19 Steffi who won 22 Grand Slam tennis tournaments

23 "Jerry ___" (Tom Cruise movie)

26 Body spray brand

27 "___ you forgetting something?"

28 Verve

30 Part of MPH

31 Roman, Inca and British

33 Talk back

35 Aware of

36 Dude

38 Run ___ (go wild)

41 Money for finding something

44 Cold War org.

45 Country with the cities of Roma and Milano

46 "___ the Wild" (Jon Krakauer book)

47 Let it ride, in gambling

48 Make the food

Down

1 Stick for a magician

2 Jai ___ (fast-moving sport)

3 Title cowboy in an Elton John song: 2 wds.

4 Dress rehearsal: 2 wds.

5 Sophomore plus two years

6 Unsigned, for short

7 British singer who was head of The Police

8 Not hers

9 Flying expert

10 "What can I do for you?"

18 Web location

20 Queens-born comedian/sitcom actor: 2 wds.

21 Rod that holds tires

22 Charges

23 Google ___

24 Vicinity

25 Sports channel

29 Best Picture set at sea

32 Long before the weekend

34 Microscopic

37 Opera tune

39 Palindromic name

40 Weirdo

41 Tear

42 Two letters after epsilon

43 More than a battle

142

Across

1 Grand ___
6 Marla of "The Jeffersons"
11 Goodbye, to the French
12 Scarlett ___ of "Gone With the Wind"
13 What students take in class
14 Coin for the bus or subway
15 Stationery with horizontal and vertical lines: 2 wds.
17 Puts on the radio
18 Several: 2 wds.
21 Color of the Beatles' submarine
26 Ravi Shankar's instrument
28 Leader of a sports team
29 Didn't leave
31 Palindromic bus driver on "The Simpsons"
32 Piece of furniture in an office
34 Puzzles that can be created on 15-across
40 Loud, metallic sound
41 Turn away, as one's gaze
42 Caribbean island nation
43 TV, radio, etc.
44 Give the house a new room: 2 wds.
45 Theater items

Down

1 Long tooth
2 Aroma
3 Hayworth or Marley
4 Steer clear: 2 wds.
5 Raw fish from Japan
6 "Can I talk to you?": 3 wds.
7 Breakfast-all-day chain, for short
8 Put in the oven
9 ___ Rabbit (tricky literary character)
10 ___ Francisco
16 Be nosy
18 Beast of burden
19 In good shape
20 Airport guess: abbr.
22 Examine: 2 wds.
23 California's largest newspaper, for short
24 After Sept.
25 "Which person?"
27 Washington football player
30 ___ Moines (Iowa's capital)
33 Place for an alligator
34 Dressed (in)
35 Quick, unexpected attack
36 Not fooled by
37 Try again
38 Faucet problem
39 Train stops: abbr.
40 "___-ching!"

143

Across

1 Blow it

6 Urge

11 Take ___ breath: 2 wds.

12 Prefix with linear

13 "Here ___" (arrival words): 2 wds.

14 "… ___ Emmanuel": 2 wds.

15 Sophisticated good taste

17 Dispatch boats

18 Smooth and cylindrical (botany)

20 "M*A*S*H" regular

24 Suffix with strict or struct

25 It goes before E except after C: 2 wds.

26 Muppet who loves pigeons

28 Deep-seated

31 1962 Wayne movie

33 Like some music

37 Blinding light

38 "Boy, Did ___ Wrong Number!" (Bob Hope movie): 3 wds.

39 Acoustic

40 Café cup

41 Silver, in Spain

42 Williams who played Potsie on "Happy Days"

Down

1 Bryn ___, college in Pennsylvania

2 Nantes notion

3 Mariner

4 Infer

5 Gift giver's command: 2 wds.

6 Teaser: abbr.

7 Cove

8 College course, casually

9 Mo.-end document

10 "Sprechen ___ deutsch?"

16 Ending for Japan or Surinam

18 Place to unwind

19 "Maid of Athens, ___ we part" (Byron)

21 Caution

22 Chemistry suffix

23 Rx instruction, initially

27 Year of ___ (2008 or 2020, to the Chinese): 2 wds.

28 Cousin in a 1960s sitcom

29 Tokyo air hub

30 Heavy leather work shoe

32 Trenton and Baltimore are on its route

33 12th month of the Jewish civil year

34 Pasternak heroine

35 "Make ___": 2 wds.

36 Normandy city

37 Cumberland ___

144

Across

1 Left work for the day: 2 wds.
7 House: Sp.
11 Rome's country, to Romans
12 Without attribution, as a poem: abbr.
13 Pullitzer Prize winning poet: 2 wds.
15 Currency unit: abbr.
16 Aegean, Red or Adriatic
17 Calf's laugh
18 Put into office
20 Grafting shoot
22 Try again
23 Plato's city
24 Coke rival
26 Lorne of "Bonanza"
29 St. Louis football team
33 Do the numbers again
34 Sound of a melon hitting the ground
35 Lang. you speak
36 "That's amazing!"
38 Number in Nicaragua
39 "Song of Myself" poet: 2 wds.
42 Hint of the future
43 Fruit that's also a color
44 Where a sparrow sleeps
45 More physically alluring

Down

1 Big beam in a building
2 Peter of "Lawrence of Arabia"
3 Put off for later, as a discussion
4 "Well done!"
5 Leading the pack
6 Destiny
7 Mazda or Mitsubishi
8 Societal rootlessness (anagram of ONE AIM)
9 "Leaving already?": 2 wds.
10 Playwright Chekhov and actor Yelchin
14 Doesn't eat, for religious reasons
19 Dealt (with), as a problem
21 Sing like a bird
23 Big primate
25 Give money to, as a university
26 Became charming to, over time: 2 wds.
27 Call something else
28 Philadelphia's NFL team
30 Grads of a school
31 Oversee
32 Pothead
34 County, in English place names
37 Cries of discovery
40 Dynamite letters
41 Money for the IRS

145

Across

1 Bakery buys

6 Baseball or blue jeans features

11 Phantom's place, in a musical title

12 Expect eagerly

13 Kind of tooth

14 "Around the World in 80 Days" author

15 Ernie who's won the U.S. Open twice

16 Santa ___, Calif.

18 "First off..."

19 Part of IPA

20 Take all of, as the covers

21 Zero, in soccer scores

22 Plays (around with)

24 Past, present and future

26 Hands over: 2 wds.

28 Lacking much money: 2 wds.

30 Word in Oscar categories

33 Longoria of "Desperate Housewives"

34 On the ___ (running from the police)

36 Fib

37 Basketball hoop

38 B-F links

39 He lost to 35-down at Gettysburg

40 "___ Mia!"

42 Best guests: hyph.

44 Didn't visit a restaurant: 2 wds.

45 "Inferno" author

46 Geeky types

47 Mystery writing award

Down

1 Attack: 2 wds.

2 Moon-landing name

3 He played Dr. Frasier Crane: 2 wds.

4 Time of history

5 Palin from Alaska

6 Brutes

7 She may have a little lamb

8 He produced "Fantasy Island" and "Beverly Hills 90210": 2 wds.

9 Mickey Mouse's mate

10 Reinforces (oneself), as for a shock

17 Tablet

23 Punk figure Vicious

25 Dull pencil point

27 Mr. Spock on "Star Trek," and others

28 Mr. Melville

29 Take to the skies

31 Nap in the afternoon

32 Harris ___ grocery stores

35 He beat 39-across at Gettysburg

41 Prefix with night or week

43 Young fella

146

Across

1 "Star ___"
5 Hairdos
10 Help, as a criminal
11 "L.A. Law" lawyer
12 City south of Hilton Head, SC: 2 wds.
14 Ziti, e.g.
15 Shampoo target
18 ___ oil
22 "Who ___?"
23 Kidney-related
24 Fix, in a way
25 Aged
26 Bouquet
29 Willing to believe anything
31 "Haystacks" painter
32 Less inept
33 Late hotelier Helmsley
35 Caribbean city: 2 wds.
40 Come to mind
41 ___-friendly
42 Goes for the gold?
43 Not crazy

Down

1 Functioned as
2 Lawyer's org.
3 Gun, as the engine
4 Piece of metal shot into paper
5 Fires
6 Henry Clay, for one
7 Breathe
8 Fruit often dried
9 Caribbean, e.g.
13 Drops off

15 "Beat it!"
16 Egypt's capital
17 Gas in air
19 One way to saute: 2 wds.
20 Opening part
21 Village leader
27 Lawyer ___ Belli
28 "Relax, and that's an order!": 2 wds.
29 "Peter Pan" dog
30 Old calculator
34 Some rolls of the dice
35 "Green Eggs and ___"
36 "Exodus" role
37 America

38 Big ___ (London attraction)
39 "We ___ the World"

147

Across

1 Letter between rho and tau

6 Lawyer's org.

9 Goodbye, in France

10 Large holder of coffee

11 Soft drink company: 2 wds.

13 Reason you couldn't have committed the crime

14 Actors Holbrook and Linden

17 Cheri formerly of "Saturday Night Live"

21 "Can ___ now?": 2 wds.

22 Hosted at one's house: 2 wds.

24 Beauty pageant title: 2 wds.

26 Mrs. ___ cow (animal that caused the Great Chicago Fire)

27 Little kid

28 Streep of "Julie & Julia"

29 Piece of glass in a window

30 Underground place for waste

33 State between Texas and Arizona: 2 wds.

37 "How very nice!"

38 Coffee that won't keep you awake

39 In favor of

40 Pleasant smell

Down

1 ___ fly (baseball play, for short)

2 Actress Lupino

3 Gershon and Carano

4 Dinner, lunch or brunch

5 German automaker

6 IRS employee

7 "It's so cold!"

8 "Is it ___ wonder?"

12 Humble homes

14 It's shouted by people who are only on TV for a few seconds: 2 wds.

15 Nimble, like a gymnast

16 Winner's victim

18 Broadway musical about a leader of Argentina

19 Spy's activity, for short

20 Very, very angry

22 Home to basketball's Globetrotters

23 Late singer Winehouse

25 "Oh yeah?": 2 wds.

29 Cost

31 Gets married to

32 Part of CEO

33 Afternoon snooze

34 One of two on your head

35 Has the power to

36 Frequently, for short

148

Across

1 Blinking pair
5 Light bulb inventor
11 Wander far and wide
12 River that Vienna and Budapest are on
13 Concept
14 Fresh water entering a lake, e.g.
15 Dessert made from an orange vegetable: 2 wds.
17 "Hallelujah" singer Leonard ___
18 State known for its potatoes
21 Vampire's killer
25 Not many
26 Gun (the motor)
27 Perspire
30 Embarrassing public fight
32 "___ Business" (Tom Cruise movie)
34 Dessert made from an orange vegetable: 2 wds.
39 Indicate
40 State known for its corn
41 Financial arrangement involving a neutral third party
42 Blood problem
43 Defeats
44 Some kids

Down

1 Mr. Clapton
2 Little green guy in "The Empire Strikes Back"
3 At any time
4 Look (for)
5 Archie Bunker's wife
6 High school social events
7 Baby
8 Mope
9 One of the woodwind instruments
10 ___ and improved
16 Tic-tac-toe line
18 Variables
19 Grass's morning cover
20 Amazement
22 "___ you joking?"
23 Barbie's buddy
24 Christmas ___
28 Puts metal plates on
29 Walk very quietly
30 Go downhill in a hurry?
31 Doubting Thomases
33 Throws off, like poll results
34 Mexican currency
35 Auntie's mates
36 Sport associated with Ralph Lauren clothing
37 Victorious cry: 2 wds.
38 Chows down on
39 Neighbor of Md.

149

Across

1 Cry like a baby
5 "Two Women" Oscar-winner Sophia
10 Ashtabula's lake
11 "Hearts ___"
12 President after Richard Nixon: 2 wds.
14 "___ moment, please"
15 Affirmative vote
16 Electric shooter
18 Challenger
23 Lunch holder, maybe
25 Dash
26 What both 12-across and 41-across have brands of in their names
30 Body covering
31 AMA members
32 Nairobi's country
34 Scarlett of "Gone With the Wind"
38 Animal house
40 Herbert of the "Pink Panther" movies
41 Comic actor known for portraying 12-across: 2 wds.
45 Certain bellybutton
46 Black cat, maybe
47 Bargains
48 Chuck

Down

1 Brought forth
2 "Gladiator" setting
3 Sends money, perhaps
4 Actress Salonga or Thompson
5 Gentleman's counterpart
6 Bid
7 2016 Olympics city
8 Make a mistake
9 Actor Beatty
13 Former NFL player in Calif.
17 Black
19 Like someone from Dublin
20 Kilmer of "The Doors"
21 Part of a royal flush
22 Guitar great ___ Paul
24 George Burns role
26 "Don't ___!"
27 Don Ho instrument
28 Metallic element
29 Untamed horse
33 Tylenol alternative
35 "Remember the ___!"
36 "The Subject Was ___"
37 Church words
39 Peepers
41 Atlantic fish
42 Color
43 In-flight info
44 Burning

150

Across

1 Publicity, casually
4 "Raiders of the Lost ___"
7 Six-pack muscles
10 Got outta Dodge
11 ___ and Jerry's (ice cream brand)
12 ___ Tuesday (Mardi Gras)
13 Neighbor of Canada
15 Time of the past
16 "Dig in!"
17 Authority
19 Cheat, in a way
21 "Don't ___!"
22 Palindromic woman's name
23 Hershey's candy bar
27 Spearheaded
28 "ER" network
29 Scottish "no"
30 Saw wrongly
32 Believer's suffix
33 DVD player's predecessor
34 Frosts, as a cake
35 Secret booze container
38 Strong tree
39 Calif. airport
40 Breakfast food
44 Good club?
45 Prefix with lateral
46 Baseball card stat
47 Take down the aisle
48 Cobb and Burrell
49 Gelled

Down

1 Lyricist Gershwin
2 "China Beach" setting
3 Volleyball player's equipment
4 Not much: 2 wds.
5 ___ center
6 Backpack
7 Not many: 2 wds.
8 Empty, like a cupboard
9 Part of a constellation
14 Sunbeam
18 Plains city, for short
19 Placid
20 "The ___ Love": 2 wds.
21 Ann ___, Mich.
23 Flatten: 2 wds.
24 Fancy pants
25 Lessen
26 "___ go!"
31 Flat-screens, e.g.
34 "How Dry ___": 2 wds.
35 Blemish
36 Shoestring
37 Fired
38 Elevator name
41 "___ Which Way But Loose"
42 Honest prez
43 Ignited

151

Across

1 Plagued, as by problems
6 Colorado ski resort, or a tree you might find there
11 Oldsmobile model
12 Switzerland's capital
13 Rude comments, in hipster-speak
14 Dr. Frankenstein's assistant, and namesakes
15 British title
16 Brynner of "The King and I"
18 Automated performer of computer tasks
19 Pen
21 Every bit
22 Section of Manhattan or London
23 Make possible
25 Farmer and author ____ Berry
27 Language spoken in Egypt and Morocco
29 Hi-Q pieces
32 Canadian city where the Blue Jays play: abbr.
33 X-ray type: 2 wds.
35 World ____ II
36 Prior to
37 Number of years you've been alive
38 Boise's state
40 Blush
42 Flax fabric
43 Scrooge
44 "It would be my honor": 2 wds.
45 Olympic racers

Down

1 Deep voices
2 Weather phenomenon that means "the boy" in Spanish: 2 wds.
3 What the police need to look through your house: 2 wds.
4 Make a mistake
5 Ginza locale
6 Texas city
7 Part of a line, in geometry: abbr.
8 What the police need to get 3-down: 2 wds.
9 Sign up, as for a class
10 Chocolate company that makes Quik
17 Auto dealership purchase: 2 wds.
20 Pop singer Lisa
24 Swiss mountains
26 "Excellent job!": 2 wds.
27 Whenever you're ready: 2 wds.
28 Person who sets up equipment for rock concerts
30 Silenced
31 Mocking, evil looks
34 They're six years for senators
39 ____ and haw (stall for time)
41 Word after olive or sesame

152

Across

1 Practices boxing
6 Like some films or change
11 Attacks: 2 wds.
12 Safe place
13 Girl who visits Wonderland
14 "___ we all?"
15 One's home country
17 Olympic Games weapons
18 First letter of "freedom" but not "Friday": 2 wds.
21 Not real quick
25 Superman's enemy ___ Luthor
26 "This tastes awesome!"
28 Amaze
29 Miss ___ (TV psychic)
31 Showed shock
33 Brother's daughter, say
35 Twinned metropolis: 2 wds.
40 ___ Rica
41 "The Governator"
42 Cereal in a blue box
43 Holiest city to Muslims
44 Tale
45 Old anesthetic

Down

1 Dog and pony show
2 ___ Alto, Calif.
3 "___ happens...": 2 wds.
4 "Friends" character
5 How prices may rise
6 Sedimentary rock
7 Bother repeatedly
8 Kitchen cooker
9 Tear apart
10 Dynamite letters
16 Tom Petty hit of 1980
18 Utah's capital, initially
19 Torme or Brooks
20 Fire
22 You lose it when you stand
23 Have red ink to clear up
24 Lead down the aisle
27 Technique with knots
30 GM brand
32 Something only a handful of people know
34 Milan's country
35 It blackens a chimney
36 Ratio phrase: 2 wds.
37 Move slowly
38 Former Vikings coach Mike
39 2011 or 2012
40 Places for trials: abbr.

153

Across

1 Critical hosp. areas, initially
5 Gardening task
11 Monsieur Descartes
12 Sang-froid
13 Iridescent stone
14 Musical shows
15 Mrs. Truman
16 Soft & ___ (Gillette brand)
17 Uncontrollable laughter
22 Shack: hyph.
24 Katy Perry's "___ of Coffee": 2 wds.
25 Suffix with ideal
26 Patriotic letters
28 H, to Homer
29 Weight used in China and East Asia
31 Sayers detective
33 Old West tourist resort: 2 wds.
35 Cambodian leader of the 1970s
36 Margosa tree
39 Three-syllable foot
42 Architect Saarinen who designed Washington Dulles' main terminal
43 Like some cats
44 They give out $20 bills, initially
45 Large migratory shorebird
46 Future atty.'s hurdle

Down

1 Ethnic group of Ethiopia
2 French chef's mushroom
3 Without remorse
4 Generator element
5 Difficult to believe: 3 wds.
6 ___ citato (the work cited)
7 Title character of Nowel Coward's "Blithe Spirit"
8 Chit sheet, initially
9 Long-running U.K. music mag.
10 Literary inits.
18 Alphabet trio
19 Polar layers: 2 wds.
20 Adorable
21 Neuter's counterpart
22 English professor's deg.
23 Granduncle of Onan
27 Department of eastern France
30 Edible seed
32 Former President of Earth on "Futurama"
34 Engine designer who partnered with Rolls
37 Late humorist Bombeck
38 Nearly all
39 700, to Nero
40 Nonprofessional sports letters
41 Stain removal product, initially

154

Across

1 ___ up (invigorates)
5 Patrick of "Dirty Dancing"
11 Light blue shade
12 More cozy
13 There are two in a pint
14 Make ___ (apologize)
15 Capsizes: 2 wds.
17 Secret agent
18 Deer meat
22 Guide
24 Give up, as territory
25 Coral island
27 Polished one's car
28 Neanderthal's "house"
29 Fur for a coat
30 Kicked out
32 Savings plan
35 With natural-born skill
37 Follower of an Eastern philosophy
40 Razor brand
41 Famous: 2 wds.
42 Feature of blue jeans or a baseball
43 High on marijuana
44 Landers and others

Down

1 Agreements between nations
2 Give material to
3 Innocent romantic crush: 2 wds.
4 Be disrespectful to
5 Used a 40-across
6 Ladies
7 Word before cheese, Indian, or "Idol"
8 Yang's counterpart, to a 37-across
9 Last letter of the alphabet, in England
10 Hospital areas: abbr.
16 Curved geometric shape
19 Seductive lady: 2 wds.
20 "___ to a Nightingale"
21 Actor Beatty
23 Voting event
25 Highest card in the deck
26 ___ Mahal
27 Far and ___ (all over the place)
29 Like the cheese on a grilled cheese
31 Have a bite of
33 Showed again on TV
34 Second U.S. president
36 Govt. arm that put up the space shuttles
37 How-___ (guides)
38 Back part of a boat
39 John Lennon's love

155

Across

1 It might be dropped
5 "Kitchen Nightmares" host Gordon
11 Kind of hygiene or history
12 Even: 3 wds.
13 Woodstock wear: hyph.
15 Call to a knocker
16 "Caught you red-handed!"
17 Produce eggs
18 Mystery writer Rankin
20 Willis's "___ Hard"
23 Last word in movies?
24 Chinese percussion instrument
25 "Hawaii Five-O" catchphrase: 3 wds.
29 Prevailing
30 Aegean island on which Homer is said to be buried
31 1980s TV E.T.
32 Mel with 511 home runs
33 "Bleak House" girl
36 What a sniggler snares
38 City steel in Europe
40 Clue weapon
43 Attack violently
44 Matinée hero
45 School assignments
46 Philosopher Descarte

Down

1 Peace Prize name
2 Ring setting
3 Like some fountain drinks
4 Glamour rival
5 End of a movie road
6 Playwright Chekhov
7 Subject with fractions
8 Used to reach a high shelf: 2 wds.
9 Prepare for a shot
10 "You got it!"
14 Liquid in a jar of pickled pigs' feet
19 Bring in
21 Lodging location
22 Swelled head cause
23 Scrape by
24 It may be natural or noble
25 Front end cover on a car
26 Crude liquid
27 Scoring ability
28 Adores, with "upon"
32 Stan Laurel's pal
33 Parenthetical bit
34 Raid rival
35 Common place for a sprain
37 Cheese in red
39 Cooking instruction
40 Siamese or Persian, e.g.
41 Industrial pollutant
42 Subway cousins

156

Across

1 "Wheel of Fortune" host
6 Revels (in), as the sunshine
11 180-degree reversal: hyph.
12 FBI worker
13 Golfer Palmer, to pals
14 Spirit in a bottle
15 Oakland football team member
17 Latvia's capital
18 Environmentalist's prefix
19 Caspian or Baltic
21 Unit of resistance
22 Zilch
24 Gives a warning to
26 Saying "Oh, that's just great!" when something bad happens, e.g.
28 Revenue minus expenses
30 Dad
33 You lose it when you stand up
34 Home for peas
36 Actress Farrow or soccer star Hamm
37 Farmland measurement
39 Send back
41 "___ We Dance?"
43 Hip and cool
44 Org. for smarties
45 Go in
46 "Take ___ off!" ("Relax!"): 2 wds.
47 Chills out

Down

1 Ray of PBS's "NewsHour"
2 Disappear without ___: 2 wds.
3 TV mobster role played by Dominic Chianese: 2 wds.
4 Like much of Arizona
5 Leg benders
6 Grocery store container
7 Ending for teen or new
8 Forgetful times: 2 wds.
9 Chess piece that leaps over other pieces
10 Prepares vegetables, in a way
16 Nuclear plant building
20 Pie ___ mode: 2 wds.
23 Clumsy fool
25 Clairvoyant's ability, initially
27 Tear
28 Blood component
29 "Friends" role
31 White ___ fence
32 Mythological half-men, half-goats
35 Put off until later
38 Actress Lanchester of "Mary Poppins"
40 When summer starts
42 Young guy

157

Across

1 Non-reactive to other gases
6 Place to play racquetball, or a 1979 hit song
10 At no time
11 Necklace component
12 Overly authoritarian
14 Do the math, maybe
15 Come into contact with
16 Hairy mammal
17 Confederate general
18 Enjoy oysters, say
19 Sea: Fr.
20 Whirlpool
22 Catches a few Z's
24 Scene of battle
26 "___ and Confused"
28 Golf scores
32 Turner who founded CNN
33 Barker or Marley
35 Two after tee
36 Palindromic woman's name
37 Mystery in the sky
38 Card with a letter on it
39 Speedy
42 Two-color cookies
43 Swap
44 Body part nicknamed the "schnoz"
45 Brought on board

Down

1 Breathe
2 Had to have
3 Avoided, as the law
4 Fire up (the motor)
5 "Give it a shot": 2 wds.
6 Money in Tokyo
7 Bovary or Butterfly
8 Brunch items
9 Kind of tree whose wood is used to smoke salmon
11 General played to an Oscar by George C. Scott
13 Averted, as a disaster: 2 wds.
21 Nickname of Red Sox great Carl
23 Put in the microwave, for short
25 Offers counterarguments against
26 Actor in "Goodfellas" and "Casino"
27 Wise old sayings
29 2009 James Cameron movie
30 Go back, as a hairline
31 Expected to place, as in a tournament
32 Claw
34 Kind of restaurant table
40 Work with the soil
41 "Either you do it, ___ will!": 2 wds.

158

Across

1 European peak
4 Ozone depleter, for short
7 Explosive stuff
10 Romania's currency
11 Chicken ___ king: 2 wds.
12 Sob syllable
13 Hearing aids?: 2 wds.
16 Bit of parsley
17 Dark loaves
18 The old man
21 Mozart's "L'___ del Cairo"
24 Western sheriffs, for example
28 Reporter's asset: 3 wds.
31 Fish hawk
32 Cut down
33 Man of morals
36 Kind of team
39 Lull: 2 wds.
43 Some lozenges: 2 wds.
46 Very long stretch
47 Honey maker
48 "___ alive!"
49 Way of the East
50 Hoosegow
51 Raft

Down

1 Brews
2 Ballet move
3 Engine sound
4 Boatload
5 Kind of shot
6 Engine part
7 He and she
8 Musical mark
9 Turn's partner
14 Restaurant calculation
15 Shrimp cousin
19 Cunning schemes
20 Scorecard number
21 Lennon's Yoko
22 Firms: abbr.
23 Cleopatra biter
25 "I'm not real impressed"
26 Lamb's mother
27 Australian state: abbr.
29 Sister of Calliope
30 Invoice amount
34 Bygone
35 A pop
36 Proof word
37 "Slow down!"
38 Florence's river
40 Drudgery
41 No later than: 2 wds.
42 Cousin of "ahem"
44 First three of 26
45 Caffeine source

162

159

Across

1 Support, as a candidate

5 Agreements

10 Powerful anesthetic

12 Patriot ___ Allen

13 Scene of battle, or basketball

14 Replay camera, for short: hyph.

15 Get ___ of (eliminate)

16 Annoy

18 Mercury or Saturn

19 "Dear old" guy

20 Hawaiian necklace

21 "Beautiful job!"

22 Cole ___

24 Unavailable for review, as documents

26 "Killing Me Softly with His Song" singer Flack

28 Green Bay football player

30 On

33 ___ Wednesday

34 Big rd.

36 Laundry detergent brand

37 Find work for

38 100 yrs.

39 El ___ (1961 Charlton Heston role)

40 "Hasta ___" ("see you later")

42 Different

44 Firing offense?

45 Piggies

46 Flowers of the future

47 Decides

Down

1 Chin covers

2 Of a part of the heart

3 Yellow dairy product: 2 wds.

4 Barbie's doll friend

5 More irritating

6 Georgia's capital: abbr.

7 Piece in a cookie: 2 wds.

8 "Hot" mexican food

9 Slept loudly

11 Train travel

17 Book, as a table in a restaurant

23 Pan used in Chinese cooking

25 One day ___ time: 2 wds.

27 Towers with warning lights

28 Comic Poundstone and singer Abdul

29 Promise

31 The ___ (eastern Asia)

32 San Diego baseball team

35 "The Dukes of Hazzard" deputy

41 Mercury or Saturn

43 Pair

160

Across

1 Fearless
5 Cash or gold coins, e.g.
10 "I had no ___!"
11 Food in a "cook-off"
12 "Some Like It Hot" actor: 2 wds.
14 Operation with a pencil
15 Clint Eastwood TV show
20 Search for water
24 Satan
25 Opera tune
26 General or corporal
27 "___ in the Night" (Fleetwood Mac album)
29 Numbers
30 One way to cook pasta: 2 wds.
32 Puget Sound city
37 Hot dog brand: 2 wds.
40 Camelot, to Arthur
41 Go a few rounds
42 Hotel posting
43 Some male dolls

Down

1 Quick meal
2 Aroma
3 Olin of "Chocolat"
4 Quite a while
5 Integra automaker
6 Slick
7 Be in session
8 Inventor ___ Whitney
9 "___ the season ..."
13 Fix
16 "My ___!"
17 "Terrible" czar
18 Little dent
19 Fraternal organization
20 Pieces of info
21 Spoken
22 Leaf-scattering force
23 Popular herb
28 Discounted: 2 wds.
29 Baseball feature
31 "___ of Endearment"
33 Job at hand
34 Sort
35 Slender
36 Blows it
37 Bobby of Boston Bruins fame
38 Baltic or Black
39 Pet with whiskers

161

Across

1. Jiffy
6. Chowderhead
11. Joust weapon
12. Occupy: hyph.
13. Daisylike bloom
14. Related on one's mother's side
15. In that case
16. Wandered aimlessly
17. Stew seasoning
19. Flowering
22. Defraud
26. Early version of a script
27. Insurance giant
28. Spanish lady
29. French pastry
30. Cart part
32. Teach
35. Eyebrow shape
39. Davy Crockett's last stand
40. Polishing abrasive
41. Fergie, formally
42. Did nothing
43. Howler
44. Floored: 2 wds.

Down

1. One way to fall
2. Punishment for a sailor, maybe
3. Some chips, maybe
4. 1992 Al Pacino film: 4 wds.
5. Part of H.M.S.
6. Fulton's power
7. 2005 Russell Crowe movie: 2 wds.
8. Top dog
9. Silence
10. Newspaper's ___ page: hyph.
16. Sock hop locale
18. Sweltering
19. Tally (up)
20. Friend in the 'hood
21. PC linkup
23. Flight board abbr.
24. Cuckoo
25. Disfigure
27. Put one past
29. Sushi order
31. Fuss: hyph.
32. Window part
33. Kind of court
34. Relative of a rabbit
36. Iran's ___ Shah Pahlavi
37. Kind of cut
38. London's ___ Park
40. Biblical high priest

162

Across

1 Do the laundry
5 Golfer's bag carrier
11 Money before a poker hand
12 Get there
13 Celebrity
14 Person who loves books
15 Brad of "Thelma & Louise"
16 Apple computer
17 Poet ____ Pound
19 Doing: 2 wds.
23 One of Santa's Little Helpers
25 Clarify in detail
27 Soccer scores
29 More than on time
30 Pilot
32 ____-Mex cuisine
33 Actress Laura of "Rambling Rose"
34 "___ Tuesday" (Rolling Stones hit)
36 Cow's food
38 In the distance
41 Money for putting a song on the radio
44 ____ Parks of the civil rights movement
45 Graduates from a school
46 Witty words
47 Put down
48 Board in a bed

Down

1 Stinging insect
2 Against: pref.
3 Fun place to go on rides and eat food: 2 wds.
4 Rival of Avis, Enterprise and Budget
5 Company that sells used autos
6 Section
7 Famous vampire
8 Performed
9 "___ been thinking about you!"
10 Suffix with mountain or musket
18 Relax
20 Spilling a beer, for example: 2 wds.
21 Scrabble piece
22 Dark mineral
23 "My goodness!"
24 Valentine's Day celebrates it
26 South American country whose capital is Lima
28 Cosmetics brand
31 Certify, as a priest
35 Root beer brand
37 Arm bone
39 Largest of the continents
40 At full attention
41 Tablet
42 Samuel Adams Summer ____
43 "That tastes good!"

163

Across

1 Pub orders
6 Weapons
10 Fit for a king
11 Unlike the kiddie pool
12 Baby's garment
14 Roy's wife
15 Finishes up
16 Without walls
17 Send a message to
19 Dusk
21 One of Frank's exes
22 Hail Mary, e.g.
23 Nice stone
24 Affirmative vote
25 Church bench
28 Snack for an aardvark
29 Mining metal
30 Respectful greeting
33 Didn't dillydally
34 Coagulate
35 Former center O'Neal, casually
37 "Portnoy's Complaint" author Philip
38 Professor's guarantee
41 "Do ___ others as..."
42 Noun-forming suffix
43 Grizzly, e.g.
44 Naps

Down

1 Sib for sis
2 Director ___ Howard
3 An optometrist administers it: 2 wds.
4 Failed to be
5 Went down in a hurry
6 Extras
7 Brings in
8 Brouhaha
9 Exhausted
13 A teacher administers it: 2 wds.
17 Make "it," on the playground
18 Night before
20 Finds a niche for
22 Breathe hard
25 A teacher administers it: 2 wds.
26 Prior to
27 Join in holy matrimony
28 Name on a book's spine
30 Wash thoroughly
31 "Home ___"
32 "Whole ___ Shakin' Goin' On"
33 ___ Domingo (capital of the Dominican Republic)
36 Principal
39 Salmon ___ (sushi bar stuff)
40 Navy rank: abbr.

164

Across

1 Color of Superman's cape
4 Lingerie item
7 Figured out
10 Inventor Whitney
11 Slough
12 "Well, lookee here!"
13 "We never had this conversation, O.K.?": 3 wds.
16 Brightly colored fish
17 Prima donna problems
18 Blood bank fluid
20 Kind of shell
23 Tennyson title character with "singular beauty"
26 Vegetable that rolls
27 1975 hit by Eric Carmen: 3 wds.
31 Hoedown participant
32 Crude group?
33 Cyberspace bidding site
35 Scintilla
39 Refreshers
42 Walk in water
43 "Getting to Know You" musical: 4 wds.
46 Scand. nation
47 Reason for overtime
48 Little jerk
49 Double standard?
50 Well-chosen
51 Get the picture

Down

1 Second chances, casually
2 Run off to wed
3 Void
4 Kind of ribs
5 Womanizer
6 Bug-eyed
7 Flips out: 2 wds.
8 Its symbol is an omega
9 Stocking's end
14 Hitchhiker's need
15 Young 'un
19 ___ Clinic
21 Cartoon collectible
22 Bonehead
24 Baseball arbiter, for short
25 Salon supplies
27 Add years to one's life
28 Test site
29 South American cowboy
30 Pronunciation symbol
34 Talk, talk, talk
36 Talks wildly
37 Comedian Izzard
38 Prepare for winter takeoff
40 Kind of sandwich
41 Sassy one
43 Explosive
44 "___ do you do?"
45 Follow

165

Across

1 Mr. Mineo
4 Make a misstep
7 Legume holder
10 U.N. member nation
11 "___ is me!"
12 "Now I see!"
13 Proves untrue, as a rumor
15 Knight's honorific
16 Rescue
17 Teacher's unit
19 Arm benders
21 "Darkness on the ___ Town" (Bruce Springsteen album): 2 wds.
23 "My goodness!"
27 Actress Thompson
28 Bank feature
30 Need to pay back
31 Table formation seen in the Southwest
33 They save the day
35 Used one's teeth
37 Gave a shock
40 Poetry event
43 Mimic
44 Combination
46 Spy novelist Follett
47 Cold, as a stare
48 KGB's former rival
49 Finish
50 Pince-___ glasses
51 Kit ___ (candy bar)

Down

1 Beer, casually
2 Largest continent
3 City for gamblers: 2 wds.
4 Woolly female
5 What your fate may depend on in 3-down: 4 wds.
6 Stitch again
7 Decide not to take your turn
8 Cincinnati's river
9 "Shoot!"
14 One-named soccer great
18 Not NNW
20 Feathery neckwear
21 Common street name
22 Actor Billy ___ Williams
24 What you say to people in 3-down: 2 wds.
25 Amaze
26 ___ Moines (Iowa's capital)
29 Kitten's noise
32 Make believe
34 Take a breather
36 Crowd uncomfortably: 2 wds.
37 Maggie Gyllenhaal's brother
38 Kind of tournament
39 Give for a while
41 Opera number
42 Mutton or venison
45 Last of the alphabet

166

Across

1 Took care of: 2 wds.
6 "___ la vista!"
11 Get ready for a marathon
12 Part of "the works"
13 Where you'll see seven dwarfs running around
15 Vietnam's capital
16 Sneaky
17 "May ___ excused?": 2 wds.
19 Biblical paradise
21 She turned people to stone
23 Kind of gemstone
27 Grads
28 Funeral song
29 "Li'l Abner" cartoonist
30 Kitchen gadgets
31 C-___ (political channel)
33 Took a chair
34 A pint, maybe
37 Antipasto piece
39 Where you'll see lots of elves running around: 2 wds.
43 Inbox contents
44 Largest organ in the body
45 John, Jane and Judy
46 Coasters

Down

1 Normal: abbr.
2 "Exodus" character
3 No longer in fine form: 2 wds.
4 Louise of "Gilligan's Island"
5 Harmony
6 Mandel of "Deal or No Deal"
7 "I'll take that as ___": 2 wds.
8 Respected gentlemen
9 Cost to drive on a road
10 Rooney or Roddick
14 Little green man in film
17 Apple product
18 Actor Lugosi
20 Pinot ___ (kind of wine)
22 Baseball referees, for short
24 Keep for the future
25 The Taj Mahal's city
26 "___ we forget"
28 Boone and Day-Lewis
30 Ashy
32 Surveys
34 "Absolutely!"
35 ___ beans
36 Dutch cheese
38 Colorado resort
40 Conk out
41 Kennedy or Williams
42 "48 ___"

167

Across

1. Actress Olivia
5. Muslim holy wars
11. Rent-___: hyph.
12. Bracelet worn around the biceps
13. Mayor of a Dutch town
15. Wood in Hollywood
16. Mountain god in Incan mythology
17. Some collars
18. Per ___ (daily)
19. Liking
20. Nonresident hospital worker
23. No-goodnik
24. Tastelessly showy in manner
26. ___ Nidre (Jewish prayer)
29. Crux
30. Late hotelier Helmsley
32. Polar toy maker
33. Western Hemisphere marsupial
35. Serving two functions: hyph.
37. Difference in years between people: 2 wds.
38. Painter Tanguy
39. Refrain sequence: 3 wds.
40. One of Sports Illustrated's "Sportsmen of the Year" in 1998

Down

1. Coleman of "Boardwalk Empire"
2. Pointed
3. "___ Fink" (Coen brothers movie of 1991)
4. Brain, e.g.
5. Gertz of "Less Than Zero"
6. Hymn "Dies ___" ("Day of Wrath")
7. Letters at sea
8. Star in Aquila
9. Grow more intense
10. Play a guitar
14. "Jimmy ___ Blues" (Spin Doctors song)
18. Prefix meaning "ten": var.
21. Marks a ballot, perhaps
22. Former U.S. president Zachary
23. Cal. col.
24. Expensive caviar
25. Tennis player Nadal
26. Autonomous area in the Balkans
27. Unwelcome obligations
28. City in Southern California: 2 wds.
29. Iron Cross, maybe
31. Annual sports awards since 1993
33. Play-of-color gemstone
34. Insect between larva and adult stage
36. J.F.K. alternative

168

Across

1 Butcher shop cuts

6 Flat, simple boats

11 Kind of ink

12 Hello, in Honolulu

13 Obeys an eight-sided traffic sign

14 "____ Christmas!"

15 Outlaw

16 Tree gunk

18 Refrigerator insignias

19 Make a choice

20 Driver's licenses and such

21 Devour

22 "You're getting on my ___!"

24 Palindromic German man's name

25 Ending for musket or mountain

26 Paris's country: abbr.

27 Chess or checkers

29 Hamster's cousin

32 New York or Tennessee, on a Monopoly board: abbr.

33 Football kicking tool

34 Yoko ____

35 Band that broke up in 2011

36 Every last bit

37 Alien's spaceship

38 Where e-mail lands

40 The devil

42 Elvis Presley hit "Blue ___ Shoes"

43 Carroll heroine

44 Groups of cows

45 Little song

Down

1 Portugal's capital

2 Caught by a videocamera: 2 wds.

3 "The details are hazy on that...": 3 wds.

4 Quick shot of brandy

5 More likely to talk back

6 Ways onto (or off) the highway

7 Beer variety

8 "No problem at all": 3 wds.

9 Fighting words

10 Tells: 2 wds.

17 TV show interruptions

23 Letter that's a symbol of victory

24 Hockey great Bobby

26 Be down in the dumps: 2 wds.

27 Showy

28 Full version of 32-across

29 Hairstyling goop

30 "Actually...": 2 wds.

31 "____ Toons" (cartoon series)

33 April 15th payments

39 Like 1, 3 or 13

41 Boxer in "The Rumble in the Jungle"

169

Across

1 Admit (to): 2 wds.
6 Bodybuilder's pride
11 Lush
12 Loan shark's crime
13 Jazz pianist Chick
14 "Peer Gynt" dramatist
15 Spots
16 Where the heart is
18 White alternative
19 Grab a bite
20 Stephen of "V for Vendetta"
23 Completely wrecking
25 Most important
28 Affirm
29 1991 Martin Scorsese film: 2 wds.
31 Resting place
32 Popular street name
33 Jack Black movie "Shallow ___"
36 Indy 500 winner Franchitti
38 Gray piece
39 Electronic game pioneer
41 Illuminated from below
43 Strange
44 Flip of a hit single: hyph.
45 Scrawny one
46 Come to pass

Down

1 Half of the Odd Couple
2 Actor Harrelson
3 Care for
4 Consume
5 Olive branch: 2 wds.
6 Practically silent: 4 wds.
7 Some PC ports
8 Vienna's country
9 Rapper Dr. ___
10 Thesaurus word: abbr.
17 Sombrero, e.g.
21 M.D.'s specialty
22 Bronze ___
23 Piece of pipe
24 Env. contents
25 Syringe amts.
26 Chance
27 Apple release of November 1, 2013: 2 wds.
30 Samuel's teacher
33 Hammerlock and nelson
34 Departure
35 Do not disturb: 2 wds.
37 Realm
39 Small batteries
40 R.N.'s forte
42 Fasten

170

Across

1 Mischief makers
5 Chicken houses
10 Not cooked very much, like a steak
11 Firetruck feature
12 Item for getting wrinkles out of clothes
13 Restaurant choices
14 Timetable
16 Month after Sept.
17 Academy Award
21 "Star Wars" director George
23 Vodka brand, for short
24 Pose a question to
25 Apprehend, like a crook
26 Sesame ___
29 Looks over quickly
31 "See what you think!": 2 wds.
32 Make a mistake
33 It shows how much something costs: 2 wds.
37 Hand-manipulated character
40 Herb used with salmon
41 Evaluate
42 Capital of Norway
43 Lions' homes
44 Pierce with a knife

Down

1 Purple flower
2 Painter Chagall
3 What Wayne Gretzky played: 2 wds.
4 One of the five tribes of the Iroquois Confederacy
5 Guitarist Santana
6 Most unusual
7 "___ to a Nightingale"
8 Each
9 Some H.S. students
11 Baseball great Brock or Gehrig
15 Some football positions: abbr.
18 Scammer: 2 wds.
19 Alda of "M*A*S*H"
20 Spare ___ (barbecue dish)
21 Final
22 Computer owner
27 The Big ___ (constellation)
28 Emphasize
29 "Hold on a ___!"
30 Statements of belief
34 That thing's
35 "It's ___ big misunderstanding!": 2 wds.
36 Amorphous amount
37 Buddy
38 Calif. and Conn. are part of it
39 Greek letter

171

Across

1 Homer Simpson exclamations
5 ___ Spring (soap brand)
10 Palin or Ferguson
11 Newspapers, magazines, etc.
12 San Antonio landmark
13 Extremely famous people
14 Bedroom chatter: 2 wds.
16 Hawke of "Training Day"
17 Slithering creature
20 Show up for
24 Be in arrears
25 Enjoyed oysters
26 Cow's sound
27 Birthed anew
29 With no clothing
30 Totally out of cash
32 What a musician reads: 2 wds.
37 Baby kangaroos
38 Make amends (for)
39 "No more for me, thanks": 2 wds.
40 Amber, once
41 Necklace parts, maybe
42 Run like a horse

Down

1 Surreal Spanish painter
2 Taken by mouth
3 Shakespeare title character
4 "Darn it!"
5 Copy
6 Take back, as words
7 "American ___"
8 Bathroom fixture
9 Is in possession of
10 Maple syrup stuff
15 This and that
17 Neither fish ___ fowl
18 Female in a flock
19 Internet
21 Big bird
22 Doze (off)
23 A deer, a female deer
25 Hauls down to the station
28 Toed the line
29 Like "das" words in German
31 Store that once had Blue Light Specials
32 Not all
33 "For ___ jolly good...": 2 wds.
34 Average
35 "What's ___ for me?": 2 wds.
36 100 yrs.
37 Triangular sail

172

Across

1 Back of the neck
5 Insignia
11 Biblical twin
12 African nation whose capital is Lilongwe
13 Drink quickly
14 Flying high
15 MacLachlan of "Twin Peaks"
16 Backboard attachment
17 Not pro
19 Bidding site
23 "Forget about it": 2 wds.
25 Song for one
26 Iron ____
27 Sandwich order, for short
29 Awful
30 Functionalities
32 Saudi ____
34 Taboo act
35 Indiana city, or a man's name
36 Meadow
38 ____-Caribbean music
41 Grooms' mates
44 Hard punch
45 Has a good time
46 Weak, as an excuse
47 Disinclined
48 "For Your ____ Only"

Down

1 Adam's apple spot
2 Far from ruddy
3 TV celebrity chef from Savannah: 2 wds.
4 Oregon city
5 TV celebrity chef from Louisiana: 2 wds.
6 African nation
7 Charges
8 Back muscle, familiarly
9 She's a sheep
10 ____-Atlantic
18 Check
20 TV celebrity chef from New York City: 2 wds.
21 Jai ____
22 "Star Wars" role
23 It may be proper
24 About: 2 wds.
28 "La la" preceder
31 Fuse two pieces of metal
33 Fit for farming
37 Congers
39 City of the Coliseum
40 Has a mortgage
41 Undergarment
42 Holy title: abbr.
43 "____ got it!"

173

Across

1 Picture puzzle
6 Athlete who uses performance-enhancing drugs
11 First letter, in Israel
12 Eat away
13 It often comes with tortilla chips
14 Become fully understood, as an idea: 2 wds.
15 Marlboro, for short
16 Sporty British cars
18 Devoured
19 Singer DiFranco
20 Take to court
21 Pull behind, as a boat
22 Advantage, in sports
24 Mistakes
26 Without a connecting flight
28 Looks for water with a stick
30 Float, as an aroma
33 One ___ million: 2 wds.
34 Snake that killed Cleopatra
36 Prefix with conservative or classical
37 Football official, for short
38 One of five on a foot
39 Has the power to
40 Embarrassing mistake
42 "Don't be a hog!"
44 Actress Page of "Juno"
45 Selfish person
46 They go downhill fast
47 Storage structures

Down

1 Mischievous type
2 "Seinfeld" role
3 Breakfast food named for a European country: 2 wds.
4 Shipping company whose nickname is "Brown"
5 Bogus proceedings
6 Last part of the meal
7 Miner's stuff
8 Food also called a "latke": 2 wds.
9 Newspaper employee
10 Extends, as a magazine subscription
17 "Seems to be the case": 2 wds.
23 Two, in Spanish
25 Aisle
27 Makes more orderly
28 Funeral songs
29 Common tie score, in baseball or soccer: 2 wds.
31 Was scared of
32 Copy machine powders
35 Irritants
41 Gave grub to
43 "Yeah, right!"

174

Across

1 Scarecrow stuffing
6 Aspirations
11 Fragment
12 Stave off
13 Roswell crash victim, supposedly
14 Bird of Celtic lore
15 Mark of perfection
16 Kind of call
18 Daughter of Saturn
19 Copycat
22 Over: 3 wds.
25 Chat room chuckle
26 Port-au-Prince is its capital
27 Dreams
29 Days ___
30 Rotten
32 Granola bit
33 "Why not?"
34 Arabic for "commander"
35 It may be glossed over
38 Can't help but: 2 wds.
41 Emulate Demosthenes
43 One way to be taken
44 Vagabond
45 Oblivion
46 Overwhelm

Down

1 Petty quarrel
2 Mosaic piece
3 This pulls a bit
4 First-class
5 Failed badly: 4 wds.
6 Fun-house feature: 3 wds.
7 Track
8 A pop
9 Go off
10 What a mess!
17 Warbler Yoko
18 Write quickly
19 Further
20 Limerick, e.g.
21 "Anything ___?"
22 Columbus is its capital
23 Granny
24 Windshield option
28 Bring into play
31 "Certainement!"
34 Leave one's mark on
35 Volcanologist's study
36 Particular
37 Bad guy
38 Shakespeare's prince
39 Actor Vigoda
40 Did nothing
42 Scrape

175

Across

1 Restraint
4 Knucklehead
7 Swell place?
10 Bustle
11 Prefix with colonial
12 End of a demonstration?
13 Succeed solely by chance: 4 wds.
16 Bar ___
17 Poet Angelou
18 Sober
20 Island near Corsica
23 Beauties
26 Contents of some barrels
27 Fly off the handle: 2 wds.
31 Lawyer's abbr.
32 "Rubáiyát" poet
33 Arrange, as hair: 2 wds.
35 Microsoft founder Bill
39 West's bridge partner
42 Labor
43 Say "Enough is enough!": 3 wds.
46 "All systems go": hyph.
47 Symbol of might
48 Sprawl
49 "Whew!"
50 Pizza order
51 Ready

Down

1 Landscaper's concerns
2 Imbecile
3 Fashion's Karan
4 To some extent
5 Coal site
6 Resting place
7 Filth and misery
8 Cry of mock horror
9 Summer drink
14 Neutral shade
15 Caustic substance
19 Art ___
21 Life story
22 Tie indicator
24 Dad's other half
25 Hose problem
27 Wielded the baton
28 Spanish bear
29 Needing oil
30 Fish with a net
34 Kit mitt
36 Slaves
37 Bud Grace comic strip
38 Shooting game
40 Ticklee's cry
41 Neighbor of a Laotian
43 Smidge
44 Friend of Pooh
45 Barely manage, with "out"

176

Across

1 Marginally acceptable: 2 wds.
8 Neighbor of Florida
9 Societal rule
12 Tourist
13 Boxing hero
14 Frigid cubes
15 Spring or autumn
17 Geeky types
20 Part of a movie or play
21 Barcelona's country
23 Street ___ (reputation)
24 Revolted: 2 wds.
26 Go round and round
28 ___ the opinion (thought): 2 wds.
30 Beer amounts
32 Will names
34 Enter again, as data
36 Prefix with classical
37 Perfect serve
38 Reagan adviser Lee ___
41 "So's ___ old man!"
42 Circus acrobat's swing
43 Men of Mexico

Down

1 "You ___ a good time?"
2 "___ Restaurant" (Arlo Guthrie song)
3 It produces documents: 2 wds.
4 Intelligence agcy.
5 Flying mammal
6 Famous ___ cookies
7 Has the nerve
9 Toy cats love to play with: 2 wds.
10 Solo
11 ___ and dined
16 Point the finger at
18 Lovely and delicate
19 Palindromic girl
22 ___ Jersey Devils (hockey team)
25 Casual turndown
26 Mist
27 Rook or bishop, in chess
29 Stop in your tracks
31 Little arguments
33 Canker ___
35 To be: Fr.
39 Not healthy-looking
40 Part of military addresses, initially

177

Across

1 ___ on the back
4 "Polythene ___" (Beatles song)
7 Stomach muscles
10 Paul Newman role
11 Vain person's issue
12 Montana or Biden
13 "The Little Drummer Boy" syllable
14 ATM code
15 Museum pieces
16 "Act your ___!"
17 Finds out new things
19 Deborah's "The King and I" co-star
20 Attention-getting shouts
21 Similar
23 "Kapow!"
25 Paquin or Chlumsky
26 Verve
28 Thin fish
29 Permitted
31 Coup d'___
33 "What ___ doing?": 2 wds.
34 Waves, perhaps: 2 wds.
37 Deeply philosophical
38 Fuss
39 Enjoy a Winter Olympics sport
41 "Lord, is ___?": 2 wds.
42 Word before gift or reflex
43 Chest muscle, for short
44 Photographer Goldin
45 Doc bloc
46 "Is it ___ wonder?"
47 Food from a hen

Down

1 Tropical fruit
2 Salad vegetable
3 Facebook format
4 Vigor
5 Catlike
6 Tourist's wear: 2 wds.
7 Almost closed, like a door
8 "___ in the USA" (Springsteen album)
9 Adjusts, as a clock
18 Make ___ (be a good vendor): 2 wds.
20 Place to get a massage: 2 wds.
22 Bending pair
24 What each of the three long entries in this puzzle begins with
27 Convention ID
30 Cloud with a silver ___
32 Clay of "American Idol" fame
34 Epic story
35 Sandler of "Big Daddy"
36 Exercise discipline with lots of stretching
40 Cold

178

Across

1 Forearm bone

5 Prepared a salad

11 Screwdriver or hammer

12 Baltimore base-stealer or bunter

13 In addition

14 Chosen by luck

15 Scoring three goals in one game: 2 wds.

17 Steal from

18 Red Square man

22 Genre for "Battlestar Galactica"

24 Eat away at slowly

25 Has the power to

26 Put a patch on jeans, e.g.

27 It may be 90 degrees in geometry class

30 Wonderful

32 Put back to 000000, as an odometer

33 Suffix with cloth or cash

34 It's worth ten times more than a "red cent": 2 wds.

38 Irish language

41 Stocking trouble

42 Intention to do harm

43 Waffle brand fought over in ads

44 Least risky

45 Condition of sale at garage sales: 2 wds.

Down

1 Six-sided state

2 Hit for The Kinks

3 They're "attached" in commitment-free deals: 2 wds.

4 Many: 3 wds.

5 Spelling of "Beverly Hills, 90210"

6 Microsoft rival, or an ancient source of knowledge

7 Tricky baseball pitch

8 Do the lawn

9 1970s band that sang "Do Ya"

10 Obama, e.g.

16 Baseball card stat.

19 Goth kids wear them: 2 wds.

20 Concept

21 2012 presidential candidate Gingrich

22 Hurt badly

23 Walking aid

28 Allow to rest, like sleeping dogs: 2 wds.

29 Morality subject

30 Alcoholic drink that's also a card game

31 Moses parted it: 2 wds.

35 "Law & Order: SVU" actor

36 "The Gift of the ___"

37 They may clash

38 Chess experts: abbr.

39 Small battery

40 Christmas creature

179

Across

1 Affirmative retort: 3 wds.
6 Singer Kristofferson
10 Schwa's cousin: 2 wds.
12 "___ Dimittis" (canticle in the Book of Luke)
13 Honorable person, slangily
14 Dame ___ Everage
15 Dark and depressing, as music
16 Less pretty
18 Treat roughly: 2 wds.
21 Dredge: 2 wds.
23 Rearward
26 Art able to
27 Mathematician who introduced the symbol e for the base of natural logarithms
29 Suffix for gran and graph
30 Captivates
32 "Am I the only one?": 3 wds.
33 Mexican cactus
36 No. 2s in the White House
39 Gulf off the coast of Yemen
40 Kitchen gadgets
43 ___ Field (baseball park)
44 Writer/director Nora
45 Related to: suffix
46 Cleansing agents

Down

1 "Woe ___!" ("Alas"): 2 wds.
2 "Uh… excuse me"
3 Spoken in a voice unchanging in pitch
4 Some upperclassmen: abbr.
5 Non-Rx, initially
6 Prepared to be dubbed
7 Gernreich who designed a shocking bathing suit
8 Tavern, old-style
9 Souvenir of surgery
11 ___ Kenyatta, Kenyan president
17 Watch wide-eyed: 2 wds.
19 Dawn deity
20 Best suited
21 Poli ___
22 Tabby, e.g.
23 Burn treatment: 2 wds.
24 Chemin de ___ (casino game)
25 ___-80 (old computer)
28 "Lemme think…"
31 Daughter of an aunt
32 Kind of column
33 Metal Couturier Rabanne
34 Copydesk change
35 Hairy Himalayan beast
37 Play thing
38 IRS IDs
41 Covert ___: abbr.
42 Plato's "P"

180

Across

1 Ford's predecessor, initially
4 ___ tree (trapped): 2 wds.
7 Prefix with friendly
8 Mediterranean isl.
9 Moo ___ pork
12 Branch cutters
14 Is no longer
15 Not expressed
17 Bond, for one
19 "I've ___ for music": 2 wds.
20 Film rating org.
21 "Bei Mir ___ Du Schön"
22 Expert with the remote control: 2 wds.
26 Hwys.
27 Fresh
28 Earlier conviction
30 Bard's forest
31 Certifies
33 Comic strip cry
34 Drink in a single draft: 2 wds.
37 180° from NNW
38 Hostile
39 U.N. member nation
40 Middle mark
41 Hangup

Down

1 CrossFit unit, briefly
2 Computer program instruction: abbr.
3 Parvenus: 2 wds.
4 "___ or lose it": 2 wds.
5 Jardin Atlantique, par exemple
6 Talk show host Hall
9 Like some Chinese food: 3 wds.
10 ___ cow (flips out, Simpsons-style): 2 wds.
11 Uzbek, Tajik, etc.
13 Extra, maybe
16 Techniques no longer commonly practiced: 2 wds.
17 Cable choice, for short
18 Agency providing printing for Congress, initially
21 Rate at which computer data is transferred, initially
23 Excommunication candidate
24 Ball raiser
25 Dominate, so to speak
28 Bear's feet
29 Some dishes on rooftops, initially
30 Window alternative
32 Charitable distribution
35 Tallahassee sch.
36 Dynamite

181

Across

1 Opening run
5 ___ Island
10 Gp. against file-sharing
11 Get ready for production: 2 wds.
12 Lift, as a log in a fireplace
13 Leg and loin of an animal
14 Hairy twin
15 Sounds of hesitance
16 Paperback publisher
18 Catchall abbr.: 2 wds.
22 Ornamental shrub
24 Cotton fabric
25 Compellingly attractive
27 Top-rated: hyph.
28 John
29 "Go ahead": 2 wds.
30 Diminish
31 Eastern way
33 Chicago daily, for short
36 Person in for the long haul
39 Caucus state
40 Where some peas may be found: 3 wds.
41 Sweet ___ (sugar substitute): 2 wds.
42 "The Merry Family" artist Jan
43 Tod D. Wolters, e.g.

Down

1 Galleria display
2 Life stories, for short
3 Natives of Montreal
4 Very early photographic process
5 Lion's cry
6 Outdoor job: 2 wds.
7 TV channel relaunched as "Versus" in 2006
8 French peer
9 Book after Galatians: abbr.
11 Final statement in a verbal argument: 3 wds.
17 Floral ring
19 What a lead actor might play: 2 wds.
20 Valentine for Valéry
21 Milk: prefix
22 Great quantity
23 "This tastes terrible!"
26 Kiwi's late kin
32 Big time?
34 Victorious shout: 2 wds.
35 Wail
36 Bro's sibling
37 Cable choice, initially
38 Professional teachers' org.

182

Across

1 Hits with the horns
6 Native American crop
11 "It's ___ thing" (easy winner): 2 wds.
12 Moray catcher
13 Caused to feel shame
15 Charlotte of 'Diff'rent Strokes'
16 French possessive
17 Widow in "Peer Gynt"
18 "I mean it!"
21 How some music is sold: 2 wds.
23 "The Beast of ___ Flats" (1961 sci-fi bomb)
27 Musical notes
28 Think (over)
29 Snooze
31 "Ready": 2 wds.
32 Bruce and Kravitz
34 Causes of some EMT calls
37 Bowl-shaped pan
38 Bunch of bills
41 Biochemical basis of heredity: 2 wds.
44 Wrinkly fruit
45 Table part
46 Poker champ Stu
47 On the chubby side

Down

1 Boxer Max
2 Cadets' sch.
3 Small, rounded projection on a bone
4 Sung syllable
5 "Perfect sleeper" mattresses
6 Contemptibly small or few
7 Loser to H.C.H.
8 Rick's "Casablanca" love
9 Snoring, in the comics
10 Earth, to Mahler
14 Bill of Rights subj.
19 Ford flop
20 Delicious, slangily
21 W.W. II org.
22 Lon ___, Khmer Republic president in the 1970s
24 Profanity, so to speak: 2 wds.
25 Ending for corpus or cuti
26 Computer key abbr.
30 Shade of silver gray
31 Mushroom with a black-edged top
33 "___ won't be afraid" ("Stand by Me" line): 2 wds.
34 Pre K.G.B. group
35 "The Hateful Eight" costar Bruce
36 Tightfitting
39 "Epitaph to ___" (Byron poem): 2 wds.
40 Disavow
42 Bambi's aunt
43 Computer heart, initially

183

Across

1 The Wizard of Oz creator
5 Creme de ___
10 Series between K and Q
12 Prayer start: 2 wds.
13 Addis ___
14 Equipped with feathers, as an arrow
15 Utah metropolis, initially
16 Capital of New Jersey
18 Less likely to fail
20 Cheer to the torero
21 "___ Mio": 2 wds.
22 College dorm. chiefs
23 Port on the Seine River, France
25 July 21st, August 8th, November 3rd, etc.
27 Piscivorous bird: var.
28 Horror movie of 2005: 2 wds.
30 Environmental no-no, initially
31 Science of the human body
34 Being afraid of
36 Never, in Nuremberg
37 Hungarian prime minister Viktor
38 Horace, for one
40 Found a new tenant for
41 Japanese-American
42 Getup
43 Written communications: abbr.

Down

1 Late Bill of fashion
2 Mosey
3 Not able to be explained
4 Out-of-control group
5 Pioneer's transport: 2 wds.
6 Jackson or Rickman
7 Acrobat who adopts unusual postures
8 Rings of color
9 Idiosyncrasy
11 Andrew to Scotland, and David to Wales, e.g.: 2 wds.
17 Fam. member
19 Get mileage out of
23 Robert who starred in "The Great Gatsby"
24 Customer
26 River islet
29 Cape ___, Massachusetts
32 Molière comedy, with "The"
33 Abominable Snowmen
35 Explorer John and others
39 Baby Pickles on "Rugrats"

184

Across

1 Fraction of a min.: 2 wds.
5 Dish alternative
10 Abruzzo bell town
11 Another name for the abalone
12 Science of good eating and drinking
14 It covers the Constitutional amendment process: 2 wds.
15 Defects
19 Encapsulate
22 Israeli oil port: var.
23 "For", in Madrid
24 Before, either way
25 Type type: abbr.
27 Organized massacre of a group
30 1942 Hitchcock thriller
32 Taras Bulba's people
36 Autos' emergency replacements: 2 wds.
38 Assign
39 Former hair removal product
40 ___ good turn (helps out): 2 wds.
41 They follow Augs.

Down

1 Serpent deity, in Indian mythology
2 Common flag symbol
3 Previously, once
4 Accustom to urban ways
5 "That's enough!": 2 wds.
6 Synthetic fiber
7 No Oscar winner: hyph.
8 Moon lander, for short
9 Suffix with fin or fish
13 Some VCRs, initially
16 Red or Cardinal, for short
17 Football kicker Yepremian
18 Pipe part
19 Christian denom.
20 ___ cloud in the sky: 2 wds.
21 Grump
26 Place
27 Spanish coin, once
28 Give the boot
29 Cereal seeds
31 Spanish bulls
33 Tribe in Manitoba
34 Not rot
35 Retired fliers, for short
36 Down
37 U.N. observer grp.

185

Across

1 Falco who played Carmela in "The Sopranos"
5 Pepé Le Pew, e.g.
10 Basketball Hall-of-Famer Harshman
11 Edible legume
12 Half-human, half-Betazoid "Star Trek" character Deanna
13 Nels of "Little House on the Prairie"
14 Fired off an e-mail
15 Style of music, a fusion of Arabic and Western elements
16 Glissando instrument
18 Nine-digit IDs
22 Spanish riches
24 Very early roughly-broken stone implements
26 1920 play that introduced the word "robot," initially
27 Mary of "Where Eagles Dare"
28 Airport info: abbr.
29 Large basin for washing up
31 "Life is Good" rapper
32 "Dedicated to the ___ Love" (Shirelles hit): 2 wds.
33 Acted the fink
35 Louvre Pyramid architect
37 GI hangouts, initially
40 Amateur, for short
43 Lion's share
44 "Enter!": 2 wds.
45 Suffix with chant or mass
46 Oxygen compound
47 Car roof variety: hyph.

Down

1 CPR pros
2 Virginia of note
3 Early term for a railroad locomotive: 2 wds.
4 1979 Broadway debut
5 Two notes on a scale: 2 wds.
6 Former NAACP President ___ Mfume
7 ___ and downs
8 "New" prefix
9 Neighbor of Mo.
11 Big company
17 Enrol again for military service: hyph.
19 Projects from a surface: 2 wds.
20 Drag racing governing body: inits.
21 Lat., Rus., and Est., once
22 "Novus ___ Seclorum" on a dollar
23 Bankrupt
25 Lantern-jawed celeb
30 Infatuated with, slangily
34 He directed "Network"
36 Cleveland's lake
38 Italian bone
39 Dance instructor's call
40 Sgt., for one
41 Certain tic-tac-toe letters
42 Having just a first and last name, initially

186

Across

1 Mexican warrior
6 Printing fluids
10 More than hate
12 Nosh
13 Involve
14 From the top
15 "What did I tell you?"
16 Spooky sounds
18 ___ Mirage, California
21 At a discount: hyph.
23 Maple syrup stuff
26 Loud chewing sound
27 Company that's also a fruit
29 Chicago clock setting: abbr.
30 Surprise for students: 2 wds.
32 Best-ever result
33 Do some arithmetic
36 Take down the aisle
39 Desktop image
40 Blood carrier
43 Pair on a mountain
44 Rookie, in computer-speak
45 Jekyll's counterpart
46 Where people "go" at night: 2 wds.

Down

1 Beers
2 "The Twilight ___"
3 French fry alternative: 2 wds.
4 Greek letter after zeta
5 Greek letter after phi
6 State bordering Montana
7 El ___ (weather phenomenon)
8 Leg joint
9 Uses a needle and thread
11 Put into political power
17 Inexpensive and low-quality
19 Biceps' place
20 Took a snooze
21 300, in Ancient Rome
22 Hesitant syllables
23 In his day, the shortest player ever in the NBA (5' 7"): 2 wds.
24 Cosell interviewed him many times
25 Candy with its own dispensers
28 O-S links
31 Indian or Pacific
32 "Lather, ___, repeat"
33 Plate
34 Gross, to a kid
35 Word stamped on a bad check
37 Buffalo's lake
38 Like some blonde hair
41 No longer working: abbr.
42 Couple

187

Across

1 Power
7 Ruin
10 Popeye the Sailor has a tattoo of one
11 ___ and aft
12 Mother ___ (noted humanitarian)
13 Onassis and Emanuel
14 Tennis star Tommy
15 Leave the union
17 Web connecting businesses, for short
18 Sailing the waves: 2 wds.
19 Prophet
20 Chaperone
21 Your planet
23 Prophet
26 Work units
30 Prejudiced person
31 Fix, as a medical condition
32 Extreme fear
34 Half-hitch or granny
35 Not new, like a car
36 Didn't dine at home: 2 wds.
38 Palindromic candy company
39 Read through casually
40 Finale
41 Person who judges food

Down

1 Singer Johnny
2 Nervous feeling
3 Minor tiff
4 1950s–70s label known for blues, jazz and rock: 2 wds.
5 ___ Angeles Lakers
6 Historical times
7 To a greater degree: 2 wds.
8 More dry and hot
9 Find a new chair for
11 They spot false claims: 2 wds.
16 "___ of Eden"
20 Previously
22 Choir voice
23 More than 90 degrees, as an angle
24 Candy company
25 "Amen!"
27 Leave in a hurry: 2 wds.
28 Complain
29 Irish ___ (big dog)
33 At full attention
37 Chai or chamomile

188

Across

1 Talk about

8 ___ Aviv (city in Israel)

11 Toronto's province

12 Pie ___ mode: 2 wds.

13 Dish with parmesan cheese and croutons: 2 wds.

15 Prepares to pray

16 Nevada senator Harry

17 Skinny fish

18 Tube-shaped pasta

19 Alcoholic's affliction, for short

20 Computer accessory

22 Finnish steam room

23 Handsome

26 ___ Perignon champagne

29 Amusing water creature

30 He lost to Bush in 2000

31 Geek

32 Beautiful ladies

34 Sandwich bread choices: 2 wds.

36 Never-proven mental ability: inits.

37 Place for F-16 fighter jets

38 "What can I do for you?"

39 Fairy-tale sister: 2 wds.

Down

1 Decreased for a penalty, as pay

2 Caught, like fish: 3 wds.

3 Strengthens (oneself), as for a shock

4 Situations

5 Risk territory named for a Eurasian mountain range

6 Respectable gentlemen

7 "Mayday!"

8 Natural skill

9 "Seinfeld" woman

10 Way up a wall

14 Scene of conflict

18 ___-pong

20 Sock grouping

21 Point, in baseball

22 Gets rid of, like extra pounds

23 Kind of animal Eddie Murphy voices in "Shrek"

24 In a relaxed state: 2 wds.

25 Pieces of bacon

26 Rival of Hertz and Enterprise

27 "You won't like the alternative": 2 wds.

28 ___ up (botched the job)

30 Boston newspaper

32 Verve

33 Goes wrong

35 Lobe's home

SOLUTIONS

1

```
R I P . A C T . B T W
E R R . D U E . O H O
H O O K O R C R O O K
A N O N . T H A T . .
B Y F A R . . G L U T
. . V I V A . E G O .
L I N E O F S I G H T
A L E . S W A B . . .
P L E A . . P I P P A
. D O L T . Z O O S .
S I N K E R B A L L S
P R O . W O E . E K E
Y E T . D Y E . S A T
```

2

```
C I T . S T A S . .
O S H . T I G H T S
E O E . R E T O O L
U N T I E . S P O O R
R E A C T S . A T P S
. E C O . H O E S .
F L A S H F L O O D S
L U R K . T E L . .
U S M A . A D I D A S
S A L T S . I C A H N
. K E E P O N . R E A
. A T R E A T . L A K
. S E K O . A P E .
```

3

```
M A G I C . C A M P S
I R E N E . O H A R A
S M O K E . W A R E S
F A R . L O B . T Y S
I N G . O N A . H O E
T I E S . E R R A N D
. . C L I E N T S . .
C O L O N Y . S T E P
O R O . H E W . E M U
R I O . A D E . W E T
G E N U S . A P A R T
I N E R T . V E R G E
S T Y L E . E N T E R
```

4

```
E L M S T . M A D T V
L E I C A . E R I E S
F I N A L . D I S C O
. E L E V E . P S P .
M S R P . E V E R . .
A T A . B Y A N O S E
C O L O R . C A P E R
Y A W N E R S . O R I
. A S A S . B R I C .
T N T . K A R A T . .
A C E O F . F R I E D
C A R L O . D R O N E
T A S E R . S E N O R
```

5

```
A C T E D . G O T H S
C A R G O . R U R A L
A M I G O . O T E R I
R E C . R O W . A P P
E L K . D A N . T O P
. Q U I T . F L O E .
C A U S E . G R I N D
A R E A . C O O K . .
R R S . T O O . E S P
L A T . O D D . D E A
O N I O N . O W I N G
A G O N Y . N O R S E
D E N T S . E N T E R
```

6

```
L A G . P E T . .
O R R . A A H . C A R
C E O . P R I M A T E
U N C L E . S U S H I
S T E E R S . T H E N
. . R O O T . T O N I
S P Y . R E P . R A N
H U S H . A L E C . .
A L T A . M A R R O W
S L O W S . S E E S A
T U R N O U T . D A D
A P E . S R I . I K E
. . A B C . T A D
```

7

```
T Y P E B . M I N D A
U V U L A . A V O I R
S E L F D E N Y I N G
H S I . D E T . D A H
. T O S I R . .
R E O R G . S A L A D
N I N O . T A R A
R O T O R . S O S A D
. P E N I N .
E D S . C F C . O L D
P E A C O C K B L U E
I E V E R . L A I N E
C R E E D . E R O D E
```

8

```
S T E P . M A S C O T
O R A L . A R C A D E
L I S A . N E A T E N
D O T S . C A N . .
. E T C H . S C A M
V A R I O U S . A L A
E R E C T . C A N O N
R I G . S P A N D E X
B A G S . A R T Y . .
. H I S . E C H O
A S S E S S . D A U B
N E E D L E . U N T O
T E A S E D . P E T E
```

9

```
A B B A . A S K F O R
C A U L . M O I E T Y
D E B T . I M L A T E
C R O I S S A N T .
. N T E S T . H M S
O P I U M . A S E A T
R E C D . T R Y A
L A P E L . D A W E S
E R L . E D U C E .
. A N G L I C I Z E
T I G E R I . A G E R
O N U S E S . T H R A
O N E S E T . O T O S
```

10

```
P E A C E . A I D E S
A L L A N . C R O U P
S P A R E C H A N G E
T A S . M A E . K E N
A S K . I N D . E N D
S O A K E D . A Y E S
. . A S Y E T . .
P S S T . C A L A I S
I O N . C A T . S N L
G O O . U N I . T H E
S T R I K E T H R E E
T H E R E . U B O A T
Y E S E S . P O S T S
```

11

```
J A P A N . A M A Z E
A W A R E . L E M O N
M E L E E . A H A N D
. . M A D A M . R E S
O W E . L O O S E .
M A T T E L . A T O M
A N T E S . I N T R O
N E O N . U N D O E S
. S T A R T . S O S .
P A T . A L E R O .
O N A I R . G O U D A
R E T R O . R U R A L
T W E E N . A T S E A
```

12

```
S O N G . C A N D O
W H O A . B E F O U L
A I N U . E N F O L D
T O U C H S T O N E .
. . R H E T O R . .
H A B E A S . D O S E
E S A . . . R E Y
R I N G . O L E A T E
. . U R G E N T . .
. G O F O R B R O K E
M U F F L E . I R A N
A N N A L S . C I R C
S N O W S . H O L Y
```

SOLUTIONS

13
```
S O G   C U P   M F R
A P O   R S T   A R A
D I O C E S E   G A P
R E D H E R R I N G S
    S E D   N E M O
S H A M A N   I T E N
H U M I L I A T I N G
A G A S   E D I C T S
L U R E   R A F
L E I S U R E T I M E
O N T   V E N E E R S
T O A   E D A   L I E
S T N   A D L   D S S
```

14
```
M S U   O F P O P
E E N   U R A N I A N
S A F E T Y M A T C H
O M A R R   P L A T S
    I N A R E A
R U R   E R R I N G
I N L I N E S K A T E
T H Y M U S   M H O
    P R E F A B
R E L O S   R E U P S
N O I S E L E S S L Y
D E S T R O Y   E I N
    A S Y L A   S E E
```

15
```
E G G   B I T
N O R   A M Y   B A G
C L E A N U P   E S E
A F A R   P E N S K E
M E T E S   O T I S
P R E   I T S G O N E
    S U N R O O F
J E T S K I S   A N A
A C H E   A B L E R
P O I S O N   A B U T
A N T   N U R T U R E
N O S   U K E   M A R
    S E T   S L Y
```

16
```
P L A N B   B O S O M
L A B O R   U L T R A
A D O R E   T I E O N
T E D   A C T O R
O D E   D I E   O L E
    S M A R T I E S
S E P I A   F I D O S
T R E S C H I C
Y E N   H E N   E B B
    G R I E G   P I E
B R U I N   E V I T A
A N I M E   R I C E D
M A N E S   S A S S Y
```

17
```
W I M P Y   A T S E A
A M O R E   C H A N G
N O N O S   M A T T E
E N D S   R E T U R N
D I A   H E S   R E D
  T Y P E S   I D E A
    M A R T I N A
S H O W   S W A Y S
C A R   M O O   N I P
R I N G I N   N I N A
A L I E N   D O G G Y
P E N N E   A S H E N
E D G E S   M E T R E
```

18
```
W I T S   A P P E A L
H A H A   T O O T I F
O M A R   D U L C E T
M A T A H A R I
    S L A W   O W N S
I N T E R N S   H I P
O O H E D   Q U A K E
U S A   C O U N T E D
S E T S   P A L S
    H O T T O W E L
S A L A M I   C H A I
I R O N I C   K A T E
B E G E T S   S T A N
```

19
```
C A P S   M E A D S
A C U R E   A G R E E
S H R I M P T O A S T
I I I   E A T   B I T
N E S   R R S   I R E
O R T E G A   A C E R
    T E C H S
Z O L A   H A H A H A
E R A   G U T   N E D
A I M   A T E   G A D
L O B S T E R R O L L
O L D I E   S P R E E
T E A R S   M A R S
```

20
```
L I M B S   S C R A M
A C U R A   C H I L I
T H R O W T H I N G S
H I D   E R E   G O S
A R E   D I M   I R E
M O R T   B E A N E D
    R O U S T
L A T E N T   M O P S
O R E   E A T   V I A
A C E   S R I   E L F
T H I R T Y T H R E E
H E N N A   L U L U S
E D G A R   E G Y P T
```

21
```
C A P R I   Q T I P S
A L L E N   U R B A N
S P A D E   A A M C O
H O T H E A D S
    A D E   H A Z Y
M A R T Y R S   L E E
A L E   O O P   E T A
Z E N   U S E D C A R
E X E S   O N E
    C O L D F E E T
J A M I N   S A W T O
A L O F T   O C E A N
R A D I O   N E S T S
```

22
```
O R D E R S   A S T I
N A R R O W   B O A R
E Q U A T E   A B B A
S U N   O D E   E L I
E E K   R E V E R E S
C L A M   N E G A T E
    S I S   N O S
T H A T O K   S A S S
R O S E H I P   J A N
A O K   O N O   U V A
U P U P   S P I D E R
M E N D   K I N G M E
A R K S   I N N E E D
```

23
```
F I T   U G H   W P M
O D E   P R O   H E E
G O L D D I G G E R S
    L O O P   L E I S
H E A T   T A L L Y
I L L   L B A R
S I L V E R B E L L S
    E A R S   A Y E
A L I G N   S P E W
B E L A   D I A L
B R O N Z E S T A R S
I O S   A L L   T O O
E Y E   P I E   A D D
```

24
```
T O T E M   K I C K S
O R A M A   A B O A T
R E B U T   N E U R O
S I L   T R Y   C E O
O D E   H O E   H E P
  A T S E A   A T M S
    H O W M U C H
S P E X   O P T E D
L E I   M F A   I E D
I R S   A F T   S R I
M U S I C   R E S I N
U S U R Y   E X U D E
P E E K S   E P E E S
```

SOLUTIONS

25

```
P R O S # I D I D I T
L U N A # R E S A L E
A L E X P K E A T O N
T E N # R I P # A V A
O R D A I N # B E N #
# P E G S # L I T #
S O R T S # A B E T S
A N A # T A M A # #
L A C # G U N N E D
A W E # E R E # O R E
M I C H A E L J F O X
I R A I S E # L A D Y
S E R V E S # O N E S
```

26

```
D O P E D # # #
O N A D I M E # S I P
C O N I F E R # T V A
E R A T # L O R E A L
# M E T A # O W N S
D E A D E N # N E H I
E T H # A C T # D O E
C A A N # H E R P E S
A G T S # O M A R #
D E T A I L # T U B B
E R I # D I G I N T O
S E E # S A U T E E D
# # M E S N E #
```

27

```
M A Y A S # A G E S
A D O B E # P E R T
D O U B L E P L A Y #
# # E L S E #
C L A Y # T A R G E T
R A T # R I N S E
I D E A # M O S S
S L U R P # M E T
S E P T I C # S E X Y
# G A G A #
T R I P L E J U M P
H E R E # M A R I A
E V E N # S K I L L
```

28

```
S K I L L # M I L A N
I N N I E # O B E S E
L E F T T O R I G H T
T W O # B I N D #
# D E L I # I W O
A P S E # S N A P O N
L I L A C # G N A R L
O P E R A S # E D D Y
T E D # P L O W #
# S T O P # A L A
T F E L O T T H G I R
S A V O R # I M U S T
P R E P S # C O A T S
```

29

```
P E P # K F C # A P P
O R E # E L L I P S E
T R A C Y A U S T I N
# A S T E R # #
H A S T # A S A P
A R I # H A V E A G O
S T E V E D A L L A S
P I G I R O N # V I E
S E E S # Y E N S
# I T S M E #
M A T T H O U S T O N
E R A S E R S # A W E
W E B # M E T # D E W
```

30

```
C H E S T # S T E P S
L I T H E # H E L L O
E L T O N # I L I A D
F L A W # H E L E N A
# O V E R T # #
D I F F E R # A W O L
A L I S T # B L A D E
B L E U # S U E D E D
# P A T C H #
S T O P B Y # E A S E
O H B O Y # C A R L A
L A I R S # D R E A R
D I E T S # S T A Y S
```

31

```
M U M M # O S B O R N
A N O A # T H I E V E
A T T N # H O A R S E
M O O N R O O F #
# R E L # I R W I N
O N C D S # N A A N S
S E A # # S T E
S A D H U # E T H I C
O L E O S # W W E
# S E A S I D E R
D M I T R I # N O R A
I A T E I T # G U A M
Y I E L D S # E T T A
```

32

```
L A P # I R K # H A Y
A L A # D U N # E Y E
T A L L S T O R I E S
E M M A # S W I G #
R O S S I # O H M S
# I P O D # H O O
D A R K S H A D O W S
U S E # O M N I #
O H I O # E A T I T
# G L E N # N A N A
H A N D S O M E S U M
O D E # P D A # K I M
G O D # N E T # S T Y
```

33

```
G O R G E # N A D A L
U H A U L # E W I N G
S N I P E # P A N T S
H O S T C I T I E S #
# E A T O U T #
A D D # U N E V E N
N O U N S # E D I T H
D E P O T S # R A L
# T E A B A G #
# L O S T C I T I E S
B E A U S # D O N N A
R E T R O # U N I O N
A S H E N # P E A S E
```

34

```
D A M P # A S S A D
M E I R # U P T O W N
A R N E # P O R T L Y
J O E P E S C I #
# S O L E # P S T S
A A H S A T # C Y A N
S P A S M # S A N T E
W I F E # S O R T I E
E A T S # O A T H
# S U B P O E N A
I N D I R A # O S E S
L E O N I D # N I T E
L U N G S # S S T S
```

35

```
A G O G # C C L A M P
D O O R # R O A D I E
S O F A # E X P O S E
# B R A # T R O N
H O R S E S H O E #
A H I # D E E P
Y O D E L # A S H E S
# D E A R # A L I
# B U G G Y W H I P
E P I C # H E R
M A D A M A # I M P S
A S I T I S # S A R A
G O N E X T # T R O T
```

36

```
M A C E # O T H E R
O P A L S # P A Y M E
C A N I T # E X P E L
H I D # R A N # E R A
A N Y W A Y # R A P
# W H I N E # A L S
T A R O T # A B C D E
A L A # S T R U T #
P U P # I N N I N G
I M P # A P E # V I E
O N E A L # S L I C E
C U R V E # T O T E S
A S S E S # P Y R E
```

SOLUTIONS

37

```
L E O . F A B . R I P
E L F . I R E . O N E
A L F A L F A . L A W
P A Y N E . M E L D S
. O T T . E V E R
S E U S S . D A R E D
P A R . . . . C A R
A R R O W . R O O M Y
. P O L E . E R A .
R I C E S . M A S S E
E E K . S T I L T E D
A C E . O W N . E G G
P E R . N O D . R A Y
```

38

```
F I B . H O T . G R U
E G O . E W E . O O P
L O C K A N D L O A D
T R A I T . A F R O
. . T H A T S
A I R . R E E S E S
S T O C K M A R K E T
S O I R E E . I K E
. . I N D I A
E D G E . D R A N K
B A R R E L O F F U N
A L I . R I N . A D O
Y E T . A P T . R E X
```

39

```
Z I P S . O T T A W A
E W A N . I R I S E S
N O R A . N I C H E S
. . K I T K A T
A P P L E . D A B S
S A L S A . S C O T T
I R A . . . A A H
F I C U S . F A R G O
. S E G A . O R D E R
. . A N D R E W
A G E N D A . N A P A
B E N D E D . A L E C
C L E A R S . S K I T
```

40

```
S P A . O F F
P E P . H A L . I A N
E P I S O D E . T W O
E P E E . E A T S A T
D E C A F . H E R E
O R E . I N R O A D S
. O B V I O U S
I N F I E L D . Y A P
D U C T . S H A L L
E R A S E S . I S L A
A S K . S H O T P U T
L E E . P O P . I R E
. N E T . E E S
```

41

```
S O L O . J O S H E D
E R I N . U M P I R E
N E T S . N E A T E N
D O T H . E N D .
. L O L A . E B A Y
P E E R O U T . I P A
E P E E S . R E G A L
C I V . S T U M B L E
K C A R . W E B E
. U S E . A R T S
D E A R M E . S T E P
U M L A U T . S H E A
G U I L T Y . Y A M S
```

42

```
I R U N . R A G E D
M A L E . A R R I D
P R E E M I N E N T
E E E . O N E C
L E S S E E . O R C H
. A G A S S I . E O S
T R O T H . N T E S T
A T L . A R D E N T
P H D S . H I N T A T
. T A U R . R N R
S T I G M A T I Z E
S H R U B . S E A S
T O S E A . R S S S
```

43

```
S O T . A B O
A T H E I S M . C R U
C H E V R O N . O O N
R E M E T . I S A Y A
U R A L I C . I S A R
M S G . G H A S T L Y
. I N H E R I T
E X C I T E D . O S F
L E W D . P E N C I L
I N O I L . N O O N E
S O R . O U T R A G E
E N D . F I L M S E T
. T E Y . T R S
```

44

```
H A M S . K I N G M E
U R E A . E P O P E E
G I R D . E A T S I N
H A C I E N D A .
. U S N A . S K I D
M A R T I N I . O S U
E R I S A . M A R A T
N I A . C O P P E R Y
A L L I . H E P A .
. N O T I O N A L
G U N G H O . I W A S
A P L O M B . N A R A
T S E T S E . T R E T
```

45

```
C O V E S . R O M P S
A R I A L . E M I L E
M E R R Y . M A N I C
E G G S . B A N N E R
R O I . T E X . E R E
A N N U A L . P S S T
. I N U T E R O
C I A O . W R E T C H
O T S . J A R . A R E
V A L L E Y . A F A R
E L I A N . S L A V E
T I M O N . I O T A S
S A S S Y . T E S T Y
```

46

```
M A T T . O S C A R S
O N U S . U T O P I A
M E N U . T O L E D O
S W A N . S P A .
. A S I . S L A P
B E R M U D A . O L E
I N S I D E S C O O P
T O V . S C H E M E S
E S P N . H E N .
. O N A . T A D A
D E M E A N . U S E R
I R O N I C . R I C E
N E E D L E . Y A K S
```

47

```
M C C V . P O L L O I
S T O A . E K B E R G
N A R C . R A S C A L
. D U M P Y . I M O
C L A U S E . D A O
S E G M E N T .
T S E . D D E . A T O
. S I L I C O N
H A L . C L O R I S
E G O . D U A N E
N U T O I L . I A G O
R E S E D A . A G R O
I S A D O R . N E A P
```

48

```
M E S H . O U T A T
A L A E . E N S I L E
M A S C . P E T T I T
O N S T R I K E .
. A A H S . D E A R
U N F R O C K . X K E
P O R E D . E L C I D
A V A . A G R O U N D
T I S A . E N G R
. D O A S I S A Y
T E R R O R . C I N E
G R A I N Y . A V I A
V E S P A . L E N S
```

SOLUTIONS

49

```
J P S . C D S . . T R Y
E A T . A R T . . H U E
S T O P P A Y M E N T .
T I L L . B E E R . . .
S O E U R . . L E G O .
. . M U S H . S E W . .
D R O P T H E B A L L .
O O H . H E E L . . . .
G Y M S . . D I V O T .
. S A S S . N O S H . .
R O L L T H E D I C E .
P D A . A O K . C A T .
M E W . R O E . E R A .
```

50

```
A S I S . T U A R E G .
S A N I . U P B I N D .
D U C T . S T U P E S .
I N U N I S O N . . . .
C A B . B L A D D E R .
. A T E E . A E O N . .
G O T A T . I N F E R .
A P O S . A L T I . . .
M A R T I N I . C T S .
. . I D E A L I S T . .
A N S E L M . E E L Y .
P H A S E I . I N O R .
E L Y T R A . A T T O .
```

51

```
R O M A N O V . L O L .
A B I L E N E . O S U .
F E L I X T H E C A T .
F R O N T . I M A G E .
L O R E . S C A L E S .
E N D . L I L I E S . .
. . P I X E L . . . . .
C R A T E S . N A B . .
C H E S T S . M O R E .
H A S T E . V I O L A .
O S C A R W I N N E R .
S T U . E A S T E N D .
E E E . D R E S S E S .
```

52

```
C H O P . S W O O S H .
L I R A . I H A D T O .
A F E W . N I T E R S .
P I O N E E R . . . . .
. . B A R B A R A . . .
I N A P O D . O V E N .
C O N A N O B R I E N .
E N D S . C A N D L E .
D E S T R O Y . . . . .
. . A N S W E R S . . .
M A R G I N . H A I L .
E V E N S O . O S L O .
T E M P E R . S T E W .
```

53

```
A L O F T . S C R I P .
C U M I N . O H A R A .
E X I S T . F I N E R .
S E T H . S A P . . . .
. . I R K . S O A P . .
C H E N E Y . A B L E .
H I R A M . G N O M E .
A H A B . E N D E A R .
R O S A . B U S . . . .
. . R I B . A B B A . .
L E A R N . A L L A N .
O G D E N . G S U I T .
T O O L S . E A R L S .
```

54

```
H A Y E S . W A Y U P .
A L O N E . H O U S E .
M A G I C C A R P E T .
S N A G . A L T . . . .
. . M O V E A W A Y . .
G I J A N E . A L E . .
A R O S E . P I N T A .
W O K . C O N D O R . .
K N E E P A D S . . . .
. . V A N . P A R E . .
U N D E R T H E R U G .
S H O R T . I C I N G .
S L A Y S . S T A T S .
```

55

```
S C A M P I . E R M A .
P O P A R T . G O O N .
Y O U L O O K G O O D .
. . E B O N . M R S . .
P A S S E . I B M . . .
A S P . A F L A M E . .
T H A T S B E T T E R .
H E R O I C . E M O . .
. K E G . A S S E S . .
P E P . N A S A . . . .
I L L D O M Y B E S T .
B L U E . P E E W E E .
B A G S . S T R E A M .
```

56

```
J A P A N . B I K E S .
A R E N A . I T A L Y .
W I T C H D O C T O R .
S A S H . A S H . . . .
. . O W W . Y M C A . .
C O N V E N T . A O L .
O B E Y S . A S I D E .
B O A . T A C K L E S .
B E T S . M O I . . . .
. . L A B . T O M E . .
M E D I C I N E M A N .
E V A D E . B A N J O .
N A M E S . A M I S S .
```

57

```
B E T . B E G . A H A .
A C E . R N A . J A B .
S H A K E S P E A R E .
K O R E A . A X E L . .
. . . A D E P T . . . .
A G A . J A I L E R . .
R A T T L E S N A K E .
C L E R I C . B E D . .
. A T T A R . . . . . .
P R O W . P O D I A . .
R O L L T O P D E S K .
A D D . E E L . A L I .
Y E S . A R E . F E N .
```

58

```
L I A R S . S O I L S .
H O V E L . S U S I E .
O N E M O R E T I M E .
. . R I P E . D S O S .
S D S . E C U A . . . .
H E I S . E N T I C E .
A D O L E S C E N C E .
G E N I U S . D I C K .
. . G R I D . T P S . .
I N C H . V E T S . . .
F E A T H E R B E D S .
A N E L E . M A L A R .
T A N Y A . O R F E O .
```

59

```
P A N D A . T I A R A .
U S E U P . A D D E D .
S L E E P E R S O F A .
H A D . L A T . R I G .
E N L . E V A . E N E .
S T E P . E R A S E S .
. . O L S E N . . . . .
T R A D E D . D I S S .
R E D . A R T . S U P .
A D J . T O O . R I O .
C O U C H P O T A T O .
E N S U E . T W E E N .
D E T E R . H O L D S .
```

60

```
P C S . M S G . . . . .
A H A . A L L . P O D .
J O H N D O E . A N A .
A R A B . B E A C O N .
M U R A L . . L I F T .
A S A . O K E E F F E .
. D A V I N C I . . . .
P R E T E N D . C B S .
L O S T . . S P O R E .
A M E N D S . E C O N .
T A R . U P T R E N D .
A N T . M A R . A C E .
. . . P R Y . N O R . .
```

61

```
R A G . T A B . C A R
O N O . E L I . O W E
A N I M A L S . M E D
M A N O R . T R I . .
. . G N U . R A N T O
B E B O P . O H G O D
E V A . . . . F E D .
T A C O S . C R O S S
A N K L E . A I R . .
. . W E D . N O W A Y
S P A . A G I T A T E
H E R . T A N . R O N
E N D . E Y E . D P S
```

62

```
D A B S . . A L I G .
I M A C S . G E N R E
T O P I C . U N T I L
C R T . I N A . H S I
H E I D E N . E S S .
. . S I N E W . S O S
M I M I C . A D A M A
E M O . E F R E M . .
S P F . U P K E E P .
A L F . E R A . V A R
B O I N G . T W E R E
I R R E G . H E I L S
. E E L Y . E N E S .
```

63

```
H A H A . C A S I N O
O M A R . A B A T E D
L E N T . R E U S E D
E N D S W E L L . . .
. . S I R E . T H E A
A T H E A R T . E L S
S H A R P . R O A M S
A O K . S T A N D O N
P R E S . A C E S . .
. . W O R K S H O P .
E A T I N G . T A D A
G L A N C E . A K I N
G A D G E T . R E N T
```

64

```
. U N T O . L O W E R
I N U R N . O N I N E
S I D E E F F E C T S
U S G . I L A . K I A
Z O E . R I T . E R Y
U N S T O P . U T E S
. . I N F E R . . . .
S C A N . L U N A C Y
C A M . B O R . M A P
A R E . A P A . A U R
R E N A I S S A N C E
P E R E Z . I N D U S
A R A C E . A S A S .
```

65

```
E L K . D P S . M E D
C A E S U R A . A C E
O N E L O O K . U H F
L I P O . F E I S T Y
. C A M I S E . . . .
I M O N I T . R P M S
C F O . G S N . O S T
C A L C . H I A T U S
. . U G A N D A . . .
L I N E A R . O T O S
A D U . D I S P O S E
T E N . D N A T E S T
H S N . A G O . S A S
```

66

```
V I S I T . A P P L E
A L I N E . C E R E S
M E E T S . E N I A C
P A G E T U R N E R .
. . . R I G B Y . . .
O N E L E G . M A E S
S A V O R . T A R A S
S P E C . E R R O R S
. . . U S E A S . . .
. M U T T O N H E A D
T A H O E . C A R B O
E L O R A . E L M E R
E T H Y L . S L A T E
```

67

```
S N A F U . D E C R Y
A E S O P . O C H E R
T H I E F . W R A P S
E R A . O W N U P . .
S U N . R A T . E A R
. . S A Y O N A R A .
C R O O N . T A U P E
D I P T Y C H S . . .
R O E . T E E . E V E
. N O H O W . L E N .
B A M B I . I C A N T
A P R O N . R O T O R
G R I E G . E N E M Y
```

68

```
T N T S . B A L D E R
A A R E . E L I N O R
M P A A . Y A S S E R
P A N B R O I L . . .
. . S E A N . E O N S
C A L E N D S . N I T
U M A . A T H . E D M
R U T . T H A T S I T
B R E E . E L I E . .
. . G O P L A C E S .
O M E A R A . R O L O
H I L L E L . A N S A
M A K E M E . S D A K
```

69

```
U N U M . . O D O R S
S O R A . D R I V E L
D E S C . I S N E A R
T S A R . S O A R . .
. . . A L G . H S I A
C H I M E R A . T M S
P I N E M A R T E N S
A L T . A C T U P O N
S T E R . E S S . . .
. . R O L F . S A D A
C A N Y O U . O B O L
U R A C I L . C A R T
P Y L E S . K A Y O .
```

70

```
T A C O S . S H A F T
A T A R I . P A L I N
C O N A N . A R E N T
K N I C K K N A C K .
. . L E E K S . . . .
B A K E R Y . S E E K
A L I . . . . E L F .
T E X T . I R O N I C
. . O S C A R . . . .
. K N O C K K N O C K
P R O B E . E A G L E
T I T A N . I T R A N
A S I D E . N E E D S
```

71

```
H A W K S . S O N G S
A V A I L . T I A R A
T E N N I S E L B O W
E N D . P E P . B O Y
R U E . S T S . E V E
S E R F . S O L D E R
. . B R A N D . . . .
B O D I E S . S C A T
O R E . S I D . R N A
W I N . I D O . A T M
W O U N D E D K N E E
O L D I E . G E N U S
W E E P S . E G Y P T
```

72

```
C A R D . . A S P C A
A P I U M . P E R O T
N A D I A . S E O U L
I C I . L E O N O R A
D E N I A L . A F T S
. G R I M M . P E E .
M A S K S . A M O R S
E T H . E S T E S . .
A T O Z . O I L I E R
T A T A M I S . T A E
P I G I T . S A I G A
I N U R N . E A V E D
E S N E S . . H E R S
```

SOLUTIONS

73
```
S M A L L █ O K I E S
C O C O A █ R E N E E
A R R O W █ D E A L T
L E E █ S H E P S █
E L S █ C A R █ P E W
█ █ C H L O R I N E
T A B O O █ F E N D S
A I R P O R T S █ █
P L O █ L A H █ C D S
█ W E D G E █ L O T
P A S T E █ D I O D E
A R E N A █ A D A G E
R E R A N █ Y O K E L
```

74
```
C A S C A █ S C O O P
O R A L S █ O R I B I
M A Y A A N G E L O U
P L A S M A █ A Y E S
█ █ S I C E M █
F I E S █ L I O N E L
I M A C S █ O F A G E
C A S H I N █ T E S T
█ █ E X T R A █
A R I D █ S E R G E I
C O N U R B A T I O N
D A R L A █ C A R N E
C R E E L █ H R O S S
```

75
```
A B B A █ F A C I A L
R O U T █ E N A C T S
M A T H █ A G R E E D
█ █ T E S T E R █
█ D E N Y █ L E F T S
R E R A N █ A L L O T
O F F █ █ U P A
S O L O S █ T I T A N
E G Y P T █ A N T Z
█ █ A R R I V E █
U N I Q U E █ A R L O
R E B U T S █ I B E T
L A M E S T █ N Y E T
```

76
```
C L O W N S █ L A P
L A R I A T █ W I F E
I M E L D A █ O M E N
█ █ D A N B R O W N
S P E W █ S A L █
C U R I E █ I D T A G
A M I L E █ T W I N E
R A N D R █ S I M O N
█ W I G █ D E N T
L A K E E R I E █
A X I S █ O N W A R D
L E N T █ S T E R E O
A D D █ S O B E I T
```

77
```
L I Z A █ Z O O M I N
E R I C █ I M P O S E
W E P T █ P E S T L E
█ W O M A N █ T E D
P A I R E D █ S T Y
E R R █ D E B █
W E E █ I E R █ Z A P
█ █ A D A █ I P A
T I C █ O U T P U T
O N O █ T O N I C █
R A N C I D █ M O N A
A N G O L A █ E D E N
H E A L T H █ D E W Y
```

78
```
W A D S █ T E L L O N
H I R E █ O R I O L E
O D I N █ F I B B E D
M E E T █ F E Y █
█ █ D O K E █ A F R O
C O F F E E S █ R A D
U N I F Y █ O P I N E
B E G █ S T R E E T S
A S S T █ R E E D █
█ █ O W E █ L E A H
W O N T O N █ O G L E
A B O A R D █ U G L I
R I D L E Y █ T S A R
```

79
```
L A G █ O T T
A V E █ I R A █ F I T
R A T T L E R █ A S A
E L S E █ K A P L A N
D O T E D █ O L A Y
O N O █ A M E R I C A
█ G E T E V E N █
O N E L A N E █ G I T
R A T E █ R E A D Y
A D H E R E █ A P O P
T I E █ I N G R A T E
E R R █ D Y E █ R O O
█ S A M █ T O N
```

80
```
W O W █ M G M █ O H O
A M I █ I I I █ P E P
W A S H A N D W E A R
A R E A █ S A D L Y
█ U N I T Y █
O M E L E T █ P G A
R I N S E C Y C L E S
O D D █ H A L O E S
█ H E Y Y A █
D R O O L █ N E M O
R E P E A T A G A I N
A B E █ T O Y █ C R Y
W A N █ E W E █ H E X
```

81
```
H A H A █ T E R E S A
E V I L █ W R A P U P
R I G S █ E N T I R E
A S H █ A L I █ C I X
█ N E R V E S █
A T O N C E █ A M I N
W O O D S █ S N I D E
N A N U █ O U T D I D
█ P A C M A N █
U H S █ F L O █ I B E
P O T A T O █ A G E S
O N E S E C █ C H A P
N E W A R K █ S T U N
```

82
```
L O S E █ C A R O B
I V A N █ B A N A N A
M E L D █ U N I T E D
B R A E █ T I M █
█ D A R T █ A S P S
G O F R E E █ L O E W
O H O █ M R S █ U S A
B I R D █ K E E P O N
Y O K O █ N E W S █
█ T M I █ I P A D
B E S T O F █ N O N E
I N H E R E █ G O N E
C L Y D E █ S N A P
```

83
```
J U M P █ A S P I R E
O N E S █ D E A D O N
E T N A █ D A L L A S
S O U L S I S T E R
█ M I N O R █
J O U S T █ N Y L O N
O A K █ E W E
G R E E T █ W H O L E
█ N A C H O █
█ B I G B R O T H E R
D O C I L E █ D I V E
D R O N E S █ O D E S
T E N E T S █ G E N T
```

84
```
A S H E █ C A M E I N
C O A L █ A T O N C E
A L P O █ L O R D E D
T O P P L I N G █
█ Y E A █ E A G L E
T E D D Y █ S N O O P
E R A █ █ O N E
E G Y P T █ L O D G E
N O S I R █ O F T █
█ G A S O L I N E
A C T O U T █ A M E R
R E S U M E █ T E A R
T O E T A P █ E S T S
```

85

```
M E M E S ▪ S A M B A
A L A M E ▪ T R A I T
X E R O X ▪ A C I D S
I V Y ▪ E R R ▪ N E E
M A L ▪ D I D ▪ E T A
U T A H ▪ P O L L ▪
M E N U S ▪ M O O R E
▪ D E U S ▪ X B O X
O R C ▪ G P A ▪ S M U
P A R ▪ G A B ▪ T A L
E V A D E ▪ A G E N T
R E B U S ▪ C U R I E
A S S E T ▪ I M S A D
```

86

```
M A G S ▪ A G L O W
A N A T ▪ G U I D E
I N G A ▪ P E N C I L
D A G G E R S ▪ E N D
▪ I S L A ▪ ▪ ▪
O F F ▪ I N N ▪ J F K
W E T ▪ S K I ▪ O R E
E D S ▪ E C O ▪ K I N
▪ ▪ A B L E ▪ ▪
P U N ▪ F L E A B A G
A N I M A L ▪ N O N O
S I N A I ▪ D O T O
S T A R R ▪ S K I N
```

87

```
A H A ▪ G A B ▪ A S K
C O D ▪ O L E ▪ P T A
T W O A N D A ▪ N A Y
▪ N E A T ▪ E R A
G A B O R ▪ S P A R K
U N I T ▪ G M A ▪
M Y T H R E E S O N S
▪ E E L ▪ S A I L
A C U R A ▪ H O T L Y
R A N ▪ C H E F ▪
S I D ▪ H A L F M E N
O R E ▪ E V E ▪ A Y E
N O R ▪ D E N ▪ Y E W
```

88

```
R A P ▪ U R I ▪ H A W
I C Y ▪ L E S ▪ I M O
M A R A T H O N M A N
▪ A V I A ▪ O O R T
R E M E M B E R M E
A R I ▪ A S P S ▪
M I D S T ▪ I E V E R
▪ A U K S ▪ A A A
▪ V E R M I C E L L I
I D L E ▪ L O N I ▪
M A R K E T P L A C E
E R O ▪ N E A ▪ N A W
D A Y ▪ E R L ▪ T R E
```

89

```
N A Z I S ▪ B U M P S
I T Y O U ▪ A S L I P
B O X U P ▪ T A K E I
B M W ▪ R A H ▪ J R R
L I V ▪ A R T ▪ I R E
E C U S ▪ R U S H E S
▪ T O T E B A G ▪
B U S S E S ▪ O F F S
E R R ▪ M T S ▪ E R E
E S Q ▪ P S I ▪ D E N
P U P I L ▪ L A C E S
A L O N E ▪ A M B L E
T A N K S ▪ S P A Y S
```

90

```
F R A M E ▪ C A S T S
R A M E N ▪ H I T U P
O V E R T H E L I N E
Z I N ▪ R E C ▪ G E E
E N D ▪ Y A K ▪ M U D
N E S T ▪ R E C A P S
▪ A S T R O ▪ ▪
N O P R O B ▪ P O R T
E P A ▪ B E E ▪ P E R
R E D ▪ E A T ▪ U S E
U N D E R T H E S E A
D E E R E ▪ A R E N T
A D D E D ▪ N A S T Y
```

91

```
I S O N ▪ S U E D E
N A N O ▪ A L L E L E
F L I M F L A M M E R
O V O ▪ L I N ▪ I G A
▪ O N E I S ▪ G I S
▪ S C H M O O Z E
K I O S K ▪ U D D E R
U N F O R M E D ▪
N A S ▪ O S S E O ▪
G L O ▪ O R L ▪ S N A
F I R S T A I D K I T
U N T I E S ▪ D E C I
▪ E S T A S ▪ T R E E
```

92

```
R I A L ▪ L U B E
A D I E U ▪ L A G E R
E A R T H M O T H E R
▪ E L I T E ▪ ▪
A I R M A T T R E S S
C R U ▪ N E O ▪ L O W
L A M ▪ ▪ ▪ I D O
E N O ▪ P E A ▪ Z O O
F I R E A N D R A I N
▪ D I O D E ▪ ▪
W A T E R S U P P L Y
P L A N S ▪ P A R S E
M E N S ▪ Y O U R
```

93

```
A P T ▪ D I E ▪ N A G
P R Y ▪ I D S ▪ E R A
H O P O M Y T H U M B
I B E X ▪ L O U T ▪
D E A L T ▪ P E R I L
▪ I O S ▪ A D O
S K I P T O M Y L O U
A I R ▪ T E A ▪
G N O M E ▪ W H E W S
▪ N A L A ▪ O A H U
J U M P A L L O V E R
O N E ▪ T I E ▪ E E L
B I N ▪ E A T ▪ S L Y
```

94

```
H A L F W A Y ▪ A S H
A M E R I C A ▪ M O O
S C O O P U P ▪ P U N
▪ O E R ▪ A L S O
P O R T ▪ A P P E A R
A X E L ▪ S I P ▪
C O C O A ▪ G L A S S
▪ O L D ▪ E R I K
S I M P L E ▪ J E D I
O T I S ▪ N B A ▪
D A N ▪ A V O C A D O
A L E ▪ P E R K S U P
S Y S ▪ T R E S S E S
```

95

```
E D E N ▪ C H E S S
L E G O ▪ A U D I O
F L O W E R G I R L
▪ A S S E T ▪ ▪
P R A Y S ▪ O P A L
L E G ▪ A V E R A G E
A L A ▪ Y A M ▪ I R A
N A M A S T E ▪ R E D
E X E C ▪ R O S E S
▪ T O U G H ▪ ▪
R I N G B E A R E R
A D O R E ▪ R O V E
P O W E R ▪ A M E X
```

96

```
B L I M P ▪ J O S S
R I S E R ▪ O N L Y
Y E S T E R Y E A R
O V O ▪ C A C O ▪
▪ N I G E R I A N
B R E W P U B ▪ A B O
L A N A I ▪ R A M I S
E R N ▪ T O O L A T E
T E A P A R T Y ▪
▪ U T A H ▪ G A I
R E F I N E M E N T
I N F O ▪ R O O T S
B O S N ▪ S P L A Y
```

SOLUTIONS

97
```
O W L . A T E . L E G
N O I . T A R . I V E
C O S M O K R A M E R
E L A I N E . P O R E
. . . L E O N A . . .
A W O L . N O R M A L
L E V I S . S T A R E
A B A C U S . F E E D
. . . E N T E R . . .
S P I N . A L O H A S
C A T T Y R E M A R K
A P E . E T C . L E E
R A M . E S T . L A W
```

98
```
B A R S . M I M I C .
I M O K . O M E G A S
T O M A T O S A U C E
E R A . I D O . A T E
R A N T S . M A N U P
S L O W . H A R A S S
. . . E R O D E . . .
S T R E E P . S I C K
T H E T A . M O C H A
E R N . C D S . I O N
P O T A T O S A C K S
S W A N E E . F L E A
. S L E D S . T E D S
```

99
```
C W T . R T S . A P R
U A R . E E E . R A E
B R E A T H E . G M T
E M A N U E L . U P I
B U S I N E S S M A N
S P U M E . . H E S A
. . R A S . N O N . .
S T E T . . O T T O S
C O C O N U T P A L M
A C H . A M P U T E E
R O E . S P A T I A L
E M S . T E S . O T T
D E T . Y D S . N E S
```

100
```
M I N I S . H A T C H
I N A N E . A T E A M
S T R A W . R E A L M
S O C C E R B A L L .
. . . A D I O S . . .
T U R N . B R E E Z E
E R A . . . L I D . .
A N G E L A . D I P S
. . M A Y B E . . . .
. H O C K E Y P U C K
M E L E E . T A L O N
O R D E R . E R N I E
D R E S S . S T A L E
```

101
```
F I F E . P A J A M A
O R A L . E N A M E L
R O C K A N D R O L L
A N T . I T S . N B A
G O O . D U O . G A Y
E R R S . P O P . . .
R E S E T . N E W T S
. . . E E K . T A R T
A S H . X E D . Y E A
A C E . T R I . T A R
R O L L I N G R O C K
O R I O L E . O G L E
N E X T E L . D O E R
```

102
```
L E N A . S H E I L A
I M A C . C O R N E D
M A N E . A M E N D S
B I C Y C L E . . . .
S L Y . H E R S H E Y
. . D E E D . C A K E
S T R A W . B A R E S
A R E S . M I N D . .
N E W Y O R K . Y R S
. . . S H E R B E T .
T R I C K Y . H O P E
U N L O A D . E Y R E
G A L O R E . A S O N
```

103
```
N U M B . . R A S P S
O T O E . P E N T U P
O N E S . O V E R L Y
P E N I N S U L A . .
. . . D I S P E N S E
E S S E N E . . G A N
R A T S O . E M E R Y
E T A . . A Z A R I A
B A C K S P I N . . .
. . . C U P H O L D E R
E T A L I I . I S E E
D O T A R D . K O L N
A P O K E . . E S S A
```

104
```
B O L O . S O S A D
O N O N . I L L G O
S C R E E N D O O R
N E G L I G E E . .
. . N A S T . S T A X
E V E N N O W . O M M
E S T E E . A P N E A
G O T . R E S I G N S
S P E E . N A N U .
. . . S L A B B E R S
. A S S O C I A T E D
S T I L T . L I N A
U S E A S . L E E K
```

105
```
. . . . . U Z I . . .
T A Z . P A R . Z I P
A V I . A C E . S R I
E I G H T H . L A K E
. A G E . A T O Z . .
S T Y X . R O U S E D
P O M . B Y E . A V E
A R A R A T . T G I F
. . . R I T A . H A L
Y E L P . Y O U B E T
A R E . A L L . O Y L
K E Y . S O D . R E C
. . . . I R S . . . .
```

106
```
M A S S . P U S H U P
A N O N . E S T A T E
I N F O . L E A D E R
N E T . M O S T . . .
E X T R A S . S H E A
. . A U D I T . A V A
F A C E T . O P R A H
E G O . V O T E D . .
W E S T . P E N C I L
. . . I D E S . I R A
C O N M A N . I D O S
B R E E Z E . M E N S
S E E R E D . O R S O
```

107
```
U S A . S O S . P I P
N O G . A R T S A L E
C A L M W E A T H E R
U V E A . . Y U L . .
T E T R A D S . A L I
. . . B R A . O V E N
C O O L M I L L I O N
H E R E . S A D . . .
I R A . B Y P A T H S
. . C A R . G O A L .
C O L L E C T E D L Y
S T E P S O N . A L E
I T S . T O T . Y E R
```

108
```
B U F F S . D D A Y
U N L I T . T O R T E
S M I T E . O M A H A
T O P . A I D . W A R
L O P . D N A . I N N
E R I K . S T A N D S
. . . N E S T E G G .
G I G G L Y . E S P N
R N A . A L G . T O E
A B C . T E A . R O W
M O O S E . R E A D E
P R I E D . B O W L S
A N N A . O N S E T
```

SOLUTIONS

109
```
O A K S   K A R A T S
D R E W   I T A L I A
D I N E   M E T A L S
S A K E   K I S S E S
    E T H A N
Y E S S I R     K E A
A R E   P D A   I N K
P R Y   A M A N D A
    O S I N G
I M P I S H   E K E S
M A I T A I   M O L E
O R T E G A   I N S T
N E T M E N   A G E S
```

110
```
R O O S T   F A G O T
E T N A S   U R A N O
C A E S A R S A L A D
E L Y   R O E   B I D
I G E T   B L E A R Y
P I A N O B A R
T A R O T   G I B E R
    T I R E S O M E
C A S E O F   A L A S
O F A   S I R   S I T
C O N F I D E N T L Y
O U T A T   C R E E L
A L A R Y   T A R D E
```

111
```
B I S O N   L A V E R
O N C U E   I R E N E
T H A T S A F I R S T
T A R   T N T   S U I
O L E   S O S   E R E
M E S S   N U R S E S
    S K Y P E
E S T E E M   V A T S
L E O   N O S   S E W
I D S   Y U M   L E E
J U S T A S E C O N D
A C E I N   L A P S E
H E R O S   T R E Y S
```

112
```
S A I N     I T I N A
A R L O   U S E F U L
D O L T   N A R I T A
R O O T S F O R
    M I L A   O S H I
C D E   O V E R E A T
A I N   S O X   L I S
S E E T H R U   F R I
K U D U   A R I D
    B O B B O O N E
N O R M A L   T U E S
S E N A T E   A B E E
C O R N Y   S T D S
```

113
```
H E A D S   O C C U R
A R G U E   B O O N E
N I E C E   A V O I D
D E S K   S M E L T S
    Q A T A R
B E A U T Y   A R E A
A G R E E   B L O W N
M O M S   E I L E E N
    T H R O B
I F F I E R   A P S E
S O L O S   U S U A L
I C O N S   S E N D S
T H E S E   E S T E E
```

114
```
C H I C   P A R I S
H E R A   A W A S H
A M E R I C A N M E
    O V E R
M A D L Y   E N A C T
O N E   Y O O H O O
U N I T E D F R O N T
T I G E R S   L E E
H E N C E   C R E S S
    C H O O
D E L T A B L U E S
U N I O N   E S A U
B E E R S   S E R B
```

115
```
S L E E P   A R P E L
S O F T A   S E R I O
I N F U L L S W I N G
  E L I S A   E N S E
M H O S   S E T T
A A R   B E R S E R K
N N E   O R A   D O R
A D S O R B S   M C I
    C H G E   Y A K S
I D E S   A B E T S
S E N T I M E N T A L
A L C O A   S T E L A
K L E P T   S E R T A
```

116
```
B A H   D E A
A V A   O R R   A R I
R I T C H I E   X E R
B A C H   C A M E R A
E T H E R   A B U T
D E E   E A C H O N E
    T A B L O I D
P E P T A L K   Y D S
E L I M   E D S E L
T I E S U P   O P R Y
E T C   C A L O R I E
S E E   L I E   A D S
    A N D   Y E T
```

117
```
A S S A M   L U R E R
O T A R U   I S O L A
R E N T E   L A S I K
T L C   Z S A   E N E
A L T   Z A C   M O E
L A I D I N   H A R M
    M E N   B A R
I H O P   H E Y Y O U
S O N   P T L   S L R
T O I   A S U   B E G
H H O U R   S L A V E
M A U L S   H E B E R
I S S U E   I D Y L S
```

118
```
G H O S T   A D H O C
R U M O R   S A U N A
A G O N Y   I N N E R
B O O G   T A C K L E
    O Z O N E
O P T F O R   M A Y O
W H O S O   J A W E D
N I N O   S E R E N E
    L O T T A
C A N O P Y   T H O M
A R O M A   C H O K E
S A V O R   H O W I E
S L A N T   I N L E T
```

119
```
  P E R I   P I T A S
I L E U M   A G A M E
B E R G S   R U R A L
O X Y G E N T E N T
    E T O N S
I P A D   M E S A B I
N A L   M I R   U A L
F L A G O N   E X T S
    O N E O N
  L E A D E R S H I P
M A R L A   N U E V O
E T A I L   O R L E S
R E S E E   T E D S
```

120
```
U N A R M E D   W I I
M I N E O L A   O N S
W H I P S A W   M T N
    O S T   T A R E
U S S R   E R E N O W
L O U T   D I S H
M A B E L   A T O N E
    A D E S   F O I E
P E L L E T   L D L S
I T T Y   R B I
T U E   D O U G L A S
C D R   S K Y H I G H
H E N   S E S T E T S
```

SOLUTIONS

121
```
L I F E S ■ A S T O
A G E N T ■ S P A R ■
B E T T Y W H I T E
S T A R ■ H E N ■ ■
■ ■ I S A ■ S A G A
A C C E P T S ■ B O X
W O R S E ■ A C U T E
E R A ■ D A K O T A S
D E M O ■ P E R ■ ■
■ ■ L O P ■ O R E O
C L I N T B L A C K
H A V E ■ A L P H A ■
I D E S ■ N A T T Y
```

122
```
D A D O E S ■ C A N
I C I C L E ■ R A Z A
G A S C A P ■ I P U T
■ A T T A G I R L
P A S S E ■ A H L ■
L U C I D ■ A T L A S
O T R O ■ W A R E
P O I N S ■ C I R C A
■ P A H ■ O N Y O U
O U T L Y I N G
E L U L ■ S V E L T E
N A R Y ■ T E R S E R
O N E ■ O Y S T E R
```

123
```
C O H A N ■ A B H O R
O R A T E ■ D I A N E
R I P E R ■ A G N E S
P O P ■ V I P ■ U S E
S L Y ■ E N T ■ K I N
■ E H S ■ R E E K E D
■ A L G E R I A ■
S O N O R A ■ N H L
I N U ■ A C T ■ H O S
E L K ■ S H E ■ A R C
N I K O S ■ A G R E E
N E A L E ■ R E R A N
A S H E S ■ S T Y L E
```

124
```
O L D S ■ K S T A R
K E E P ■ N E T M A N
L O C I ■ S I R I U S
A V E R S E T O ■
■ P I T C H D A R K
M A T T S ■ S E T A N
S C I ■ H M O
G R O I N ■ H O L S T
T E N D E R I Z E ■
■ O U T V O T E D
P L A T T E ■ N I D I
H O B O E S ■ I C U S
O N E O R ■ C S C H
```

125
```
S M U G ■ C O U P
H O M E S ■ O W N E D
R U B L E ■ P E D R O
A L I ■ R E P ■ E M U
N I L ■ B R O ■ R I G
K N I T ■ E L E C T S
■ C H I C A G O ■
F L A U N T ■ O V A L
A O L ■ H O V ■ E V A
L U C ■ A R C ■ R I P
S N O B S ■ R E C A P
E G R E T ■ S M O T E
■ E D G E ■ O P E D
```

126
```
A B E L ■ R I V A L S
P E L E ■ O N E S I E
E A S E ■ W A N T O N
S U E G R A F T O N
■ R E N E ■
D E C A Y ■ W H A L E
I R O N ■ U H O H
S A N T A ■ E X A M S
■ M E L T ■
■ S I O U X F A L L S
R E S I S T ■ B E A T
H E L L E R ■ L I M A
O D E S S A ■ E S P N
```

127
```
G S O ■ E D H ■ E W S
T I N A M O U ■ N E U
O L D K I N G C O L E
S K E I N ■ H O L L Y
■ T E L S T A R ■
P I R A N A ■ E G E R
A T E ■ T D S ■ A A S
C A V S ■ L L O Y D S
■ L E A V E I N ■
V I R E O ■ P I E R S
C A S S I U S C L A Y
R N A ■ C L U E S I N
S O L ■ E M P ■ A L S
```

128
```
A L U M ■ K N I C K
C A N S O ■ E E N I E
H D Q R S ■ P A D R E
■ U P L I T ■ I O N
A R E ■ O T O E S ■
B O S N ■ S U P P E R
A L T A R ■ T E E N A
D E I C E R ■ E N T S
■ O L A N D ■ S R A
M A N ■ D A R L A ■
O P I U M ■ E U B I E
A I N T I ■ I S L E T
B E G E T ■ T E R A
```

129
```
E S C ■ A M I ■ P T A
N I L ■ D E N ■ Y E S
T E A ■ A D S ■ R E P
A S S ■ M I T ■ A P E
I T S ■ S C I ■ M E N
L A S S ■ A L L I E S
■ C H I L L E D ■
A T H E N S ■ O S L O
C H E ■ V C R ■ C O N
T E D ■ O H O ■ H O E
I C U ■ L O N ■ E N D
V A L ■ V O N ■ M E G
E N E ■ E L Y ■ E Y E
```

130
```
U S N ■ I R E ■
S O U P C O N ■ H E A
B A R R E L A L O N G
■ S I L L ■ O R D O
T W I G ■ E G G S O N
E E N ■ F R E E D
M S G ■ O C D ■ O L A
■ H E R O S ■ E D D
M Y O P I A ■ A U L D
D O M E ■ S C T V
S H E E R T E R R O R
E O S ■ R E L I E V E
■ R R S ■ S O W
```

131
```
D E B T S ■ T A R A S
O M A H A ■ A R O M A
C I T E D ■ K E B A B
E L M ■ A W E ■ I Z E
N I A ■ T O O ■ N O R
T O N S ■ K N O W N S
■ F A R ■ E L I ■
S H O W E R ■ E L S E
E A R ■ W E T ■ L U X
E V E ■ A D O ■ I M P
S A V E R ■ A L A M O
A N E N D ■ S E M I S
W A R E S ■ T A S T E
```

132
```
D E C A L ■ A G A P E
E R A S E ■ B A N A L
M I S S T H E M A R K
I N E ■ M O L E ■
■ G E M ■ S O F A
P H R A S E S ■ M E L
H O U S E ■ I D E A S
I L L ■ E A T I N T O
L E E K ■ R U G ■
■ I K E A ■ C O O
S H A N I A T W A I N
H E R D S ■ E A G L E
E X I S T ■ D R E S S
```

SOLUTIONS

133
D	I	S	C	O		U	N	F	I	T
O	T	H	E	R		Z	O	R	B	A
W	A	R	N	S		I	F	O	L	D
	L	E	T	O	N		A	S	E	A
B	I	D	S		U	N	I	T		
L	A	D		A	D	O	R	E	R	S
O	N	E		M	I	D		D	O	O
G	O	D	D	E	S	S		F	A	D
		W	E	S	T		A	L	D	A
H	A	H	A		S	O	L	A	R	
E	X	E	R	T		D	A	K	A	R
L	L	A	M	A		O	M	E	G	A
P	E	T	E	R		R	O	S	E	S

134
L	A	G		P	K	G		G	T	O
A	T	L		L	I	A		A	O	L
M	H	O		O	N	R	A	M	P	S
B	O	B	O		E	R	N	E	S	
S	L	A	P	A	T		N	O	O	R
		L	E	N	I		O	F	I	T
D	A	I	R	Y	C	A	T	T	L	E
I	T	Z	A		E	V	A	H		
S	W	A	T		N	A	T	R	O	N
	A	T	O	N	E		E	O	N	S
S	T	I	R	F	R	Y		N	E	Y
O	E	O		L	G	E		E	A	N
A	R	N		D	Y	S		S	L	C

135
A	P	E		P	R	O		M	E	H
P	I	N		D	O	W		A	V	A
R	E	D	S	Q	U	I	R	R	E	L
I	T	E	M		T	E	A	K		
L	A	D	E	D			W	I	N	O
			L	I	S	A		N	A	P
W	H	I	T	E	K	N	I	G	H	T
E	O	N			M	I	N	D		
D	E	A	L			A	I	O	L	I
		S	I	A	M		O	M	A	N
B	L	U	E	J	A	S	M	I	N	E
O	U	I		A	Y	E		T	A	P
A	G	T		R	O	W		S	I	T

136
	F	R	O	C	K		Y	S	L	
	S	E	A	R	L	E		O	E	O
S	A	N	F	E	R	N	A	N	D	O
T	E	N	T	O		N	D	A	K	
U	N	E	S		C	I	V	E	T	S
D	S	L		S	A	T	I	R	E	
		L	A	P	E	L				
	G	M	I	N	O	R		L	A	A
D	A	E	M	O	N		T	A	U	R
A	L	A	E			D	R	U	R	Y
C	O	N	D	I	T	I	O	N	A	L
H	S	T		N	O	D	I	C	E	
A	H	A		I	W	I	S	H		

137
D	E	F	S		R	E	M	A	D	E
I	C	E	T		E	V	E	N	L	Y
S	H	E	A		B	I	R	D	I	E
H	O	L	Y	M	O	L	Y			
		O	A	R		L	I	K	E	
S	E	Q	U	I	N	S		S	A	G
K	L	U	T	Z		P	I	N	T	A
I	M	A		E	V	I	C	T	E	D
D	O	D	O		A	C	E			
		R	O	L	Y	P	O	L	Y	
K	A	R	A	T	E		A	S	I	A
I	G	E	T	I	T		C	L	A	W
N	O	L	E	S	S		K	O	R	N

138
L	O	T		S	U	B		P	U	B
A	M	A		U	S	A		E	P	A
P	A	P	T	E	S	T		P	A	Y
U	H	O	H		R	H	E	T	T	
P	A	N	E	L		S	T	A	R	R
			M	A	P		C	L	E	O
R	A	P		W	I	N		K	E	Y
A	L	O	E		P	E	G			
J	A	P	A	N		W	R	O	T	E
	S	T	R	I	P		I	C	O	N
A	K	A		P	U	P	T	E	N	T
C	A	R		P	R	O		A	T	E
T	N	T		Y	E	T		N	O	R

139
F	A	T	T	Y		S	T	R	I	P
A	T	A	R	I		E	R	A	S	E
T	O	X	I	N		R	E	I	N	S
E	P	I	C		R	I	A	L	T	O
			K	R	A	F	T			
T	O	R	Q	U	E		W	A	C	O
O	D	I	U	M		E	I	G	H	T
M	E	M	E		B	E	L	O	I	T
		S	T	I	L	L				
T	A	T	T	O	O		I	N	K	S
E	Q	U	I	P		S	A	I	N	T
E	U	R	O	S		E	M	C	E	E
D	A	N	N	Y		A	S	K	E	W

140
S	A	R	I	S		S	I	D	E	S
Q	U	O	T	H		A	K	I	R	A
U	S	L	T	A		N	E	G	E	V
A	S	L		R	C	A		I	N	A
S	I	E		P	H	A	E	T	O	N
H	E	R	N	I	A		T	A	W	T
			S	T	E	N	C	I	L	
S	A	K	S		S	O	C	C	E	R
A	T	A	B	L	O	W		A	V	E
H	O	T		U	N	B		M	E	A
A	N	I	O	N		A	M	E	N	D
R	A	N	D	A		R	A	R	E	D
A	L	G	E	R		N	E	A	R	S

141
W	A	R	T		S	A	S	H	A	Y
A	L	O	E		E	N	T	I	C	E
N	A	Y	S		N	O	I	S	E	S
D	I	R	T		I	N	N			
		O	R	S	O		G	R	A	F
M	A	G	U	I	R	E		A	X	E
A	R	E	N	T		S	T	Y	L	E
P	E	R		E	M	P	I	R	E	S
S	A	S	S		O	N	T	O		
			M	A	N		A	M	O	K
R	E	W	A	R	D		N	A	T	O
I	T	A	L	I	A		I	N	T	O
P	A	R	L	A	Y		C	O	O	K

142
F	O	R	K	S		G	I	B	B	S
A	D	I	E	U		O	H	A	R	A
N	O	T	E	S		T	O	K	E	N
G	R	A	P	H	P	A	P	E	R	
			A	I	R	S				
A	F	E	W		Y	E	L	L	O	W
S	I	T	A	R		C	O	A	C	H
S	T	A	Y	E	D		O	T	T	O
			D	E	S	K				
	C	R	O	S	S	W	O	R	D	S
C	L	A	N	K		A	V	E	R	T
H	A	I	T	I		M	E	D	I	A
A	D	D	O	N		P	R	O	P	S

143
M	I	S	D	O		P	R	E	S	S
A	D	E	E	P		R	E	C	T	I
W	E	A	R	E		O	C	O	M	E
R	E	F	I	N	E	M	E	N	T	
			A	V	I	S	O	S		
T	E	R	E	T	E		S	W	I	T
U	R	E					A	N	I	
B	E	R	T		I	N	B	R	E	D
			H	A	T	A	R	I		
	E	L	E	C	T	R	O	N	I	C
G	L	A	R	E		I	G	E	T	A
A	U	R	A	L		T	A	S	S	E
P	L	A	T	A		A	N	S	O	N

144
G	O	T	O	F	F		C	A	S	A
I	T	A	L	I	A		A	N	O	N
R	O	B	E	R	T	F	R	O	S	T
D	O	L		S	E	A		M	O	O
E	L	E	C	T		S	C	I	O	N
R	E	D	O		A	T	H	E	N	S
			P	E	P	S	I			
G	R	E	E	N	E		R	A	M	S
R	E	A	D	D		S	P	L	A	T
E	N	G		O	O	H		U	N	O
W	A	L	T	W	H	I	T	M	A	N
O	M	E	N		O	R	A	N	G	E
N	E	S	T		S	E	X	I	E	R

SOLUTIONS

145
```
C A K E S . S E A M S
O P E R A . A W A I T
M O L A R . V E R N E
E L S . A N A . O N E
A L E . H O G . N I L
T O Y S . T E N S E S
. . G I V E S U P . .
H A R D U P . B E S T
E V A . L A M . L I E
R I M . C D E . L E E
M A M M A . A L I S T
A T E I N . D A N T E
N E R D S . E D G A R
```

146
```
W A R S . C O I F S
A B E T . A R N I E
S A V A N N A H G A
. . P A S T A . . .
S C A L P . O L I V E
C A R E S . R E N A L
R I G . . . . O L D
A R O M A . N A I V E
M O N E T . A B L E R
. . L E O N A . . .
H A V A N A C U B A
A R I S E . U S E R
M I N E S . S A N E
```

147
```
S I G M A . A B A
A D I E U . U R N
C A N A D A D R Y
. . A L I B I . .
H A L S . O T E R I
I G O . H A D O V E R
M I S S A M E R I C A
O L E A R Y S . T O T
M E R Y L . P A N E
. . S E W E R . .
N E W M E X I C O
A A H . D E C A F
P R O . S C E N T
```

148
```
E Y E S . E D I S O N
R O V E . D A N U B E
I D E A . I N F L O W
C A R R O T C A K E .
. . C O H E N . . .
I D A H O . S T A K E
F E W . . . R E V
S W E A T . S C E N E
. . R I S K Y . . .
P U M P K I N P I E
D E N O T E . I O W A
E S C R O W . C L O T
L O S S E S . S O N S
```

149
```
B A W L . L O R E N
E R I E . A F I R E
G E R A L D F O R D
O N E . A Y E . . .
T A S E R . R I V A L
. . B A G . R A C E
A U T O M O B I L E S
S K I N . D R S . .
K E N Y A . O H A R A
. . D E N . L O M
C H E V Y C H A S E
O U T I E . O M E N
D E A L S . T O S S
```

150
```
I N K . A R K . A B S
R A N . B E N . F A T
A M E R I C A . E R A
. . E A T . P O W E R
C O P Y . A S K . .
A N A . K R A C K E L
L E D . N B C . N A E
M I S T O O K . I S T
. . V C R . I C E S
F L A S K . O A K .
L A X . O A T M E A L
A C E . U N I . R B I
W E D . T Y S . S E T
```

151
```
B E S E T . A S P E N
A L E R O . B E R N E
S N A R K . I G O R S
S I R . Y U L . B O T
E N C L O S E . A L L
S O H O . E N A B L E
. . W E N D E L L . .
A R A B I C . P E G S
T O R . C A T S C A N
W A R . E R E . A G E
I D A H O . R O U G E
L I N E N . M I S E R
L E T M E . S L E D S
```

152
```
S P A R S . S H O R T
H A S A T . H A V E N
A L I C E . A R E N T
M O T H E R L A N D .
. . E P E E S . . .
S M A L L F . S L O W
L E X . Y U M . A W E
C L E O . G A S P E D
. . N I E C E . . .
. S I S T E R C I T Y
C O S T A . A R N I E
T O T A L . M E C C A
S T O R Y . E T H E R
```

153
```
I C U S . H O E I N G
R E N E . A P L O M B
O P A L . R E V U E S
B E S S . D R I . .
. H Y S T E R I C S
L E A N T O . A C U P
I S M . U S A . E T A
T A E L . W I M S E Y
D U D E R A N C H .
. N O L . N E E M
D A C T Y L . E E R O
C A L I C O . A T M S
C U R L E W . L S A T
```

154
```
P E P S . S W A Y Z E
A Q U A . H O M I E R
C U P S . A M E N D S
T I P S O V E R . .
S P Y . V E N I S O N
. L E A D . C E D E
A T O L L . W A X E D
C A V E . M I N K .
E J E C T E D . I R A
. T A L E N T E D
T A O I S T . A T R A
O F N O T E . S E A M
S T O N E D . A N N S
```

155
```
N A M E . R A M S A Y
O R A L . I N A T I E
B E L L B O T T O M S
E N T E R . O H O .
L A Y . I A N . D I E
. E N D . G O N G
B O O K E M D A N N O
R I F E . I O S . .
A L F . O T T . A D A
. E E L . E S S E N
C A N D L E S T I C K
A S S A I L . I D O L
T H E M E S . R E N E
```

156
```
S A J A K . B A S K S
U T U R N . A G E N T
A R N I E . G E N I E
R A I D E R . R I G A
E C O . S E A . O H M
Z E R O . A L E R T S
. S A R C A S M .
P R O F I T . P O P S
L A P . P O D . M I A
A C R E . R E J E C T
S H A L L . F U N K Y
M E N S A . E N T E R
A L O A D . R E S T S
```

157

```
I N E R T . . Y M C A
N E V E R . P E A R L
H E A V Y H A N D E D
A D D . M E T . A P E
L E E . E A T . M E R
E D D Y . D O Z E S .
. . A R E N A . . .
. D A Z E D . P A R S
T E D . B O B . V E E
A N A . U F O . A C E
L I G H T F O O T E D
O R E O S . T R A D E
N O S E . . H I R E D
```

158

```
A L P . C F C . T N T
L E U . A L A . H O O
E A R T R U M P E T S
S P R I G . R Y E S .
. . P O P P A . . .
O C A . L A W M E N
N O S E F O R N E W S
O S P R E Y . H E W
. . A E S O P . . .
S W A T . L E T U P
T H R O A T D R O P S
E O N . B E E . I T S
T A O . C A N . L O T
```

159

```
B A C K . . P A C T S
E T H E R . E T H A N
A R E N A . S L O M O
R I D . I R K . C A R
D A D . L E I . O L E
S L A W . S E A L E D
. . R O B E R T A .
P A C K E R . A T O P
A S H . A V E . E R A
U S E . C E N . C I D
L U E G O . O T H E R
A R S O N . S W I N E
S E E D S . . O P T S
```

160

```
B O L D . A S S E T
I D E A . C H I L I
T O N Y C U R T I S
E R A S U R E . . .
. . . R A W H I D E
D O W S E . D E V I L
A R I A . R A N K .
T A N G O . S O N G S
A L D E N T E . . .
. . . S E A T T L E
O S C A R M A Y E R
R E A L M . S P A R
R A T E S . K E N S
```

161

```
F L A S H . S C H M O
L A N C E . T I E U P
A S T E R . E N A T E
T H E N . G A D D E D
. . T H Y M E . . .
A B L O O M . R E A M
D R A F T . A E T N A
D O N A . E C L A I R
. . W H E E L . . .
S C H O O L . A R C H
A L A M O . E M E R Y
S A R A H . L A Z E D
H Y E N A . I N A W E
```

162

```
W A S H . C A D D I E
A N T E . A R R I V E
S T A R . R E A D E R
P I T T . M A C . .
. . E Z R A . U P T O
E L F . E X P L A I N
G O A L S . E A R L Y
A V I A T O R . T E X
D E R N . R U B Y .
. . C U D . A F A R
P A Y O L A . R O S A
A L U M N I . Q U I P
D E M E A N . S L A T
```

163

```
B R E W S . . A R M S
R O Y A L . D E E P
O N E S I E . D A L E
. . E N D S . O P E N
T E X T . S U N S E T
A V A . P A S S . .
G E M . A Y E . P E W
. . A N T S . O R E
S A L U T E . S P E D
C L O T . S H A Q .
R O T H . T E N U R E
U N T O . A T I O N
B E A R . D O Z E S
```

164

```
R E D . B R A . G O T
E L I . B O G . O H O
D O N T Q U O T E M E
O P A H . E G O S . .
S E R U M . . T A C O
. . M A U D . P E A
A L L B Y M Y S E L F
G A L . O P E C . .
E B A Y . . S H R E D
. N A P S . W A D E
T H E K I N G A N D I
N O R . T I E . T I C
T W O . A P T . S E E
```

165

```
S A L . E R R . P O D
U S A . W O E . A H A
D I S P E L S . S I R
S A V E . L E S S O N
. . E L B O W S . .
E D G E O F . E G A D
L E A . A T M . O W E
M E S A . H E R O E S
. . C H E W E D . .
J O L T E D . S L A M
A P E . M I X T U R E
K E N . I C Y . C I A
E N D . N E Z . K A T
```

166

```
S A W T O . H A S T A
T R A I N . O N I O N
D I S N E Y W O R L D
. . H A N O I . S L Y
I B E . E D E N . .
M E D U S A . O P A L
A L U M S . D I R G E
C A P P . P A R E R S
. . S P A N . S A T
A L E . O L I V E .
M I D D L E E A R T H
E M A I L . L I V E R
N A M E S . S L E D S
```

167

```
D A B O . J I H A D S
A C A R . A R M L E T
B U R G O M A S T E R
N A T A L I E . A P U
E T O N S . D I E M
Y E N . E X T E R N .
. . S N E A K . .
. B R A S S Y . K O L
M E A T . L E O N A
E L F . O P O S S U M
D U A L P U R P O S E
A G E G A P . Y V E S
L A L A L A . S O S A
```

168

```
L O I N S . R A F T S
I N D I A . A L O H A
S T O P S . M E R R Y
B A N . S A P . G E S
O P T . I D S . E A T
N E R V E S . O T T O
. . E E R . F R A .
G A M E . G E R B I L
A V E . T E E . O N O
R E M . A L L . U F O
I N B O X . S A T A N
S U E D E . A L I C E
H E R D S . D I T T Y
```

169

```
O W N U P . Q U A D S
S O U S E . U S U R Y
C O R E A . I B S E N
A D S . C H E S T . .
R Y E . E A T . R E A
. . T O T A L I N G .
C H I E F . S T A T E
C A P E F E A R . . .
S P A . E L M . H A L
. D A R I O . O D E .
A T A R I . U P L I T
A L I E N . S I D E B
S C R A G . E N S U E
```

170

```
I M P S . . C O O P S
R A R E . L A D D E R
I R O N . O R D E R S
S C H E D U L E . . .
. . O C T . O S C A R
L U C A S . S T O L I
A S K . . . . N A B .
S E E D S . S C A N S
T R Y I T . E R R . .
. . P R I C E T A G .
P U P P E T . D I L L
A S S E S S . O S L O
L A I R S . . S T A B
```

171

```
. D O H S . I R I S H
S A R A H . M E D I A
A L A M O . I C O N S
P I L L O W T A L K .
. . . . E T H A N . .
N E W T . A T T E N D
O W E . A T E . M O O
R E B O R N . N U D E
. . B R O K E . . . .
S H E E T M U S I C .
J O E Y S . A T O N E
I M S E T . R E S I N
B E A D S . T R O T .
```

172

```
N A P E . E M B L E M
E S A U . M A L A W I
C H U G . E L A T E D
K Y L E . R I M . . .
. . A N T I . E B A Y
N O D E A L . S O L O
O R E . B L T . B A D
U S E S . A R A B I A
N O N O . G A R Y . .
. . L E A . A F R O .
B R I D E S . B L O W
R E V E L S . L A M E
A V E R S E . E Y E S
```

173

```
R E B U S . D O P E R
A L E P H . E R O D E
S A L S A . S E T I N
C I G . M G S . A T E
A N I . S U E . T O W
L E A D . E R R O R S
. N O N S T O P . . .
D O W S E S . W A F T
I N A . A S P . N E O
R E F . T O E . C A N
G A F F E . S H A R E
E L L E N . T A K E R
S L E D S . S H E D S
```

174

```
S T R A W . H O P E S
P I E C E . A V E R T
A L I E N . L A R R Y
T E N . T O L L . . .
. . J U N O . A P E .
O N T O P O F . L O L
H A I T I . M U S E S
I N N . N O I S O M E
O A T . S U R E . . .
. . E M I R . L I P .
H A S T O . O R A T E
A B A C K . R O V E R
L E T H E . S W A M P
```

175

```
L I D . A S S . S E A
A D O . N E O . Q E D
W I N B Y A F L U K E
N O N E . M A Y A . .
S T A I D . E L B A .
. . G E M S . O I L .
L O S E C O N T R O L
E S Q . O M A R . . .
D O U P . G A T E S .
. E A S T . W O R K .
D R A W T H E L I N E
A O K . O A K . L I E
B O Y . P I E . S E T
```

176

```
H A L F B A D . . . .
A L A B A M A . L A W
V I S I T O R . A L I
I C E . S E A S O N .
N E R D S . S C E N E
. S P A I N . C R E D
. . R I S E N U P . .
S P I N . W A S O F .
P I N T S . H E I R S
R E T Y P E . N E O .
A C E . A T W A T E R
Y E R . T R A P E Z E
. . S E N O R E S . .
```

177

```
P A T . P A M . A B S
A R I . E G O . J O E
P U M . P I N . A R T
A G E . L E A R N S .
Y U L . H E Y S . . .
A L I K E . B A M . .
. A N N A . E L A N .
. . E E L . L E G A L
. . E T A T . A M I .
S A Y S H I . Z E N .
A D O . S K I . I T I
G A G . P E C . N A N
A M A . A N Y . E G G
```

178

```
U L N A . T O S S E D
T O O L . O R I O L E
A L S O . R A N D O M
H A T T R I C K . . .
. . R O B . L E N I N
S C I F I . E R O D E
C A N . . . . S E W .
A N G L E . G R E A T
R E S E T . I E R . .
. . T H I N D I M E .
G A E L I C . S N A G
M A L I C E . E G G O
S A F E S T . A S I S
```

179

```
I A M S O . K R I S .
S H O R T U . N U N C
M E N S C H . E D N A
E M O . U G L I E R .
. . T E A R A T . . .
S C O O P U P . A F T
C A N S T . E U L E R
I T E . E N A M O R S
. . I S I T M E . . .
P E Y O T E . V P S .
A D E N . C O R E R S
C I T I . E P H R O N
O T I C . . S O A P S
```

180

```
R M N . U P A . . . .
E C O . S A R . S H U
P R U N E R S . W A S
. . V O I C E L E S S
A G E N T . N O E A R
M P A A . B I S T . .
C O U C H P O T A T O
. . R T E S . A N E W
P R I O R . A R D E N
A C C R E D I T S . .
W A H . T O S S O F F
S S E . I L L . U S A
. . . C E E . R U B .
```

181

```
A B C D . . R H O D E
R I A A . T O O L U P
T O N G . H A U N C H
E S A U . E R S . . .
. . D E L L . E T A L
S P I R E A . P I M A
C H A R I S M A T I C
A O N E . T O I L E T
D O S O . W A N E . .
. . T A O . T R I B
S T A Y E R . I O W A
I N A P O D . N L O W
S T E E N . . G E N L
```

182

```
B U T T S . M A I Z E
A S U R E . E E L E R
E M B A R R A S S E D
R A E . T E S . A S E
. R E A L L Y . .
O N C D S . Y U C C A
S O L S . . M U L L
S L E E P . I M S E T
. L E N N Y S .
O D S . W O K . W A D
G E N E T I C C O D E
P R U N E . A P R O N
U N G A R . P U D G Y
```

183

```
B A U M . . C A C A O
L M N O P . O L O R D
A B A B A . V A N E D
S L C . T R E N T O N
S E C U R E R . O L E
. O S O L E . R A S
R O U E N . D A T E S
E R N . S A W I I .
D D T . A N A T O M Y
F E A R I N G . N I E
O R B A N . O D I S T
R E L E T . N I S E I
D R E S S . L T R S
```

184

```
N S E C . C A B L E .
A T R I . O R M E R .
G A S T R O N O M Y .
A R T I C L E V . . .
. . F A I L I N G S
E N C Y S T . E L A T
P O R . . E R E .
I T A L . P O G R O M
S A B O T E U R .
. . C O S S A C K S
S P A R E T I R E S
A L L O T . N E E T .
D O E S A . S E P S .
```

185

```
E D I E . S K U N K
M A R V . C O W P E A
T R O I . O L E S O N
S E N T . R A I .
. H A R P . S S N S
O R O . E O L I T H S
R U R . U R E . A R R
D I S H P A N . N A S
O N E I . T O L D .
. P E I . U S O S
N O N P R O . M O S T
C O M E I N . E U S E
O X I D E . T T O P
```

186

```
A Z T E C . I N K S
L O A T H E . D I N E
E N T A I L . A N E W
S E E . E C H O E S
. R A N C H O .
C U T R A T E . S A P
C H O M P . A P P L E
C S T . P O P Q U I Z
. R E C O R D
D I V I D E . W E D
I C O N . A R T E R Y
S K I S . N E W B I E
H Y D E . T O B E D
```

187

```
M U S C L E . M A R
A N C H O R . F O R E
T E R E S A . A R I S
H A A S . S E C E D E
I S P S . A T S E A
S E E R . E S C O R T
. E A R T H .
O R A C L E . E R G S
B I G O T . C U R E
T E R R O R . K N O T
U S E D . A T E O U T
S E E S . P E R U S E
E N D . T A S T E R
```

188

```
D I S C U S S . T E L
O N T A R I O . A L A
C A E S A R S A L A D
K N E E L S . R E I D
E E L S . P E N N E
D T S . P R I N T E R
. S A U N A .
D A S H I N G . D O M
O T T E R . G O R E
N E R D . B E L L E S
K A I S E R R O L L S
E S P . A I R B A S E
Y E S . R O S E R E D
```